GAFFS

About the author

Rory Hearne is an Assistant Professor of Social Policy in Maynooth University, specialising in housing policy and housing rights. He makes regular appearances on national TV and radio as an expert on Ireland's housing policy, including *Prime Time, The Brendan O'Connor Show,* and *The Blindboy Podcast.* He has written articles for *The Irish Examiner, TheJournal.ie and The Irish Times.* He is the author of *Housing Shock: The Irish Housing Crisis and How to Solve It* (2020) and *Public Private Partnerships in Ireland* (2011). Rory completed his PhD in Trinity College in 2009, and subsequently worked in social housing regeneration, as policy analyst in economic inequality, and researcher in social policy, before joining Maynooth University. Rory is also host of the current affairs podcast 'of hope', *Reboot Republic.*

GAFFS

Why No One Can Get a House, and What We Can Do About It

Rory Hearne

HarperCollins*Ireland*

HarperCollins*Ireland*
2nd Floor Macken House
39-40 Mayor Street Upper
Dublin D01 C9W8
Ireland

A division of
HarperCollins*Publishers* Ltd
1 London Bridge Street
London SE1 9GF

This edition published by HarperCollins*Ireland* 2023

1

First published by HarperCollins*Ireland* 2022

A catalogue record for this book is available from the British Library

ISBN: 978-0-00-852961-1 (PB)

Typeset by Palimpsest Book Production Ltd, Falkirk, Stirlingshire

Printed and bound in the UK using 100% Renewable Electricity
at CPI Group (UK) Ltd, Croydon CR0 4YY

For the children we have failed as a nation.
No more.
Let us create a new path.

Contents

Preface, 2023

'I want to own a gaff by the sea, I want to see if dreams can be made, I want to see what real life is about' – Meryl Streek

This is a book of hope. Despite the housing crisis worsening since I wrote the first edition back in 2022, a dramatic change can already be seen taking place across Irish society in how we talk and think about housing. There is a sense that we've undergone a shift in our understanding of what the real purpose of housing is. I am proud that *Gaffs* has helped contribute to the reshaping of this national conversation. From seeing housing as a property investment or financial asset, many in Irish society now realise its fundamental role: providing us with a home, a place of shelter, stability and safety, somewhere to live. This shift is nothing short of a cultural revolution, and will surely result in a major change in how housing is treated in politics, policy and within the economy. Ultimately my hope is that it will lead to the catastrophic housing emergency being solved. This is the idea central to this book, that the most fundamental function – the *true* value – of housing is as a home. It is a human right that must be available to everyone.

As I highlight throughout this book, the reason we are in this housing crisis is because we lost our way and started thinking about housing only as an asset with investment value. This transformation of housing into a financial commodity has benefitted mainly already-privileged groups, while its fundamental and essential role as home was abandoned – with disastrous consequences for younger generations.

If we can dislodge the dominance of the 'housing as property' ethos – which I like to believe we are doing – and reassert the primary purpose of delivering housing (that is, to meet the housing needs of the population, not the profit demands of investors) then we *will* get out of this crisis. Central to this change will be the Irish State's return to doing to what it did right in the past: building social and affordable housing on a massive scale.

A Change in the National Conversation

Over the last ten years I have been researching and campaigning for a major change in ideas and policy around housing, but successive governments and policy-makers have dismissed or ignored my recommendations. Unsurprisingly, private-property interests actively opposed me. But their market- and investor-obsessed approach has utterly failed, and people are realising that we need a new approach. The core ideas and values of treating housing as a human right – that housing should be available as a public service like health and education – are now being taken up by growing numbers of people. This view was seen as radical just a few years ago, but now it is, thankfully, seen as completely necessary. And that is where the hope for solving this crisis comes from.

The reaction to the ideas within this book has been incredible, with an increasing awareness of the housing crisis inspiring real citizen action on housing. There is a cultural explosion happening, communicating the different dimensions of the housing and homelessness crisis and expressing the desire for change. It's visible in the work of so many artists: the artist-led Féile Housing/Féile Tithíocta group; Blindboy Boatclub; Spice Bag's provocative eviction picture; Asbestos's giant gable-end mural in Cork; Martin Leahy's fiery song 'Everyone Should Have a home'; plays such as Emmet Kirwan's *Accents*, and films such as Clare Dunne's *Herself*.

This cultural revolution is rippling across communities, through towns and villages. From the large trade-union-supported Raise the

Roof protests, to the new tenants' union supporting renters, CATU, to the on-line campaigning group Uplift, those affected by the housing crisis are coming together. And it is having real impact.

The highlighting of the scandal of derelict and vacant buildings by these campaigns, opposition parties in the Dail, the innovative work of Frank O'Connor and Jude Sherry, as well as the contribution of this book, has resulted in the government – despite initially refusing – introducing a vacant property tax and grants for renovating derelict buildings. These measures are still insufficient, but they do show how social action on housing is forcing a change in policy.

People are also acting directly to deliver community and co-operative affordable housing, like Common Ground in Wicklow and the Cork Student Housing Co-operative. Local authorities and housing associations are working hard to deliver social and affordable housing.

This desire for change was visible at the multiple events I have been asked to speak at around the country in the last year. I'm contacted daily by people from across society who are suffering from the housing crisis – teachers, community workers, tech workers, students, musicians, artists, childcare workers, nurses, doctors, one-parent families, disabled people, victims of domestic abuse, Travellers, refugees and those not affected directly but disgusted by the crisis. All of these people express the same feeling – that they cannot take any more and they have had enough. They are no longer accepting being silenced, shamed, stigmatised, hidden and ignored. Like a Phoenix rising from the ashes, this generation – Generation Locked Out – is speaking out and acting for change. Tenants are staying in their homes refusing to be evicted into homelessness, campaigning for a right to a housing referendum and demanding support to get what should be a right for all – a home of their own.

Big changes in societies often happen like this. A small movement spreads through the grassroots. Initially hidden from view, it quietly grows in influence, outside of establishment processes, media and politics. Then it erupts, capturing the zeitgeist and attention of a nation, expressing a core idea. This is what is taking place around housing right now. It's happening in conversations, in families, among friends, and this is where society and culture is changing. Irish society is deciding a new direction is needed in housing.

A Generational Issue

Older generations are starting to get it too – if a little belatedly – that it's not millennials drinking too many lattes that's stopping them from moving out, but government housing policy, along with landlords and investor funds, locking the younger generations into their childhood bedrooms and rent traps. You can't afford a home when half your income is eaten up by rent gone to a landlord's 'pension' investment, when house prices are ten times your income and banks won't lend you a mortgage, or when you are outbid by vampire funds or previous generations buying up all the properties. Those previous generations never had to pay the levels of rent, coupled with the cost of living crisis, facing today's younger generations. They didn't have to face being outbid by investors. Landlords don't want to hear that their 'rental stream' is actually a person, a tenant, who is being denied the privileges they had, but that fact can no longer be ignored.

Over the last three decades the profits of landlords, developers, banks and investor shareholders have risen dramatically. And who's been facilitating those profits? Generation Stuck, through ever higher rents and house prices. This is one of the main reasons rents and house prices are now disproportionately high. This is 'rentier' capitalism, economic activity that makes profit without working for it, without contributing to society. They extract profit (rent) from other people's income earned in the real economy doing real work, while the rentiers just gain more wealth through their 'investments' (property). The re-emergence of rentiers is part of why we are returning to feudal levels of inequality.

But many among the business community also now recognise this rentier capitalism and broken housing market is jeopardising the real economy. They can't recruit staff because potential employees can't find affordable housing. In short, the housing crisis is undermining Ireland's economic growth.

Generation Locked Out is the first generation since the foundation of the state to be financially worse off than their parents. But who are the real people behind the crisis? What is their experience? Why is this happening, and how have we become one of the wealthiest countries in the world, yet fail to provide the most fundamental human need – shelter, a home, a place to be?

As I write this, monthly rents are at an average of €1,413 nationally, and €2,169 in Dublin, up almost 7 per cent in the last year. An average nurse's monthly take-home salary after tax, for example, is €2,196. The maths speaks for itself. This is why hospitals face wards closing due to lack of staff, just as crèches, schools and many businesses all face similar crises of recruitment. The housing crisis is affecting the ability of our essential services to function, threatening the continued functioning of our health system, our education system, our economy, our very society.

Lifting the Ban, Removing the Lifejackets

The large vested interests, such as private developers, landlords, banks, investor funds, landowners, estate agents and professional 'consultants' make huge money from the private-market approach to housing. They do not want house prices or rents to fall. They do not want a huge supply of social and affordable housing. But these interests and their lobbyists have a tight grip on politics, government and the State: in fact, many of those in government are and have been landlords and have close relationships with the property industry. The housing crisis is not an accident or something that just happened – it resulted from decision after decision by successive governments that prioritised their interests over those of renters, the homeless and ensuing generations who would need a home. The lifting of the eviction ban was the starkest example of this prioritisation.

The eviction ban had offered some respite from these conditions, yet the government – in one of the cruellest decisions made in Irish political history – and in the midst of an unprecedented crisis, ended the ban in March 2023, taking away a crucial life jacket for thousands of renters. The immediate effect of this was that 11,868 Notices to Quit (NTQs) were issued to renters in 2022, compared to 3,033 in 2021 – a 290 per cent increase in just a year. But unlike many European countries where a tenant stays in place when a landlord sells up, here in Ireland a landlord can evict the tenant when selling. As a result, renters across the country are in a state of panic, fear and anxiety about where they are going to go if they receive a notice-to-quit from their landlord.

The public argument made to justify lifting the ban was the need 'to keep landlords in the market'. But if landlords want to leave, why not just let them? The property doesn't vanish into thin air. The government should use its surplus billions to buy up the property of any landlord that doesn't want to be a landlord anymore. Renters can be kept in their homes, and supported to buy it themselves, or stay there as permanent social or cost rental housing. It's a win-win.

Another reported reason for lifting the eviction ban was to benefit the cuckoo funds – the new large institutional landlords who are taking over Dublin – who want to be able to evict tenants as neces-sary and squeeze out ever higher rents. Why do we prioritise these funds over a generation in need of a home?

Renters are now facing an unprecedented crisis as landlords sell up their 'investments'. Even since the initial publication of this book in September 2022, the scale of landlords selling has accelerated dramatically as property prices continue to climb. But a landlord's investment asset is also a tenant's only home.

11,868 evictions translate into around 30,000 people, including families and children, being forced to leave their homes. Many will go into homelessness, couch-surfing, even emigration. To put these numbers in stark historical context, during the Famine, from 1849 to 1854, 48,740 families were permanently evicted out of their homes, an average of 8,123 per year. So, the 11,868 NTQs issued in 2022 will lead to more evictions this year than took place in some years during the Famine period.

The Faces Behind the Figures

These are not just numbers, these are real people. Take Erica and Paul. Erica is a nurse in the National Maternity Hospital, Paul works for a homelessness charity. They have two kids, Emma (7) and June (5). They happily go to school around the corner from their house. Emma and Paul have rented the house for eight years – it's the only home their kids know. The neighbour's kids are their kids' best friends. It's their community. But Erica and Paul are hiding a terrible trauma from the kids. The landlord is selling up, they're being evicted, and they can't find anywhere else to rent. Paul is sick with worry and stress. Erica is trying to hold it together. But they both know that in a few months they are likely to be homeless. Two parents in full-time jobs, yet in Ireland today even they will be made homeless.

Sean is twenty-nine, he's in a high-paying tech job, but he's being evicted too. He has no option but to move back in with his parents for his thirtieth birthday. It's that or emigrate. He feels his generation has been sold out, sold a lie.

Jen is forty and living in Mayo. She's been three years trying to buy a home. Every time she is outbid by someone buying a house as a holiday home or Airbnb. She's finding it very difficult not to internalise it all as a personal failure. She feels constantly on the edge of rage at the selfish behaviour of older generations. She has worked her whole life, and now finds herself living with the constant fear of homelessness and an increasing sense of hopelessness.

From March 2022 to March 2023, 2,734 families – including 5,700 children – lost their home. In April 2023 Ireland reached a shameful milestone when the highest-ever number of people homeless was recorded, over 12,000. There were 12,259 individuals living in homeless emergency accommodation, which included a shocking 3,594 children homeless with their families – an increase of 28 per cent since March 2022. All are experiencing the trauma of losing their home.

One mother describes how during their time in emergency accommodation her 'children have all got pale and skinny, the joy has left them'. Children living in homeless hubs are getting ill from living in cramped conditions. Chronic stress has a major negative impact on children because their brains and bodies are still developing. Their development and behaviour are compromised. This crisis has life-long negative consequences, which will be felt for generations to come.

Generation Stuck at Home

Half a million young – and increasingly, middle-aged – people are living in their parents' home – this is Generation Stuck at Home, and they are largely invisible in the housing discussion. In Ireland 75 per cent of 20- to 29-year-olds are still living at home with their parents. In Denmark it's just 12 per cent. And this trend continues on to people in their thirties: 41 per cent of 25- to 34-year-olds in Ireland live with their parents. It wasn't like that ten years ago. In 2013 just 19 per cent of that age group lived at home.

Joanne didn't think, at thirty-one, that she would be living back in Ennis in her childhood bedroom, wondering when her life will start. She would love children, a family of her own, but how can she even start that journey without a home of her own? In her thirties she can't even play her music loud as her parents knock on the door – 'keep it down', they say. Then there's the degrading inquisitions over going out – 'text us when you're home', 'where are you going?' her parents ask. Though her parents mean well, she feels like she's regressed to being fourteen again. Her mental health is deteriorating as she finds it hard to see a future. It's impossible even to have a serious relationship, as she is embarrassed about telling people she's still living at home.

Sinead is thirty-two and from Waterford – she spoke on my podcast *Reboot Republic* about what it is like living with your parents in your thirties and how hard it is to talk about this. She clings on to the hope of being able to buy a home of her own. She even has a box put away under her bed that she calls her 'box of hope'. She puts into it little things that she dreams will go in the kitchen of her future home; cups, plates, napkins, table settings, a teapot. That's her way of coping. She pulls out the box and looks at the pieces of her 'home' inside. She feels these fragments of the home dream, but then has to put them back under the bed and leave them there. It's symbolic of how the dreams of an entire generation are being destroyed, hidden away, just clinging on to fragments of home hidden under their bed.

Generation Emigration

And then, recurring all too frequently in Irish history, there is Generation Emigration, taking flight from our shores, this time because of the housing crisis. Michael is twenty-seven, and he's loving Australia. Can't beat playing hurling with the lads in 24-degree heat – in the middle of winter. He's a teacher, left Dublin last year because he was sick of paying most of his wages in rent to a landlord who never fixed anything and wasn't even registered with the RTB. But yesterday Michael found out his mum has cancer. He's in shock, not sure what to do. He just wants to give his mum a hug. He's thinking about moving back to be with her, but there's no room at home as his sister and her kids moved back in when they were evicted from their rental home. So where would he even live?

Laura is from Kerry, she's thirty-four and a nurse in Canada. She has two kids but per parents never see them. She always dreamed of living in Killarney with her kids going to the local school, but now she sees no point in moving back home. She just couldn't afford the rent or to buy a home on a nurse's wage. She and her parents are heartbroken.

We are losing our youth, our energy, our future, the country's soul and spirit, to emigration once again. Emigration bears a huge emotional toll, for those who leave and those left behind, that we cannot and should not repress. The government might accept this emigration as a handy political pressure valve, but as a society we should not accept it. These are the people – along with hundreds of thousands like them – at the heart of this crisis. This is their deep personal loss, grief and trauma.

Generation Shafted

This is a generation that has gone to college, worked hard, taken out loans to cover education, have been made suffer from austerity and short-term contracts, have worked professional careers and yet are now being priced out of Ireland. It is a generation that doesn't see a viable future here. Of 25- to 34-years-olds, 40 per cent are living with parents, 33 per cent are renting. Just 27 per cent own their own home. Almost three-quarters of this generation are in some form of being stuck, locked out of having their own home. And it's not their fault. They really are Generation Shafted. Their housing needs were sacrificed by successive governments since 2009 in order to 'recover' the economy after the crash. They were made pay for bailing out the banks, property developers, NAMA and the privileged older groups who invested in, and own, property. One has to wonder – what is the point of all the economic growth and wealth if we cannot provide a home for our younger generations and for everyone living in this country?

The New 'Toxic Normal' and the State of the Nation

A core concern of this book is the emotional, psychological and mental-health impact of the housing crisis. The well-known trauma expert Dr Gabor Mate states that we now live in a society of a 'toxic normal'. We have come to tolerate previously unimaginable levels of homelessness as well as couch-surfing, adults stuck living at home in their childhood bedrooms, evictions, massive rents and emigration. Yet this quasi-normalised housing crisis is a major cause of chronic and toxic stress and will continue to have huge social costs, including an increased demand for already overstretched health services and a negative impact on work, family life and relationships. The Irish government, the State and the property investors are giving no consideration to millions of people, to a generation living in permanent housing insecurity. These human stories of Ireland's housing crisis only scratch the surface of a social catastrophe that is destroying the lives of people. It is an individual and collective trauma, a hidden epidemic that will have huge implications for decades to come.

The solution to this is clear – we need to significantly escalate the delivery of social and affordable homes beyond what is currently being done. In 2022 there were 30,000 new homes built, but that is nowhere near the real need of over 50,000 per year. And almost a third of all newly built homes in 2022 (9,000 homes) were investor fund build-to-rent properties at unaffordable rents. Less than a third (8,000) were actually homes bought by ordinary home-buyers. A further 7,500 were social housing (mainly bought from the private market). Incredibly, we are actually going to see a fall in new builds in 2023 by 10 per cent less than 2022's output, to 27,000 homes. Yes, you read right: at a time of unprecedented housing need, the number of new homes being built will decrease. Some parts of the country have seen a dramatic slowdown in new home starts; Cork City is down 38 per cent, Galway city is down 68 per cent, Kildare 43 per cent, Limerick, 8 per cent.

Because of inflation, rising interest rates and economic uncertainty, private developers, investors and financiers are deeming it unviable to finance and build. This shows the inherent instability and unreliability of the market to provide housing. There are now 70,000 homes with full planning permissions that remain unbuilt. The government is using public money to waive the levies for developers and investor funds who own such planning permissions – it's a bail-out blank cheque with no affordability requirements. What should be done is to use public money to compulsory purchase the land with the planning permission off the investors and rapidly build on them as social and affordable housing.

The government claimed that the 7,500 social homes built this year is the highest since the 1970s. There are several issues with this claim – firstly, our population at that time was just 3.8 million, today it's over 5 million. In order to build an equivalent level of social housing per head of population as in 1975, the government would need to have built 13,718 social housing units last year. That is close to the numbers of social housing units (15,000) we should be building each year. Secondly, most of this new social housing is not actually being delivered by local authorities but is being bought from private developers through 'turnkey' developments, which is taking housing supply from those looking to buy a home. Rather than taking houses from the market the State should be delivering its own additional supply of social and affordable housing. To do this, there should be the establishment of a national home building agency, along with an increase in capacity of local authorities and housing associations (like Respond, Cluid and O Cualann) to develop and deliver housing themselves.

Just over a thousand affordable homes were provided in 2022 (684 cost rental and 323 local Authority Affordable Purchase). While it is a start, it is a drop in the ocean compared to what's needed. There should be 25,000 affordable rental and purchase homes being delivered each year, and they need to be delivered at rents and house prices that are *actually* affordable.

A Time for Action
There are some actions you can take to help make an impact in this regard. If you are looking to get an affordable or social home from these new affordable housing schemes, you should contact your local authority to see if you are eligible for any of them. Ask to put your name down on any waiting lists – be they social housing, affordable purchase, or cost rental. The more people who put their name down, the more apparent the actual level of housing need will become to authorities. Your housing needs can't be hidden and dismissed as easily then. And you might just be fortunate to be allocated an affordable home to rent or buy. Another thing you could do is identify empty land or derelict empty buildings around you and contact your local authority to ask are they taxed, fined or why isn't the local authority acquiring them with compulsory purchase orders. You can also contact elected TDs, councillors and politicians and ask what they are doing to tackle the housing crisis, such as bringing these into use as homes.

The solution to this crisis is not more landlords. The solution is supporting Generation Locked Out to become homeowners and public housing tenants; it is more tenant protections and lower rents. Turn the landlord-owned properties into affordable home-ownership and public housing.

In the immediate term, the eviction ban should be reinstated for three years and the tenant in situ scheme expanded to buy up from any landlord that wants to leave and keep the tenant in their home. That avoids the huge social costs and trauma of people having to leave their home, the cost of emergency homeless accommodation and the need to subsequently acquire additional social homes to house them. Keeping renters in their homes is a simple way to reduce housing demand.

The government and others have been claiming the housing crisis results from 'population growth', COVID pandemic shutdowns, inflation and refugees from Ukraine. But the truth is that the housing crisis pre-existed all of these. Many countries have experienced population growth and refugee arrival, yet they do not have the scale of our housing crisis. The evictions into homelessness are being done by Irish landlords, not refugees.

As this book explores in greater detail, the main causes of our housing crisis are the shift over thirty years away from building social and affordable housing by local authorities, the over-reliance on the market to deliver homes, and handing housing over to global investor funds. Ireland is not full. We have 166,000 vacant homes, and hundreds of thousands of derelict and vacant buildings, and we are one of least densely populated countries in Europe. That is a huge potential supply of housing we could quickly unlock. It is so sad and wrong to see vulnerable migrants and refugees being blamed for the housing crisis. And let's be clear – those orchestrating the 'house our own' protests do not actually care about the homeless and housing victims here in Ireland. They are jumping on the housing issue to spread hate and division. They offer no real solutions to get us more housing or to prevent homelessness. They claim to be standing up for housing yet do not believe in housing as a human right. They only take attention away from the real causes of the crisis.

Since I wrote this book an economic game-changer has emerged that can and should help solve the housing crisis – and that is the massive budget surplus of up to €34 billion due to the exchequer in the coming years. A significant proportion of that money should be put into massively expanding social and affordable housing that is green and environmentally sustainable including modular housing, retrofitting existing homes and bringing into use derelict and vacant ones.

It is scandalous to only put that money away into a Future Reserve Fund. There is no future if we can't provide homes for our nurses and doctors, or teachers and childcare workers, our artists, cleaners and bus drivers. It is immoral, while children are being scarred, losing their homes, growing up in emergency accommodation. And it is economically illogical, when we can't currently get workers due to the lack of housing, to refuse to invest billions we have readily available in housing.

An immediate €8 billion of that should be put into housing through the setting up of a national sustainable home-building agency to directly build social and affordable homes, retrofit and refurbish vacant and derelict properties. This would create a permanent capacity of housing construction skills within the public sector. It would not replace the private building market but would provide additional capacity and a guaranteed supply of social and affordable housing additional to market provision. Investment is also needed in public transport links to make land and housing around the country accessible.

We need big, bold, brave ideas and measures that will have a real impact on massively increasing the supply of affordable housing – not tinkering about trying to make the private market 'work' when it will never do so. We need a new road map for housing, and my hope is that this book goes some way to drawing that map.

We need to stop normalising the housing crisis. Secure, affordable, sustainable homes for all are at the core of a compassionate and just society.

The market cannot be allowed to dictate people's housing needs. The State must guarantee homes for all in a fresh approach. There are local elections, a general election and possibly a housing referendum all to take place within the next year and a half. These are, in many ways, the most important elections of a generation, where it will be decided whether we continue the housing inequality catastrophe, or take a new path.

The housing crisis won't change for the better unless the people of Ireland stand up and demand we take a new path in housing. Thankfully this is starting to happen, people are finding their voice and power. You too can play your part. This is hope, this will bring the change needed.

Rory Hearne
June 2023

Chapter 1
The Housing Crisis:
A Generational Faultline

There is a generational fissure growing in this country, a divide unlike anything we have seen for a long time. It is a generational inequality in housing. A generation is being locked out of one of the most basic human needs – a home. The crisis has reached the point of inflicting major social and economic damage to this country and its people, and is even causing a mental health crisis of its own.

If you are in your twenties or thirties and early forties, you are part of the millennial generation Y. You worked hard to get to college, or complete your Leaving Cert, or get an apprenticeship; you got a degree, a PhD, a job; you pay your taxes, you vote, you do everything society tells you to do. And yet here you are, locked into paying massive rents, unable to save. Or locked in your parents' box room. Or locked into homelessness. You are locked out of buying a home of your own, and you might even be considering leaving Ireland (or have emigrated already) because you are locked out of a future here. You are locked out of getting the most basic fundamental human need – shelter. A stable, affordable home of your own.

But your parents, just like you, went to school, worked hard, got an apprenticeship, a trade or a degree, and then found a job. They saved. Still in their twenties, they bought their home or got a council house (which they probably later bought) from the local authority. Many did have to emigrate because of the lack of jobs, but some returned and they were able to buy a home. This was the experience of the Baby

Boomer Generation and early Gen Xs from the 1960s to the 2000s. But it is certainly not your experience when it comes to housing. You are part of a new generation – Ireland's Generation Locked-out.

This book is about the story of your generation – how it has had its future robbed by decades of failed policies that handed housing to the private market and investor funds. It is about the new generational divide – housing. The housing crisis has been compounded by other changes and policies that disproportionally impacted on you – austerity, stagnant earnings, the shift to contract work and the gig economy. You are the generation that can't imagine a future. A generation relying on precarious, insecure work and precarious, insecure housing. A generation that has been turned into a rent-generating asset for global real estate investor funds – Ireland's new vulture landlords.

I wrote this book to show you that you *can* have a future in this country, that there is a way in which you can have a secure, affordable home of your own. There is a future where you can plan your life and do the wonderful creative jobs and hobbies you want, whether teaching, nursing, accountancy, photography, journalism ... whatever. You deserve that future: a home in your country. And this book will show you that your housing situation is not your fault. It will explain how and why governments made decisions that led to you being stuck where you are. But it will also explain how we can solve the crisis – together. It will explain, I hope in a straightforward way, why we are in this crisis. The situation we find ourselves in is multi-layered: so this book takes you on a journey through our housing history, politics, social policy, the psychology of home, and more. But my vision and purpose in writing it is to put the heart back into home and help bring about a new future of affordable, decent, life-time secure, environmentally sustainable homes for all in this country.

Listening to and reading a lot of the discussion on the housing crisis, you would think that it appeared out of nowhere, that there is no reason for it – it 'just happened'. But this narrative is utterly untrue. Most important, this crisis can be solved. My hope is that with the information in this book you will understand why we are in this situation and how we can get out of it. I also hope it will help you to feel confident and motivated to talk about the real reasons for the crisis and the solutions that can work, to your friends, work colleagues, family members, on social media, and even to politicians when they come knocking on your door. This is a book to inform, engage, educate and inspire real change in housing.

It all starts with home. This is not about property or investments or crude demand and supply estimates, it's about us realizing that what we must provide people is affordable, secure and stable homes of their own. That is what should be the goal of our housing system and economy, not the bottom lines of investor funds, estate agents, big property developers, or the bank's balance sheets, or landlords' incomes.

We need to turn the dominant property economics approach to housing in Ireland on its head. We need to put the heart back into home. The emotional importance of secure, affordable, decent standard housing should be central to housing policy. Our understanding should be that housing is, first and foremost, a home.

Generation Locked-out has been given no choice in housing. Either you accept the investor fund micro-apartments – the tenements of the twenty-first century – the expensive build-to-rent and co-living apartments – with no possibility of buying any of them, and no homes big enough for families; or you get to 'choose' to stay with your parents or leave the country. It's a 'choice' between unaffordable rents, insecure housing, homelessness and emigration. But where are families of the future supposed to live? Where are single people supposed to live?

We all need stability, security and hope to live fulfilled lives. As humans we need to feel that we are a valued part of our tribe, our society, our community – the backbone of a country. But younger generations are being alienated from their own country. The social contract has been broken. This will lead to divisive inequality, isolation and endemic loneliness. But there is a way out of this crisis. There is hope and there are solutions. This book shows that through a change in direction in housing policy, through new ideas and new ways of providing affordable, decent-quality homes on a massive scale (and this country has done it in the past), homes that are also environmentally sustainable, we can solve this housing crisis. Yes, we can solve the housing crisis and help the climate too. It really is a no-brainer. We can give this generation a home of their own, either owned or rented – affordably and secure for life. We must give them that future here in Ireland.

You can have a central role in making this happen – in raising your voice, in putting pressure on politicians, in making this an issue they have to act on. In this, and in other practical ways, you can be part of making your home, your community, your country. History shows that nothing changes unless people make some noise and put energy into solutions. You can contribute in so many wonderful, creative and important ways. There is lots you can do that I will explain in the book, from signing online petitions to highlighting vacant and derelict properties, being part of the new renters' union, and getting involved in housing co-operatives. We all have a part to play in solving Ireland's housing emergency.

Too many of those affected by the housing crisis feel ashamed and unable to talk publicly about it. They are worried that it will upset their families. They feel that it is their failure, their responsibility, their fault. They feel stigmatized. Yet they shouldn't. We really need to start talking about this. We need to break the stigma and silence around how the housing crisis is impacting on people. There's also a sense of despair and hopelessness, a feeling that the housing crisis is unfixable. That is the myth the investor funds, banks and developers want you to believe. If you just accept this crisis as the way things are, it will be the reality for the future. You will continue to pay astronomical, unaffordable rents and crazy house prices. But if you see that there are solutions, and if you do not accept that the current situation is the new normal in Ireland, the future can and will be different.

Let's be clear – the housing crisis is not your fault. An affordable, decent, secure home is a legitimate aspiration. The crisis is not the fault of millennials eating too much avocado toast. The housing crisis is not something that just happened; it resulted from bad policy choices – mistaken decisions made by governments, over decades, to stop local authorities building homes, telling them to get out of housing and hand it over to the private market.

It resulted from governments prioritizing the banks, developers, landlords and vulture investor funds over the housing needs of younger generations. Generation Locked-out has been used as the sacrificial lamb for the recovery of the Irish banks and property market. This is where generational inequality really bites. The policies the government was putting in place back in 2010 – austerity, cuts in housing, NAMA, bringing in the investor funds – were about cleaning up the mess caused by the crash. But they cleaned it up by putting the cost of the crash on to the people who didn't cause it – you, millenials, Gen Z, children growing up today, and future generations to come.

The housing crisis is also having a serious impact on the economy, jeopardizing the entire future of the country. Businesses will not locate and grow in Ireland if their workers have nowhere to live and settle. The failure to realize this reveals a serious misunderstanding of the role of housing in the economy. You cannot have a functioning economy without a stable and sufficient supply of affordable homes. The private market (the developers and investors) on its own will never provide that. There is no country in the world where it does. The big global investor vulture funds do not want to provide a supply of affordable homes that would lead to lower rents because high rents are the basis of their profits. Large-scale involvement of the State (local authorities delivering homes) and not-for-profit housing providers (associations such as Respond, Clúid, the Ó Cualann Cohousing Alliance) is the only way to ensure a sufficient supply of affordable homes. We appear to have forgotten the lessons of the past. It was not private investors or developers that built our stock of affordable homes from the 1920s to the 1990s, it was Irish governments, the State – through our local authorities.

The destruction of the social contract

The property ladder has been pulled up out of the reach of Generation Locked-out. At the same time, the social contract has been ripped apart. Younger generations do not have access to a home of their own or to council housing, which was available to previous generations. But increasing numbers of those in their forties, fifties and sixties who are stuck in the private rental sector are also affected. And this is the potentially disastrous future facing Generation Z, now in their teens to mid-twenties. If you have young children, this could be their future too, unless we change the housing situation rapidly.

The number of people who are able to buy their own home – the level of home ownership – has collapsed among adults in Ireland since the financial crisis in 2008. Out of all EU countries, it was Ireland that has had the biggest fall in home ownership rates over the last decade. Unfortunately we are top of the class in the wrong areas. In 2005, a large majority of Irish households (82 per cent) owned their own home. However, that fell by 14 per cent to just 68 per cent of households in 2020. Home ownership levels have not been as low as this since the early 1970s. People are also older now before they are in a position to buy. In 2004, 60 per cent of people aged 30 or under had bought a home, but in 2020 that figure was just 27 per cent.

Social housing (or council housing) provided by local authorities was a vital source of affordable and secure housing for Irish families since the foundation of the State. But delivery of this much-needed housing has fallen off a cliff. In 1950, Ireland was a much, much poorer country. Much of rural Ireland still didn't have electricity, and secondary education was still only available to those who could pay the fees. Yet local authorities built an impressive 7,787 houses. In 1975, almost a third of the Irish population was below the poverty line, but still local authorities built almost 9,000 homes in that one year, at a time when the population was just 3.2 million. How many social homes did local authorities and housing associations build in 2019? Just 2,000.

While there have been many positive changes in Ireland in recent decades, we have gone backwards in terms of housing affordability and the number of homes available for people to buy and rent. We have lost fifty years of housing progress.

The housing market is a fire that government has poured fuel on, rather than quenching the flames. It has handed the market over to vulture funds. House prices and rents have more than doubled in the last decade while wages have only increased by a fraction of that. How can people afford a home if house price and rent increases are multiple times the rate of wage growth? For example, the minimum wage increased by just 13 per cent since 2011, while rents have increased by 89 per cent.

The real shame is that in 2013, less than a decade ago, housing was actually affordable in this country. This belies the claim you often hear – made by people who either benefit from the housing market, or are just cranky – that 'Sure things were always like this, house prices were always expensive, and nothing ever changes anyway.' In fact, in 2013 the national average house price was €171,000. In Kildare it was €177,000, in Galway City it was €159,000, in Cork City €167,000. Even in Dublin City it was just €185,000. House prices were four times the median income (i.e. the income that is the halfway point, with 50 per cent of people having an income higher than the median, and 50 per cent having an income lower). But by 2020 house prices had jumped to seven times the median income. That is classed as 'severely unaffordable' housing under international definitions of housing affordability. House prices have increased by 125 per cent nationally since 2013. The average house price in Kildare is now €354,000, in Cork City it's €311,000, in Dublin City €510,000 and in Galway City €345,000. While the cost of housing materials is increasing now, it did not increase by 91 per cent over the last decade. So something else happened. And a large part of what happened is that different parts of the private housing market simply increased the amount of profit they took out, whether through charging higher rents, higher land costs, or higher house prices at point of sale.

We need to get under the bonnet of the housing crisis and see what is wrong with an engine that is constantly running too fast, too slow, or hurtling over the cliff. If we take apart the engine to find the blockages, the missing parts, the parts that shouldn't be there, we might see that in fact things are not as they seem, that the problem is not only with the engine but also the driver.

The government makes many decisions that affect housing. We call this public policy or social policy. They can relate to planning laws (such as what should be the minimum size of new apartments or what percentage of developments should be affordable and social housing); or tax measures (such as what benefits and perks it gives to global vulture funds that make them want to come here and buy up homes); or legislation for the private rental sector (such as capping rents at 2 per cent annual increase in a Rent Pressure Zone, or what penalties it puts on landlords who breach the rules); or fiscal and budgetary measures (such as how much money it decides to spend each year on building new social housing). These decisions interact with each other and impact on housing supply (especially the supply of social housing, since that is what the government controls directly), but it also impacts on the private housing market, influencing what landlords, developers and investors do. Property and finance economists in the media often criticize the government for 'interfering' in the market, and claim that if the market were left alone it would do a better job of delivering homes. But of course what they really mean is that the government should interfere, to help them, but not to make housing more affordable by reducing house prices and rents. Bad public policy decisions made by governments have been the major factor in causing the housing crisis. It is shocking to realize that many policy decisions were made with the actual intention of creating the housing crisis such as inflated house prices and rents. They were clearly bad policy decisions from the perspective of those seeking an affordable home – but they were hugely beneficial for those profiting from higher house prices and rents, and they suited the political agenda and ideology of the political parties in government. The difficult truth is that the massive increase in house prices and rents over the last decade has actually been government policy. Bizarre as it might seem, your unaffordable housing is the policy 'success' of recent governments. It has been government policy for over a decade to make housing unaffordable. Let me repeat that. Government policy for the last ten years has been trying to increase house prices and rents, making housing unaffordable to you, in order to make it more profitable for vulture funds, corporate landlords, the banks and private developers.

The crisis, from the viewpoint of the new landlord class in Ireland – the global real estate, vulture and cuckoo investor funds – is a business opportunity. Their investment strategies are based on the housing crisis continuing. It is their business model. These 'institutional investors', backed by the government, are taking over our housing system, especially in Dublin and the commuter counties. These new large corporate landlords bought just 76 units in Ireland in 2010, but in 2019 they bought 5,132 homes, 44 per cent of all new purchases in Dublin. That same year they bought 95 per cent of all new apartments built in the country. They now own over 45,000 homes in this country. The largest landlord in Ireland is IRES REIT, a Canadian-funded Real Estate Investment Trust that has its shares traded on the stock market. The entry of this 'shareholder' capitalism business model in housing is an unprecedented change in the nature of housing. It transforms the housing system from providing homes to being taken over by faceless financial investment companies focused primarily on maximizing the returns to their shareholders and global wealth investors, all through sweating their asset – you, Generation Rent.

I will let them explain in their own words who they are and what they are doing here.

Greystar is one of the new giant global real estate investment and development companies to come into Ireland. It is headquartered in the USA. It manages more than $50bn in assets, owns more than 186,000 apartments and student accommodation in countries across the world. It is focused on, as it explains, 'generating attractive risk-adjusted returns on behalf of institutional partners through the acquisition and development of rental housing properties globally'. In 2019, it entered the Irish housing market with the aim of delivering 'a new approach to rental housing investment in Ireland'. So what is this new approach? Well, Greystar explains that it's 'prioritizing development opportunities along with the acquisition of assets under forward purchase structures and operational platforms'. And it points out that 'Dublin's strong demographics and sustainable economic growth has resulted in an acute housing shortage offering a tailwind for future investment prospects'. So your housing crisis is their 'tailwind for future investment prospects'. And their ultimate aim is? To provide affordable homes to their tenants? Who are you kidding? They explain further: 'by investing intelligently with a global capital allocation strategy . . . Greystar aims to maximize investment returns for our investors.' Yes, their priority is maximizing the return (i.e. rent) for investors. Generation Locked-out, watch out – these global and Irish investor fund REITs are coming for you. And this is shown clearly in their involvement in a new development in Dublin. Griffith Wood, on Griffith Avenue, which has just been completed, includes 382 apartments. Some locals were excited about the opportunity for their children to buy a home there, or even downsize to a smaller home themselves and free up their home for their kids. But in 2021 Greystar bought the entire new development, and is going to rent all the apartments out. Not one apartment is for sale. And the rents are shockingly high. A two-bedroom, two-bathroom flat is available for €2,445 a month, while a three-bedroom, three-bathroom flat can be rented for €3,600 a month. So all the dreams of the locals for new homes for their kids have gone up in smoke.

So it's clear that these investor funds, these faceless piles of global cash, want to turn us and our homes into assets that maximize the return to global investors. It's a scary future.

Generation Rent

It's in the rental market where housing costs in Ireland have become really unbearable. Rents have doubled in the last decade. In Dublin, they are now 52 per cent above the highs of the Celtic Tiger.

For 90 per cent of earners, the average rent in Ireland is now unaffordable under international definitions of affordability.

Rents are an average of €1,415 a month nationally. You would need to be earning €75,000 a year (be in the top 10 per cent of earners) for this rent to be considered affordable (that is defined as where the rent is less than a third of your net income). In Dublin, it is even more severe. You need to be earning €115,000 a year (which would put you in the top 5 per cent of earners) for the average rent of €1,972 per month to be affordable. A teacher or a nurse on a starting salary in Dublin would have to spend almost their entire take-home income (83 per cent of it) to rent an average-priced home. It is these inflated rents that the investor funds are here for. And they want them to continue to rise even further.

In December 2021, Dublin was the sixth most expensive capital city in the world to rent in, the third most expensive capital city in Europe after London and Monaco. Little old Dublin, a small capital on the edge of Europe, with some of the biggest rents in the world. The Irish housing market is clearly very badly broken.

Rents are critical because today in Ireland a whopping 20 per cent of all households (up from just 10 per cent of households in 2006), equating to 1 million people, live in the private rental sector. They are Generation Rent. All types of household are there: singles, sharers, couples, many with young children, migrants, carers, teachers, doctors. The private rental sector is now people's home, and for many it will be their home for life. Older people too are stuck in the private rental sector and are terrified about how they will be able to afford the rent when they retire. This social issue is a ticking time bomb for the future.

High rents are pushing renters into poverty. Many are struggling in the private rental sector, and combined with the rising cost of living renters are being forced into choosing between paying essential bills, medical costs, education, even eating, and paying the rent. That's not even including trying to save for a deposit. The lack of long-term security (leases are generally no longer than a year or two and a landlord can evict people for lots of reasons not the fault of the tenant) means that renters are desperate to leave the private rental sector. A third of private renters would like to go into social housing, but there is hardly any available. So the desire to buy your own home is not just a fanciful whim or the result of some ambitious property gene, it is a fundamental requirement in order to get a permanent, affordable, secure home. It's more expensive to rent than to pay a mortgage. More people would be happy to rent if there was real security and affordability; and there should be no difference between renting and owning in terms of security or affordability. But the Irish private rental sector is neither secure nor affordable.

A massive 3,038 notices to quit (eviction notices) were issued to tenants in 2021, a 62 per cent increase in evictions on the previous year. This is the highest number of evictions of tenants to take place in a single year in this country since the foundation of the State. Two-thirds of eviction notices were issued to tenants outside Dublin, showing how the crisis has spread across towns, cities and rural areas around the country. Ninety per cent of the evictions were 'no fault' of the tenant but because the landlord decided to sell or refurbish the property or to move a family member in. But it was the tenants' home. They had no choice but to gather up their belongings and try to find somewhere else. The lack of affordable rental properties means that many are forced to move back to their parents' home, sleep in cars, couch surf, sleep in cars, or become homeless.

Renters are in a state of continual anxiety and stress, with devastating mental health impacts, as a result of rising rents and fear of eviction. A generation is stuck, their lives on hold, because they cannot plan ahead as they don't know where they will be living in a year, six months, two months . . . Will the landlord sell up and evict them? Will they be able to afford this ever-rising rent in the years ahead? Will they have to uproot their children again, move them away from their friends, school and community, to try to find another rental home? No matter how hard you try, you just cannot make a home in the Irish private rental sector.

Tenants can't paint their walls, hang a picture, have a pet, and often have to up and leave their home before they have long enough to get involved in the local community, so vital for children and families. Only 15 per cent of renters are renting by choice – 44 per cent want to own their own home and 32 per cent want to live in social housing. A quarter of all children are growing up in the insecure private rental sector. That is 281,000 children living in a housing situation with their families that is unstable, where they might have to leave their home. This is a fundamental flaw in the Irish housing system that places massive pressure on the housing market. Everyone is trying to get out of rental and buy. This pushes up prices. But this dysfunctional system does benefit some. Especially the investor fund/corporate landlords who have this growing 'market' of limitless demand – renters stuck renting with no escape route and left with the option of paying ever higher rents, or becoming homeless. It profits the private developers who sell the houses at higher prices; and the banks cash in on it when they get to approve ever-higher mortgages; and, of course, estate agents get higher commission.

But the madness in the housing market is plain to see for everyone. A shed in Galway was recently advertised at €100,000 to buy. Three-bedroomed homes in a new development in Dublin were advertised for €330,000 in 2020. Just over a year later the next phase advertised the same homes for €390,000, a 18 per cent increase. There was an apartment advertised in Dublin for €2,000 a month where you could pop your chips into the oven from your fold-out bed. US real estate fund Kennedy Wilson is renting 2-bedroomed apartments in Capital Dock for €3,500 a month, but the *Business Post* reported in 2021 that nearly half of the 190 apartments in the 22-storey build-to-rent tower in Dublin's Docklands were vacant. 'Win a home' competitions have also become commonplace across the country. It has reached a bad state when people know that they will raise the most amount of money for their local charity or GAA club if they offer not a big cash prize, but a home, the most sought-after prize of all.

There is also a massive hidden homelessness crisis of half a million adults living at home with their parents because they cannot get a home of their own. The sheer number is staggering: 350,000 young adults aged 18 to 29 and 100,000 adults aged 30 to 49 are still living at home. Most of these (250,000 in total) are working. Those stuck at home feel infantilized, frustrated, depressed and rightfully angry at the unfairness. Moving out of the family home is a key life stage towards independence. Their parents' generation had a forever home by their mid-20s, but because successive governments have failed to deliver affordable homes, millennials are stuck at home, lives on hold, a stalled generation.

Younger generations are now emigrating in increasing numbers because of the housing crisis. Throughout Irish history it has been poverty and the lack of jobs that forced people to emigrate. But now, for the first time in this country's history, it's not jobs but rather the lack of housing that is causing people to leave these shores.

The psychological importance of home

We have forgotten in this country what the true value and meaning of home is. It's not the price of property but shelter, a place of protection from the elements (and we need it in this rain-sodden country) and security, a place of safety, of warmth. Home provides our personal and private space to enable us to live a life of dignity as human beings, as citizens of this country. Home is our sanctuary. Housing is a fundamental need – we cannot live without it. It is where we express ourselves, our personal identity. It is intimate to us. We fill our homes with who we are.

Homes are the places that create communities. They are the most important place for children. It is where they grow and develop, both physically and psychologically; a secure base from which they can confidently explore the wider world, create, dream, crawl, have birthdays, have friends over to play. The psychosocial role of housing in our lives – the psychology of home – is vital. Our home impacts on our wellbeing – our health, both physical and mental. The link between housing and health is a given. Children in poor housing have poorer health; dampness and mould, for example, lead to asthma and bronchitis. Without a secure home we are in a state of ontological insecurity. Persistent stress, in relation to things we have no control over, causes physiological damage – it leads to raised cortisol levels and significantly impacts our physical and mental health. Housing insecurity is a major contributor to stress and anxiety. Yet an entire generation has no place they can call home. We are failing to provide a secure base for a generation of children and exposing them to the damaging stress of insecure housing.

The Covid pandemic made many of us re-evaluate our lives and the importance of our homes. Housing inequalities were starkly exposed during the pandemic. Those with plenty of space, inside and out, could work from home, isolate and endure lockdowns a lot better than those in overcrowded and smaller homes, without multiple toilets and living rooms, or without any green space. Covid revealed the damaging physical and mental health impacts of inadequate and overcrowded housing.

It is crucial to see the connections between the pandemic and the origins of our modern welfare state. The welfare state was developed by governments in the early twentieth century as part of a response to squalor, poverty, ill health and pandemics. It was set up because the private market and businesses failed to provide essential human needs of housing, health, education and a basic standard of living such as welfare for growing populations living in cities in the first half of that century. The welfare state aimed to achieve greater equality and social justice in the context of populations devastated by world wars and economic depression. Housing was a central plank of this welfare state. Public and social policy developed social housing, and local authorities were tasked to build affordable housing for working people and the poor. The State's key responsibility was to deliver health, housing and education for everyone, regardless of income. The private market would not provide for all, because it would not be profitable. The social policy understanding, learned through harsh experience, was that the key social and human needs, and social rights, of health, education, welfare and housing have to be guaranteed by the State in order to address poverty and inequality and ensure stable economic growth and social cohesion. These basic human rights were recognized and understood as essential for an adequate standard of living in the 1948 United Nations Declaration of Human Rights. Throughout the twentieth century countries across Europe built a massive amount of social or public housing. Some countries did it better than others, but it was an area in which Ireland did very well. Until the 1980s. That's when it all went wrong.

Since then, a pernicious ideology has emerged that cast aside the lessons of social policy, health and Keynesian economics and put a free market economics ideology at the heart of housing policy. This 'neoliberal' thinking (driven by Thatcher, Reagan and free market economists like Friedman and Hayek) saw government as the problem: council housing created lazy, delinquent people; social housing was a failure; and the government would no longer have a role in such enterprises. Ireland embraced that ideology in housing policy and the State stopped building local authority housing. In the late 1960s, 20 per cent of our total housing was social housing; now it is just 11 per cent. That was the big mistake. It was a failure to grasp the true nature of markets and how they work and assuming that housing need would be met by the 'invisible hand' of the free market. This property market and 'real estate' economics approach to housing as investment asset has taken over since then. It views housing as a 'unit', a commodity, where supply is to be determined by financial demand and profitability. 'Demand' does not actually express the real housing need that people have, but only what people can afford to pay, so if you can't afford the market prices, you are not included in the 'demand' figures, and you become invisible in the property market economics approach to housing.

But that approach has obliterated the social, health and psychological importance of home, and has led to this worsening crisis. To get ourselves out of this crisis we have to take a different approach to housing. We need to think differently about housing, property and economics, to understand that housing's fundamental role and value is its use as a home, not its value as a financial asset to be profited from.

The property economics approach to housing is also based on the *homo economicus* view of housing: that it is the individual's responsibility to source it in the marketplace. There is no role for society or the welfare state. In this view people are assumed to be individualistic, rational, utility-maximizing and profit-oriented. But this is a flawed understanding of human beings, especially when it comes to housing. People need a home; they cannot live without it. It's not like deciding to buy a car or a TV. That is why there is such apparently irrational behaviour when it comes to spending so much on buying or renting a home. People are desperate for a secure home, so they will pay what they have to, and can, and beyond that, to get a home. The investor funds know that. That's why they want to get into housing.

The social impacts of the crisis

Using a social policy, health and psychological lens to view housing, we put a greater focus on considering the human impact and devastation of the housing crisis. We take a deeper look at the social costs, not just economic value and Excel sheets of supply and demand. The long-term health and broader economic costs and implications emerge, such as the growing inequalities in society. But treating housing this way also reveals a potential for decent, affordable housing for everyone to help address our key societal challenges – including mental health, physical health, inequality – and of course the climate and environment.

Inequality has become one of the biggest concerns in public and social policy. It has profoundly negative impacts on people and societies, and it destabilizes economies. We have seen the political and social implications of this generational inequality in the USA, and we are starting to see it here too. The current house prices and rents are unsustainable economically and socially. This is the first generation since the foundation of the Irish State in 1921 to be worse off than their parents. At a time of unprecedented wealth and technological advances, that is an utter failure of policy, economics and politics.

Ireland has a world-class public education system that gives every child an equally high quality education, regardless of economic background, with additional resources targeted in schools in areas of disadvantage. We have a public health system that provides healthcare, with challenges, gaps and delays, but on an increasingly universal basis. However, it is in our housing system that inequality in Ireland really grows like poison ivy. It is ripping apart the social cohesion and sinews of society that bind us together. It was exposed during the Covid pandemic, when we were not 'all in it together'. Levels of Covid were highest where housing problems were worst.

Inequality is also growing as global wealth funds make hundreds of millions in rent from tenants who are pushed into poverty. Inequality is growing between those who can get a deposit from the bank of mum and dad and can buy a home, and the majority of people stuck in private rental transferring their income to become wealth for investors, or delaying adulthood and independence living in their parents' home.

Looking at housing from the social perspective puts a greater focus on the harshest inequalities that have emerged in the housing crisis, most especially homelessness. A staggering 15,000 children have been made homeless with their families in the last eight years. They are forced to live for months, even years, in inappropriate homeless emergency accommodation – hotels, B&Bs and Family Hubs. It is estimated that close to 30,000 children and their families suffered the trauma of the loss of their home in Ireland in recent years. They experienced some part of the many aspects of homelessness, either being evicted, going into overcrowded housing, or going into hidden homelessness, even on a temporary basis. Homelessness is identified in psychology as an adverse childhood experience (ACE) that has potentially lifelong implications. Babies don't have enough space to learn to crawl, children don't have the room to develop, they are filled with shame, they don't admit to their friends where they live. They don't invite friends to their birthday parties. They become anxious, withdrawn, feel 'out of control', consumed with worry and unable to focus on and enjoy their childhood.

How is it acceptable that the Irish State allows this trauma to be inflicted on tens of thousands of children in this country, one of the wealthiest in the world? It is utterly unacceptable. As a society we should not tolerate even one child being homeless. The high numbers of children being made homeless in Ireland today is a case of state failure and a violation of the basic human rights of these children.

We also have to consider the hugely devastating impacts on the mental health of people stuck in their parents' home. Their housing situation hangs like a dark cloud over them; they have less independence; their ability to develop into a full adult, to have a family of their own, is stalled, possibly indefinitely, because of the housing crisis. There are major mental health implications of not having control over your own life. Among 21- to 30-year-olds living at home with their parents, an overwhelming 93 per cent would prefer to be living separately from them. Most feel their parents won't treat them as an adult until they move out. Seventy-six per cent of 21- to 30-year-old women living at home said they do not have enough privacy. And their parents are suffering too, watching their adult children suffering from the fear that they will never have a home of their own.

The housing crisis also has other social impacts that are often not adequately thought about or considered in policy. Those working in domestic abuse services highlight that the crisis impacts on the ability of victims to leave situations of domestic violence. They are trapped in abusive relationships, in part because of the lack of availability of homes. People are being put into situations of risk in overcrowded rental housing, and disgustingly some landlords have advertised 'sex for rent'. Couples have spoken about putting off having children until they have a secure home of their own, and then reaching the point where it is too late. Other couples have put all their savings into IVF and then been unable to afford a deposit. The very fundamental desire to have a child, the ability and capacity to feel secure enough to start a family, to bring a child into the world, to build a future, has been taken away from people because of the lack of a secure, affordable home.

Then there are the multiple crises within the housing crisis. People with disabilities locked out of accessible homes, waiting for years for appropriate housing. Travellers suffering discrimination, being made homeless or stuck in substandard accommodation sites. Asylum seekers granted refugee status and permission to remain in Ireland but unable to leave the inhumane direct provision system because of the lack of affordable housing.

Ending the property addiction

It might appear that there is no end in sight to this crisis. But I believe we are at the beginning of the end of the crisis. That is because a profound value shift is under way in Irish people's attitude to housing that will, in the coming years, lead to a transformative change in policy and housing delivery. The question is how long this will take to translate into politics and policy, and how much of a change it will bring about. This is the hope, and challenge, for the coming years.

What is this shift in attitudes to housing? It is a dramatic change in the way we look at and think about housing. It is fundamentally different from the view of housing as an investment asset. People now do not care about a mythical 'property ladder' or potential future property values; many do not even want to own a property. What they want is a home of their own, in a place where they want to live, that is affordable and secure for as long as they need it. They don't care if their house doubles in value or whether landlords are making sufficient profit to invest. They are not looking for an investment asset. They want a home. And this is a seismic change in attitudes to housing in Ireland. But this new value shift clashes with the way housing is talked about and treated in Ireland – as your property investment. This is a clash of values. And we need to talk about it, because this generation is the one that has it right. Its view of housing as a home, as a human right, is the one that can get us out of this crisis and set us on a path so that we never see a repeat of the Irish housing disaster that has been ongoing for twenty years now, one of boom (1990s–2007), bust (2008–2013) and boom (2014–202?). We know what comes next.

The value clash is not as divided across the generations as it might seem. Older generations are also undergoing a major values shift. Even homeowners who until recently might have considered rising prices positively are seeing them through their children's eyes. You might be in your fifties, sixties or seventies, and your adult children could still be living at home. Increasingly, the homeowner generation is realizing that their children have no prospect of finding a home in this current approach to housing. What is the point in knocking around in a house worth half a million when your kids are paying €2,000 rent a month with no prospect of stability or affordability, not to mention the prospect of not having grandchildren owing to your own children's reluctance to start a family when without a home of their own.

Many homeowners were also burned during the Celtic Tiger years and they know that things have to change. When the Celtic Tiger was in full swing, everyone who had a bit of money was told to go and buy a property – the banks shoved money at everyone. As a nation we were trained to watch the value of our property. Middle-class homeowners became property speculators and investors. We were going to win big on the property market gamble. But the financial crash taught Irish people a harsh lesson about what happens when you treat housing as an investment commodity and as an asset – thousands of people lose their homes, the economy crashes, and society is devastated.

Now we need to move this value shift that is going on in people's hearts and minds into a national conversation and social movement. We need to change the national conversation about housing. Too many of us still think of it as property, an investment, an asset. We think of the property ladder and how much our house is 'worth'. But the property ladder is the problem. There are no rungs on it for the current generation. The question for us all now is – is this the type of country we want our children to grow up in? Is this the type of country we want to grow old in?

Taking action

The locked-out generation who are being denied a secure, affordable home of their own are standing up for themselves and taking innovative action, despite the huge personal toll the crisis is taking, and despite the narrative that both blames and ignores them. We have protested and highlighted the crisis and younger generations increasingly vote for non-traditional political parties. In 2016, young people were central in the Apollo House occupation that converted the NAMA building into a homeless shelter; the Take Back the City movement of 2019 saw young people occupying derelict buildings in Mountjoy Square to highlight the injustice whereby thousands of properties are left vacant while many people do not have a home. For the first time in Ireland a renters' union has been set up to organize private renters and others affected by the housing crisis into a community and assert their rights. Walking tours of dereliction in Cork and Dublin have captured the public imagination. Younger generations are making housing a major political issue, seeking alternative policies, and a value shift to treating housing as a human right. We have seen similar movements in relation to the issues of marriage equality and abortion, as well as in our changing attitude to prioritizing and de-stigmatising mental health. Younger generations have driven a profound change in Irish society's values and priorities. Housing, as a human right for all, is the new equality movement, and it is badly needed.

Solutions

We are still at a point where the crisis can be stopped and where we can avoid a housing dystopia before it's too late. For most of the twentieth century the Irish State built homes for people and actively subsidized people to buy their home. If the State did it before, why can't it do so again? The Irish State still has a huge amount of land on which it can build affordable homes. The investor funds can be stopped. We can make housing a human right, and ensure that

everyone has an affordable home of their own that is also environmentally sustainable. But the housing ship needs to be turned
quickly. That demands a societal shift in how we understand, think
about and treat housing. It needs Generation Locked-out to realize
they do not have to accept this. This is not normal. This is not okay.
It does not have to be like this. It can be very different.

We have an unprecedented opportunity to really tackle the biggest
societal and environmental challenges facing us – through housing.
Housing can play a part in addressing three of the major existential
crises – climate change, mental health and social inequality.

Through a new vision for our housing system, based on ensuring
environmentally sustainable, affordable, high-quality homes for all,
we can make a major leap forward to meet our climate targets in a
socially inclusive way. There is a real danger that in the transition to
a zero carbon future, those most suffering from housing inequalities
will also have to pay the highest price – those unable to afford the
cost of retrofitting their homes, and tenants in the private rental
sector who have no input in retrofitting and landlords with no obligation to retrofit. They will be pushed further into energy poverty.

Through housing we can address isolation and give people hope
and a stake in the future, by involving them in creating places, in
creating community, in overcoming the alienation of the age of
social media.

We need a referendum to put the right to housing in the
Constitution, to have a national conversation, to decide our priorities.

An alternative policy path is required. We must develop a new
vision for an active and inclusive role for the State in delivering
housing, making the State central once more to home building. The
vision must be built on the recognition that the treatment of housing
in policy, public narrative, the economy, politics and societal values
as a financialized commodity, as an investment asset, results in our
hamster wheel of a housing system in constant crisis and worsening
inequality.

In this post-Covid stage we have to address the social inequalities
the pandemic highlighted. People have come to realize that they

want access to outdoor space, to nature; to live closer to family; to be able to work remotely.

We must revalue and recreate housing into what it was for many years in this state – and what it must become again – a home. A home that provides a secure base for everyone; for children, families, individuals and communities to develop and flourish, to be healthy and secure, to fulfil their potential. That is what is possible and necessary. We must come together to achieve it.

Ultimately this comes down to you, and all of us raising our voice and taking action. It is up to us to decide that the current situation is not acceptable, that it is not right. Talk to your family, your friends, your work colleagues about how the housing crisis is impacting you and those around you, and others. There are solutions. We cannot just accept this as normal.

We have changed Ireland. We have achieved marriage equality, we repealed the Eighth, we are challenging mental health stigma and wider social inequalities. We are a country that prides itself in being caring, inclusive and holding dear the value of social justice. It is time to make these the dominant values in housing. Everyone should have a home, a gaff of their own, a place where they can feel secure, where they can feel they have a future. You have the right to a home – you can make it happen. As Nelson Mandela said, 'It always seems impossible until it's done.' So let's get this done.

Chapter 2
How Did We Get Here?

Ireland hasn't always had a housing crisis. Our current state of affairs is far from normal. Ireland made incredible achievements in delivering social and affordable housing from the 1950s to the 1970s. But to get there, we went through a lot of housing hardship and learned some important lessons. This housing story starts with the Land League in the late 1880s.

Ireland's long struggle for a home

The struggle to have a home of our own is one with a long history in this country. It is deeply connected to our independence as a people and a nation. Anyone who went to primary school here will have etched into their minds an image of the eviction of a tenant farmer and his family, and the destruction of their thatched cottage, by armed police and British soldiers using a battering ram. You look at it and see the human suffering caused by being dispossessed of your home. What have you left? A few scattered possessions.

Many tenant farmers who faced rent hikes and evictions by absentee British landlords organized in the Land League. They campaigned for the 'three Fs' (fair rent, fixity of tenure and free sale). They organized rent strikes. They got local communities to band together and ostracize the landlords. This is where the term 'boycott' originates, from actions by the Land League in 1881 against Captain Charles Boycott, a landlord who was evicting farmers in south Mayo. If you are a renter it will no doubt be intriguing to recall that boycotting landlords, along with the rent strikes, became one of the most effective methods of campaigning by tenants. An idea for dealing with rogue landlords in the twenty-first century, perhaps. The Land League was successful, and the Labourers (Ireland) Act 1906 was passed, which resulted in some of the first 'public' housing being built by the Irish State as county councils were funded to build over 40,000 new rural cottages, each on an acre of land.

In the nineteenth and early twentieth centuries, our cities, especially Dublin and Limerick, had some of the worst slum housing conditions in Europe. James Connolly described 'the housing accommodation of the Dublin workers' as 'a disgrace to the City', with 'high rents and vile sanitary arrangements'. A fascinating report from 1914, *An Inquiry into the Housing Conditions of the Working Classes of Dublin*, shows how bad things were. There were tenement houses all over Dublin, from Francis Street and The Coombe to Gardiner Street and Dominick Street. The report found 1,518 tenements with 22,701 people living in them. They were classed as 'unfit for human habitation', and landlords were criticized for their poor treatment of tenants. The report found that tenements developed in houses 'which were built to accommodate one family' but 'have been taken over by landlords who farm them out, without in any way making them suitable for the purpose, in one-, two-, or three-roomed dwellings'. So landlords were maximizing the rent they could make, with no consideration of the impact on the tenants. Those living in the worst tenements explained they couldn't find anywhere else because 'having a family of young children rendered it very difficult to get a good class of dwelling, landlords having an objection to take in tenants with young families'. It is sad to see history repeating itself today; some families in Dublin become homeless because some landlords do not want to rent to families with children. It is an important lesson – relying on 'for profit' private landlords for housing means that low-income households, particularly families with children, suffer.

Another parallel with today's housing crisis is the strong links between politics and housing that was also evident back then. Some elected politicians, just like today, were also landlords. In 1914, some of the elected members of Dublin Corporation were landlord owners of tenement houses classed as 'third class property' and 'unfit for human habitation'.

Back then, too, state bodies were reluctant to tackle mistreatment of tenants by private landlords. Laws on rental standards were not rigorously enforced. The 1914 report mentioned widespread 'non-enforcement of the sanitary laws', which 'permitted dwellings which are not fit for habitation to be inhabited by the poorer classes'. And this lack of state oversight created owners with 'little sense of their responsibilities as landlords'. This is an important part of our history. We need to relearn the lessons of our housing past from a century ago. Poor housing standards, exploitation and unaffordable homes is what you get if you leave housing up to the market.

The other lesson is how fundamental housing is to our health. In the late nineteenth century, the Irish State, and other governments around the world, built housing as a public health measure. The link between bad conditions and overcrowded housing and ill-health and disease was being established. The 1914 report pointed out that there was little point sending patients with tuberculosis to 'sanatoria fitted with all modern appliances' and then 'allowing them back to housing conditions' that had caused the disease in the first place. It also highlighted the financial savings from providing proper housing: 'if decent and proper houses were provided for the people, much saving might thereby be effected both to the State and Municipality by the . . . almost certain consequent reduction in crime and sickness.'

And just like the property industry lobbyists of today, back in 1914 the private business interests and landlords argued that city councils and the State should not take on building homes on a major scale. They argued that 'every encouragement should be given to private enterprise' to do it. But the report concludes by making a point that is as relevant today as it was then. It said that while private enterprise 'would have to some extent supplied the deficiency of housing', there was, in fact, 'little hope that it would be . . . sufficient to grapple with the present needs' for housing. It is incredible to see the same debates today about letting the market economics of supply and demand fix housing. The report noted, 'We are aware that it is held that from a strict economic point of view the sound attitude [would be] to allow the problem to be solved by the ordinary law of supply and demand.' It concluded, however, that the 'strict economic treatment of the [housing] question does not meet the necessities' of the crisis. In other words, the private market failed to provide homes to people because the economics of the free market doesn't ensure housing for working people and the poor. Therefore, the State, as the 1914 report makes clear, 'has a duty' and a 'responsibility' to provide housing.

The rise of the State as home builder

The new Irish Free State responded to the 1914 report recommendations and the lessons of the tenements by building homes on a huge scale. The 1922 'Million Pound Scheme' supported local authorities to construct 2,000 houses for purchase in just two years. As part of this scheme Dublin Corporation built the famous Marino estate, on the model of the garden city, as public housing for the working classes in 1924. Today the Marino estate is sought after by those with families for its green space and community design. Three-bedroomed terraced houses there are regularly sold for over €450,000.

Between 1914 and 1945, Europe and the USA experienced two world wars and a massive economic crash. A new school of economics and thinking about how economies should work, led by economist John Maynard Keynes, was growing in influence. Keynesian economics became the dominant way in which governments ran their economies for the next thirty years. Keynes argued, as did many trade unions, socialists and social democratic parties, that governments' core responsibility were to ensure that people had access to the basic needs of healthcare, education, housing and social welfare support. Central to Keynes' economic theory was that if you rely on the market – the private sector – to provide things like housing, health and education, you will have regular economic crashes (booms and busts), unmet social needs and rampant inequalities. That is because leaving these sectors of the economy to be run for private profit will result in the provision of services that only make a profit, and services that are not profitable, such as housing for lower-income households, will not be delivered. So the *State* must ensure that there is sufficient funding for the provision of the core social areas of the welfare state – housing, health and education. They are essential to providing everyone's basic human needs. Ireland did not adopt this Keynesian approach to the delivery of health and education services, leaving them largely up to the Church, but it did implement an Irish version of it in the delivery of housing.

What the Irish State achieved in housing from the 1940s to the 1970s was nothing short of astounding. For example, in 1950 alone, 7,787 houses were built by local authorities and 4,518 by private enterprise. That is over four times the number of social houses that the government built in 2018. In the same year, the population of Ireland was just 2.8 million. Today, with a population of 5 million, the State would need to be building around 14,000 social housing units per year to be at the equivalent level we were building back in the 1950s, but it only builds about 3,000 social homes per year. Back in the 1950s and 1960s, local authorities were building housing from scratch themselves, often directly employing their own trades-people. In this way, the new social housing was adding a supply of affordable housing that was additional to the supply of homes coming from the private house-building market. This is a funda-mental role that social housing should play, and it did play that role for a long time – until the 1980s. And, as we will see later, this move away from social housing being built by the State is at the heart of why we are in crisis today.

Through the 1950s and up to the 1980s, the Irish State provided home ownership to a wide section of the population through grants and low-cost loans to builders, tax relief and low-cost mortgages to home purchasers; and it sold local authority homes to tenants at a discounted rate. Public utility societies and co-operatives were given state grants to build homes. A home purchaser could recoup almost 30 per cent of the cost of a standard suburban house from the government. Grants and government-backed home-purchase loans continued until the 1980s. These policies resulted in the level of home ownership increasing from 52 per cent in 1946 to 59 per cent in 1961 and to 68 per cent in 1971. This can be described as a 'de-commodified' form of home ownership; there was very little profit-taking and private market involvement in the financing and building of housing. Housing is delivered like a commodity when all parts of the housing process, from lending finance, to the sale of land, to building and selling, are treated as profit-making business enterprises. But the State had removed large parts of this private profit-making business from delivering housing, so it was treated not as a commodity but more like a public good or public service. Provision was based on meeting housing and social need, not on profitability.

As a result, at this time, there was a major decline in private renting and private landlords. When people had other options – social housing and state-provided affordable home ownership – they chose these, not private rental. In the 1940s, 25 per cent of households were in the private rental sector. This declined to 17 per cent in the 1960s, and just 13 per cent in 1971. The withdrawal of private landlords was not seen as a bad thing, as it is today. People either owned their home or were in local authority social housing. These homes were more affordable, secure, and had higher standards than much of the private rental sector. Policymakers of today should take note.

Between the 1950s and 1970s local authorities and the National Building Agency built hugely successful housing estates across the country that provided good-quality and, importantly, life-time secure homes. People did not have to worry about the landlord evicting them. In every town and village across Ireland, from Tramore to Tralee, from

Clonmel to Carrick-on-Suir, from Ballina to Bray council houses were built and families had a place to call home. Places like Mahon in Cork, Moyross in Limerick, and Ballymun, Ballyfermot, Tallaght and Clondalkin in Dublin were built. Communities were created and thrived.

Through local authorities building homes on a huge scale, the State provided quality secure social housing and facilitated home ownership across the social classes in Ireland. The extent of this achievement, from a social and economic perspective, is very well described in an RTÉ news report from 1962 by reporter RJ Dowling. In the black and white TV clip, RJ is wearing a distinctive dark-rimmed pair of glasses and reads his notes from a slip of paper. He's reporting from a newly built corporation housing estate. He says, 'There's nothing special about these houses behind me, they are ordinary corporation houses, three bedrooms, sitting room, dining room cum kitchen, bathroom, lavatory, gardens back and front, you see them everywhere – whole towns have been built of them for the last thirty or forty years.' He looks down at his notes and reads, 'They've aroused the admiration of many people from other countries.' Then he looks to the camera and says something very profound. 'There's nothing special about them, as I said, but *they symbolize the finest thing that Ireland has ever done.*' He goes on to interview a tall man with slick black hair, wearing a neat suit, who talks to camera in a proud and confident way, his arms folded and a lit cigarette in his hand. This man is Colm O'Doherty of the Department of Local Government and head of the National Building Agency. He explains, 'The local authorities, by which I mean the corporations, the county councils, they have built some sixty thousand houses since 1948, private enterprise, in the same period, that's privately owned houses, has built fifty-eight thousand houses, that's 120,000 houses. In the same period there have been 67,000 houses reconstructed, that's rebuilt or modernized with state and local authority assistance. That gives a total of over 180,000 houses newly built or reconstructed since 1948 . . . giving roughly half a million people in the new houses.' He explains that the funding for all this housing came from the government. No reliance on private investors here. The camera gives us a wide-angle of Mr O'Doherty, a man proud of his country and its housing achievement. What would he say to us now?

Sowing the seeds of today's housing crisis: the 1980s

The Irish housing story changed drastically and for the worse in the 1970s and 1980s, when the seeds of today's housing crisis were sown. Internationally, Ronald Reagan was elected President of the United States and Margaret Thatcher became Prime Minister of Britain. They had a political belief – an ideology – that saw the state, big government, and the huge role it was playing in areas of the economy, from making cars to building houses, as a major problem. They argued that the state and public services were inefficient, and the private sector, because of its profit motivation, was much better at delivering all aspects of the economy. They wanted public services opened to private business. Margaret Thatcher had a conservative, right-wing view of society. In fact, she did not believe in society at all. She believed achievements in life came from the individual's hard work and she ignored the role of inequalities in affecting life opportunities. She blamed people in receipt of social welfare for being in poverty. She ignored the uneven playing field that exists for those born into lives of disadvantage, those struggling with poverty, ill health and discrimination. The derogatory 'welfare scroungers' narrative had begun. Thatcher believed that council housing, local authority housing, was creating welfare-dependent and lazy people. Social housing was deemed a failed form of housing for a lower class of citizen. She wanted the state to cut back support and welfare, to stop building council housing, to force people to take responsibility for themselves, stop relying on 'handouts', and become homeowners. The state was to stand back and let private enterprise take over. This neoliberal economic approach was in direct contrast to Keynesianism. Neoliberalism stemmed from an ideology that blamed and criminalized the poor for being in poverty, and placed the responsibility for poverty on the individual, rather than on structural inequalities resulting from the market economy.

In Ireland, this right-wing neoliberal thinking started to take hold in the 1980s and really took off in the 1990s. The big change happened in the mid-1980s, when in response to economic stagnation, Fianna Fáil- and Fine Gael-led governments implemented austerity budget cuts. In 1987, a newly elected Fianna Fáil government led by Charles J. Haughey cut funding for local authorities to build social housing. The new Minister for Finance, Ray MacSharry, announced in the 1987 Budget the ending of housing grant schemes and the cutting of capital spend on new building of social housing. The system where local authorities were able to borrow to build social housing was ended and replaced with grants from central government.

Responding to MacSharry's budget in the Dáil, Barry Desmond of the Labour Party described this 'slashing of the local authority house building programme' as a 'drastic step'. Another TD, Tomás Mac Giolla of the Workers' Party, outlined that the previous year's cuts under the Fine Gael–Labour government had meant all house building by Dublin Corporation had stopped; 'They are building almost no more local authority houses. They might build 15 to 30 but the 1,500 houses they used to build are a thing of the past.'

The extent of the cuts is shown by the collapse in new social housing built by local authorities from 7,002 units in 1984 to just 768 units in 1989.

At the same time, the sale of social housing to tenants continued at pace. But now, with not as many new social homes being built to replace the ones being sold, the overall social housing stock reduced significantly: 43,000 new local authority homes were built in the 1980s, but 46,000 were sold to tenants, a net loss of 3,000 social homes. With less social housing on offer, it became less available, and therefore social housing became restricted to those most at need, who were the most marginalized. This narrowing of the social mix of households in social housing is described as a process of residualization. In previous generations, social housing had been available to a much wider mix of working people.

Alongside this narrowing of provision of and access to social housing, the 1980s heroin epidemic, unemployment crisis and rising poverty were devastating disadvantaged areas. This was compounded as areas of social housing became more concentrated with those most severely affected by social and economic disadvantage. Social housing estates received increasingly negative media coverage and were labelled 'no-go areas', 'ghettos', and 'sink estates'.

It was a self-fulfilling prophecy of conservative neoliberal politics and policy. Restricting the eligibility of social housing meant that it increasingly housed only the most vulnerable and marginalized, the most poor. Then politicians, free market economists, commentators and the media further demonized social housing and the areas it was in. As a result, governments further reduced social housing budgets, broke up social housing communities, and stopped building social housing estates. All because of an ideological belief that social housing had 'failed'. Yet the evidence was not there to back that up. Social housing hadn't failed. Social housing continued to provide homes for people. What had failed was neoliberal economics that resulted in widening inequalities, poverty and fundamentally reduced social housing to a residual role that no longer housed a socially mixed population.

Rather than addressing real issues in social housing estates, such as the inadequate maintenance of social housing by local authorities, poor design and layout, the lack of community and social facilities, playgrounds, shops and transport (e.g. building homes on the outskirts of Dublin), social housing as a form of housing for those who could not afford housing from the market was demonized. The positive contribution of social housing in providing secure, quality homes and nurturing strong communities was dismissed in a full-frontal ideological assault on the very existence of public housing. It was a return to the Victorian ideas of deserving and undeserving poor. Those in (and in need of) social housing were 'othered' as undeserving. Therefore, governments stopped building social housing because 'those welfare scroungers didn't deserve it'. This stigmatization of social housing and those who lived in it was driven by an ideology and political belief that saw private business and the private market as king and saw no role for local authorities to build social housing.

But if those in need of social housing were the losers, who were the winners? They were, of course, those for whom the right-wing politicians made their policies (and who, not coincidentally, funded their political parties) – the expanding private market and private enterprise in housing, the new 'real estate' business of property speculators, private developers, banks, landowners and landlords.

Unfortunately, from the 1980s onwards, Irish policymakers and politicians took up the language and policies of neoliberal politicians in the USA and the UK and handed housing over to the private market. This policy and ideology expanded to a new level in the Celtic Tiger period.

Chapter 3
The Celtic Tiger:
Boom to Bust

Former Fianna Fáil Minister for Finance Brian Lenihan was being interviewed by RTÉ in November 2010 about the economic crash that had engulfed the country from 2008 onwards and his government's role in it. He was in defensive mode and made it clear that while mistakes were made by those in power, it was the Irish people who needed to shoulder the blame. Lenihan said, 'Let's be straight, I accept there were failures in the political system. I accept I have to take responsibility as a member of the governing party during that period for what happened, but let's be fair about it – we all partied.'

'We all partied'? This was an attempt to place the responsibility for the economic crash on the Irish people, and not on the policies and actions of big developers, banks and governments. It worked. Many people think it was our credit splurge that caused the crash. Austerity was the medicine we deserved. But that's not the truth. The truth of what actually happened is a story that helps explain why we are in the housing crisis today.

Everyone knows that if you want to fix a problem the first thing you need to do is figure out what is causing it. If there's water coming through your ceiling, you don't just put tape across the crack where the water is coming in, you go up to the attic and work out what it is. Is it a broken pipe? Or is the water tank overflowing? We have to do the same with the housing crisis. We need to really investigate it and find out how we ended up where we are. Politicians and media economists and commentators spout a lot of spin and nonsense about why and how we got here, and much of it is an attempt to deflect us from the decisions that caused the crisis. A lot of the blame lies with government policy during the Celtic Tiger boom and in the crash that followed it. There was a housing crisis then too. And it was not an accident; it didn't just appear out of nowhere. It resulted from decisions made by government and the actions of the private housing market – developers, builders, land-owners, banks, property investors, estate agents, financial advisers and investors, and landlords – all of whom were trying to maximize the profit they made from the housing market at the expense of those who needed a home. The thing is, you can't fully explain what is going on today without going back and looking at what happened then.

During the hype of the Celtic Tiger, it was not unusual to hear people (in the media, at least) talk about weekend shopping trips to New York, getting limos for first communions, buying a second house in Dublin, a holiday home in Leitrim and maybe even two in Bulgaria. Or to see advertisements for chandeliers on the back of Dublin buses. The big developers were flying by helicopter to attend the Galway Races. This was the sort of crazy exuberance that was seen during the years of the Celtic Tiger, a period of unprecedented economic growth in Ireland from 1995 to 2007.

In the mid to late 1990s, there was a real economic expansion in employment, population and wage growth, driven by export-led economic expansion in pharmaceuticals, finance, computer IT, with multinational firms playing a big role. Adding to this was a major public investment in expanding free third-level education, and building new hospitals, schools and transport infrastructure, such as motorways and the Luas, which started in 2004. But then in the early 2000s, so the story goes, the Irish people lost the run of themselves, overborrowed, and splurged, leading to a massive crash. The crazy exuberance led to ever-rising house prices.

But that's not the real story behind the crash.

The Celtic Tiger housing boom

At the heart of the Celtic Tiger was a massive housing boom fuelled by excessive lending by the banks and driven by government policy and the private property industry – in particular a small number of private developers and banks, but also small-time individual 'property investor' landlords purchasing homes to rent.

The policies that reduced the building of social housing by local authorities, which we looked at in the previous chapter, were extended further by the Fianna Fáil–Progressive Democrat (PD) government that was in power from 1997 until the crash in 2008.

Bertie Ahern was Taoiseach at the time. He wasn't much into critical self-reflection or learning from social policy analysis. In 2006, he said he didn't see a problem with the high levels of borrowing to buy property, there was no indication of difficulties, and people should keep buying houses.

The government further encouraged the shift from housing as a home to housing as an investment asset. They told people to speculate in the property market and gave tax breaks for landlords to buy a second, or third, home to rent out. These became the 'buy-to-let' investors. The banks lent massively, which added fuel to the fire of rising housing prices, until the inevitable crash.

New housing output (or supply) in Ireland grew from 19,000 new houses a year in 1993 to 39,000 in 1998. It rose again to 68,000 in 2003 and reached a staggering high point of 88,000 new homes built across Ireland in 2006. At the same time, and despite the huge increase in the supply of new houses, prices also increased by a whopping 292 per cent from 1996 to 2006.

To give a sense of the scale in increase in house prices, let's look at averages over time. In 1995, house prices were four times the average wage. Just four years later, in 1999, house prices had jumped to seven times the average wage nationally, and in Dublin house prices had spiked to nine times the average wage. By 2003 house prices had grown nationally to eight times the average wage and in Dublin to almost 11 times the average wage.

Here is an important lesson. A huge rise in the supply of housing doesn't necessarily lead to lower house prices and more affordable homes. It shows the claim by the property economists that rising supply leads to falling house prices is not always true.

Banks were fuelling the boom by throwing mortgages at home buyers. They were giving out 110 per cent mortgages – they would lend you the entire cost of the home, and give you 10 per cent extra on top for investing in the home, a car, a holiday, no deposit needed.

But the really important untold story is that the banks weren't just throwing money at young couples to buy a home, as we will see later, they were massively lending to people to buy a second, or third (or fourth) property to buy and rent out, through a buy-to-let mortgage. These were Ireland's first round of landlord property investors. The banks also lent to developers to build offices, hotels, golf courses, and to buy up land and property in Ireland and around the world. The borrowing of the six main Irish banks – Bank of Ireland, Allied Irish Banks, Anglo Irish Bank, Irish Life & Permanent, Irish Nationwide Building Society and Educational Building Society – grew from less than €16bn in 2003 to approximately €100bn by 2007. This was like adding rocket fuel to the engine of house prices from 2003 to 2007.

And what was the Taoiseach's view of those who criticized the policies that were supporting the housing boom of the time? In July 2006, Bertie Ahern said, 'Sitting on the sidelines or on the fence, cribbing and moaning, is a lost opportunity. I don't know how people who engage in that don't commit suicide because, quite frankly, the only thing that motivates me is being able to actually change something.'

The Fianna Fáil government had become very close to many of the big developers who were driving the building boom of new houses – most were giant new estates on the outskirts of towns, cities and in commuter belts – as well as shopping centres and offices across the country. There was a famous fundraising event at the Galway Races where developers and other big business types paid up to €4,000 a table to have dinner with Bertie Ahern and the Fianna Fáil ministers.

Fianna Fail's coalition partner, the PDs, led by Mary Harney and Michael McDowell, were close followers of Margaret Thatcher's neoliberal agenda and were notoriously anti-state and anti-social housing. Michael McDowell argued that inequality was beneficial as a way to motivate people. 'A dynamic liberal economy like ours demands flexibility and inequality in some respects to function,' he stated. Such inequality 'provides incentives . . . Driven to a complete extreme, the current rights culture and equality notion would create a feudal society.' He believed that inequality is not only acceptable, but actually serves a function to motivate people. Therefore, the PDs were not supportive of policies to reduce inequality, such as social and affordable housing.

Of course, inequality needed to be justified during the Celtic Tiger period because it was rising rapidly as Ireland saw the emergence of a super-wealthy club of businessmen, bankers and developers. A lot of their wealth was made off the backs of people getting saddled in debt trying to buy a home and the increasing numbers of people having to rent from private landlords as they couldn't afford to buy and there was no social housing available.

Bankers' pay reached outlandish levels as the top executives of the banks were rewarded handsomely for overseeing a huge expansion of lending. That lending grew as house prices increased. The boss of AIB was paid €2.4m in salary and bonus for 2006. The CEO of Anglo Irish Bank had a total remuneration package of €3m at the time, including a bonus of €1.8m. In 2007, Bank of Ireland's chief executive, with a total wage package of €4m, was one of the highest paid people in Ireland.

The higher the house prices, the more the banks could lend and the more they benefited. It was a virtuous cycle for the banks, but a dangerous and toxic cycle for Irish society. In 2007, the average new mortgage was €266,000, nearly double the 2002 figure. The total mortgage debt in Ireland increased from €47.2bn in 2002 to over €139.8bn at the end of 2007. Higher house prices. Higher mortgage lending. Higher profits for the banks and salaries for the CEOs. But more debt for Irish home buyers.

Developers

The others to make the most of the housing boom were the Irish developers. The banks, particularly Anglo Irish Bank, were lending billions to developers to invest in property from housing to hotels, offices, shopping centres, golf courses and, of course, land. Lots of land. It was reported that twelve developers owned 90 per cent of the land in and around Dublin at the height of the Celtic Tiger.

Here is what we know about some of the developers at the time.

Developer Liam Carroll reportedly had €1bn in assets and was Ireland's tenth wealthiest person in 2006. Carroll's Zoe Developments was responsible for developing a lot of apartments in Dublin. They were criticized as being very small. Building smaller apartments maximizes the number of units you can get on a site within height restrictions, and therefore increases profits. Planning laws were changed after the crash to try to make apartments bigger with a liveable space. But then the developers leaned again on the Minister for Housing and apartment guidelines were reduced in 2016.

It is interesting that developers and real estate property tycoons always want to build big. High rise means you can squeeze more units onto the site. High rise means high profit for property developers. It's also about wealth. Historically, wealth was held mainly in property, and property size was a symbol of wealth and power.

Another developer, Sean Mulryan, then the thirteenth richest person in Ireland, had €820m, and owned Ballymore Properties. At its peak, Ballymore had a £15bn development plan in Britain, Ireland and Europe.

Trailing after Mulryan were Johnny Ronan and Richard Barrett, with €620m. 'They jointly owned Treasury Holdings Group as well as the National Treasury Management Agency (NTMA) headquarters (the agency that manages the assets and liabilities of the Government of Ireland) on Grand Canal Street, Dublin 2. Treasury controlled more than 131 property projects with a total value of over €4.6bn. In 2004, Treasury bought a 60 per cent stake in the €595m Battersea Power Station in London.

The Sisk family, Ireland's biggest building contractor, came in at number 24 in Ireland's rich list with €455m. Joe O'Reilly and Liam

Maye were worth a mere €230m; the Longford duo ran Castlethorn Construction, which built Dundrum Town Centre, Ireland's biggest shopping centre, and developments in Adamstown, west Dublin. O'Reilly's company, Chartered Land, sold the retail element of the South King Street scheme in Dublin 2 to Anglo Irish Bank for €101m at the peak of the property boom.

Bernard McNamara, a resident of Dublin's plush Ailesbury Road, one of the best-known Irish property developers, built up debts of about €1.5bn during the boom. He part-owned a number of hotels, including the Shelbourne Hotel, and development properties and was involved in the disastrous €400m purchase of the Irish Glass Bottle site in Dublin's Docklands. The Dublin Docklands Development Authority, a state agency, was also in the consortium.

Gerry Gannon, another developer, giving evidence at the 2014 trial of three former directors of Anglo Irish Bank, was asked if he had been one of Ireland's biggest property developers in 2008 and whether his net worth had approached €1bn. 'Probably, yeah,' he replied. He co-owned the K Club golf resort at Straffan, County Kildare, with businessman Michael Smurfit. The two acquired the resort for €115m from the then Jefferson Smurfit Group in 2005.

Cork developer Michael O'Flynn, chairman and managing director of O'Flynn Construction, developed the high-end residential development the Elysian in Cork City, at 68 metres Ireland's tallest building at the time. The company had an estimated €1bn worth of projects under way in Ireland and abroad.

Developers also engaged in buying up land on a speculative basis. They would buy the land under agricultural or other zoning, and seek to get it rezoned as residential or retail, which would massively increase the value of the land. The local council, planners and councillors made the decisions on rezoning land in their areas. So, as the planning tribunals revealed, developers would sometimes grease the planning decision wheels with bribes to elected councillors and officials. Developers also speculated by bidding with each other for prime land, which also inflated land prices. Higher land prices means higher house prices.

The media, estate agents and financial 'advisers'

Developers weren't the only ones making huge profits from the rising cost of housing. The media and estate agents also made big money off the property boom. Weekend newspapers had expansive, full-colour spreads on housing and property (we can see today that the property sections in some newspapers have returned) and they sold advertising space in these property sections.

Estate agents act as intermediaries, arranging the buying, selling, renting and leasing of property and land. They are paid on a fee or contract basis, often in commission, and so are incentivized to get higher prices. More transactions (house sales) in the market and higher house prices lead to higher revenue and profits. For example, the housing and letting website MyHome.ie was set up in 2001 by estate agents Sherry FitzGerald, the Gunne Group and Douglas Newman Good. MyHome.ie had a turnover of €6.2m in the mid-2000s. In 2006 the Myhome.ie property website was bought by the *Irish Times* for €50m.

Irish estate agents and property advisers are also global businesses. In 1998, Sherry FitzGerald joined with the global property advisory firm DTZ Holdings, which in 2016 was taken over by Cushman & Wakefield. Remember the name Cushman & Wakefield – it will come up again when we look at the entry of the investor funds. Another example of the dizzying heights the property real estate sector reached is that the directors of one estate agent, Lisney, were paid €5.9m in 2006 – an almost 50 per cent increase in one year.

Another, Hamilton Osborne King, reported a turnover of €35.7m and pre-tax profit of €7.8m in 2005. It was bought for a cool €50m by UK-based property advice firm Savills in 2006, when Ireland was viewed as having one of the 'most dynamic housing markets'.

The range of stakeholders making a tidy profit during the boom included mortgage brokers, financial advisers, financial investment firms, property analysts and fund managers, who invest and advise on investing. Mortgage brokers and financial advisers make money when people are taking out mortgages or investing in property. They work on commission, so the higher the prices, the higher the lending, the higher the mortgages, the more they make. The more buying and selling and investing, the better.

Another example is Davy Stockbrokers. Davy is Ireland's largest stockbroker, wealth manager, asset manager and financial adviser. Property investment and advice is a big part of its business. It has had a well-documented controversial history with claims of tax evasion, bribery and payments to politicians, and insider trading.

These businesses do well in a high-turnover, high-value sales market. It is not the case that all estate agents and brokers are money-chasing, property-fuelling agents – but that's how their business makes money. And so, when they give advice in the media on what the government should or should not do, we should always be wary and question their motives. They are not impartial; understandably, their priority is the financial interest of their business. They rarely promote affordable housing or more social housing – for many of them, that would mean less business and less profit. Because when you are in the business of housing as property and real estate, essentially more affordable housing and more government building of housing is bad. Higher house prices and a bigger private market is good. It's just business for them, it's not about homes. It's about real estate. So the more housing is turned over to the private market, and the higher house prices rise, the more money can be made by all the different private businesses involved in the housing chain, from land to finance to development, as they turn our homes into money-making commodities.

The Celtic Tiger housing crisis

The Celtic Tiger is generally thought of as a property boom, but it was also a housing crisis. And it has remarkable similarities to today's housing crisis. This should make us sit up and think about what actually happened then. Just like today, it didn't appear out of thin air. It was caused by policy failure and market success. A housing crisis is not market failure – the market is just doing what the market will always do. It will be as successful as possible for private developers and property investors, but it will always be a failure for those in need of a home.

Why did house prices get so high? A big part of the story is because there were no alternative ways for people to get a home other than to buy one from the private developers in the market. There was no choice of lending, other than to get it from the commercial banks. There was no social or affordable housing provision on any significant scale that would have taken the pressure off the housing market, or government-provided affordable lending. Fianna Fail and the PDs together drove the nails into the coffins of social and affordable housing delivery in this period and handed housing over to the market, the private developers and landlords, who were also, surprise surprise, active funders of both parties. The production and availability of housing was handed over to be controlled by those whose only ultimate interest was profit, not meeting the social need for housing.

In the 1970s, the Irish Government built 61,953 social homes. In the 1990s, just 20,184 social homes were built. In 1975, local authorities were providing one-third of total new housing being built in the country. But at the height of the Celtic Tiger, just 6 per cent of new housing built in the country was social housing.

If housing was a game of hurling, what happened between 2002 and 2007 was that the private sector lined out with a full team of fifteen Kilkenny hurlers while the Irish State sent out just one player. But in fact they weren't even on opposing teams. The private sector was given a walkover to take over the housing game in Ireland. The market (banks, developers, investors) was handed the complete provision of housing. The private sector built and financed 92.5 per cent of all homes in those years. The State all but withdrew, building a miniscule 7.5 per cent of all homes. This was the lowest amount of social and affordable (public) housing built in Ireland since the days of the tenements. It was a return to the Victorian days of private dominance and state failure to deliver housing. And just look what resulted when the market (the private banks and developers) was given complete control of our housing system. It wrecked the country.

Additionally, the ongoing policy of selling local authority housing to tenants meant that, with virtually no new social housing, there was an overall decline in social housing stock. More than 240,000 local authority houses were sold under the various tenant purchase schemes. With very little social housing available, those locked out of buying a home had nowhere to go but into the private rental sector. And so private rents rose in this period, from €600 a month in 1997 to €870 in 2002 – a 45 per cent increase in just five years. And given the lack of social housing, higher rents and house prices, there was a massive 40 per cent jump in those on the social housing waiting lists, from 27,427 households in 1997, to 39,176 in 1999, to 50,715 by 2004, an 85 per cent jump in just seven years.

There was a further big change in the early 2000s, when the Irish State, through local authorities, started to become a big purchaser and renter of homes from the private market. This added to house price pressure as it was an additional housing 'demand'. It began using the private rental sector for social housing. This was a fundamental shift in social housing delivery and policy from bricks (building social housing) to benefits (getting social housing from the private rental sector through welfare payments – housing benefits – being paid to private landlords).

In 2003, local authorities built 4,000 homes but bought 900 homes from the market, and got 500 from the rental market. So in 2003 just over a quarter of new social housing was coming from the market. But in 2007, they built 5,000 but bought 2,000 from the market, and got 3,000 from the private rental market. By 2007, then, half of all new social homes were coming from the market.

Rent supplement was a state payment to cover rental costs for those who were unemployed or on low incomes and who couldn't afford the rent in the private rental sector. But as social house building declined housing need was increasing dramatically (as we saw in the rise in social housing waiting lists). This meant that those on low incomes in need of social housing were churned into the private rental sector using the rent supplement payment. And increasingly, those in the private rental sector who couldn't cover rising rents also needed this payment. As a result, the number of people receiving rent supplement increased by 110 per cent between 1994 and 2003 (from 28,800 to 59,976). By 2006, over a third of all private rental households were in receipt of rent supplement.

In 2004, these payments to landlords to house tenants in the private rental sector became classified as an actual form of permanent social housing. A new scheme, the Rental Accommodation Scheme (RAS), was set up whereby the local authority and the landlord would make an agreement for long-term rental. The meaning of social housing was fundamentally altered. It was no longer local authorities building social homes that offered tenants a lifetime tenancy in local authority council housing; instead, private landlords were being paid for tenants to stay temporarily in the private rental sector.

This is the big shift in housing policy that no longer gave a role to local authorities to build housing and decided that the private market should be given the monopoly of delivery of housing, for all sectors of society, from high earners to the lowest incomes.

The government's other main response to the housing crisis at the time was the introduction of Part V of the Planning and Development Act 2000. This new measure required, as a condition for planning permission, that private developers transfer up to 20 per cent of the land or housing in a new-build housing development to local authorities for social and affordable housing.

Noel Ahern, the Minister of State for Housing and Urban Renewal from 2002 to 2007, and brother of Bertie Ahern, introduced Part V to the Dáil. Speaking in February 2000 he argued that the measure was needed as the 'trends in house prices are, in the long run, profoundly damaging to social cohesion and future economic well-being'. He went on to explain the need for the State to provide social and affordable homes:

> The provision of adequate housing for all members of society has been a major issue of public policy for Governments of all shades since the State gained its independence. It has further been a

traditional aim of Government to facilitate people in buying their own homes where this is possible. This has had a beneficial stabilizing effect on society, and home ownership is an aspiration which the vast majority of people hold dearly. . . . [T]he State also has a responsibility to assist those who cannot afford to house themselves and this has been done through the provision of local authority or other social housing. Part V is designed to underpin these two planks of the housing policy.

A big part of the justification for Part V was the idea of social mixing and integrating social and affordable housing with private housing estates to achieve 'more inclusive communities'. Some used the derogatory language of avoiding 'developing ghettos of local authority houses'. A Fine Gael senator explained their support for Part V: 'We must ensure no more ghettos are built, such as those in the 1970s where all those in the social housing sector were confined to specific areas.'

The other argument for Part V was that as land went up significantly in value when it was rezoned by planners for development, landowners and developers gained that value increase. They also gained from the infrastructure (water, roads, etc.) that was put in to make land useable to build homes. So the State should recoup some of that gain by getting 20 per cent of the land, but not at the market value of the land (which would be expensive) but at its existing use value (i.e. cheaper). This was a way to provide local authorities with cheaper land to build social and affordable housing.

But then, through the latter half of 2000 and into 2001, in response to Part V, developers undertook a form of 'strike' by stopping putting forward sites for planning permission. They were flexing their muscles, showing who was boss and who controlled housing delivery in Ireland. And they were showing where their interests really lay – in maximizing profit from housing.

Some counties, like Cork, Limerick and Kerry, saw planning applications dry up completely; others, such as Meath, Wicklow and Kildare, saw planning applications fall by as much as 60 per cent. The developers engaged in massive lobbying of government politicians (and of political parties they funded). It was argued that building social and affordable housing in private estates would lead to a drop in prices of the houses nearby because of the stigma attached to it.

'Who would want to buy next to social housing?' they said. It would force down house prices and therefore profits. So what happened? The government capitulated to the developer and land-owner lobby and, as always with policy, the devil is in the outcome and delivery. Or, in this case, the lack of delivery. Never be wooed or fooled by nice words in policy. The Fianna Fáil–PD government changed Part V in December 2002 to allow local authorities to opt out of enforcing the on-site 20 per cent rule and instead allowed developers to give the local authority the equivalent in cash or land or houses somewhere else.

This is how the developers won the housing battle of the Celtic Tiger. If it had been implemented, Part V could have played a role in avoiding the crash. Businessman and senator Feargal Quinn spoke in the Seanad about what happened: 'The builders seem to have won once again. There is a price for letting builders off the hook. However, we can be sure they will not pay the price. The customers will pay, as they have always done.'

It's a pity the government did not listen to Senator Kathleen O'Meara of the Labour Party:

Part V is fundamental because it attempts to tackle one of the most significant problems thrown up by the failure to address the housing problems in this country and represents a very important aspect of social policy, namely that we must provide affordable housing for those who cannot compete in the market.

She went on to say, just as the 1914 report had recommended:

The State has a duty and responsibility to intervene to ensure social and affordable housing is provided where the market fails to do so. It is not surprising that there was massive resistance to the provision from the building industry, which has been doing extraordinarily well from the current boom. I am surprised at the rapid and extraordinary capitulation of the Government to the resistance of the building industry to Part V of the Act.

Part V ended up playing an almost negligible role in the delivery of social and affordable housing. If it had been left in place it could potentially have provided 50,000 social and affordable homes. Instead, it provided just 2,400 social housing and 5,000 affordable units over 2004 to 2007.

The regeneration game

At the same time the government was claiming it wanted to increase (through Part V) the amount of land local authorities had to build social housing, it was actually forcing local authorities to sell off public land to developers through another new policy, public–private partnerships (PPPs). In 2001, the Department of Housing sent a circular to local authorities telling them to:

[C]onsider the extent to which additional housing supply can be brought on stream through PPPs between local authorities and private developers utilizing suitable local authority lands. These lands would primarily be lands in areas where there is already a significant concentration of social housing.

In these PPPs, the private developer was given the land on which long-standing working-class communities were living. In return for rebuilding a smaller number of new social housing units on the land, the developer could build huge numbers of private houses and retail units. From the government's perspective it was a win–win; it got new social housing for free (as it placed no value on the land, or the communities). The government also got to break up what it called the 'ghettos' and disperse the community (i.e. poor people); through the 'regeneration' residents had to leave to facilitate demolition and rebuilding. But the reduced number of new social housing units meant they couldn't return. So the local authority would no longer be responsible for dealing with what it called the 'headache' of managing social housing estates. PPPs were a win–win for the developer too – they got the land and would make a huge profit from selling the private development they built on it.

Twelve social housing estates ended up being part of PPPs with developers, including some very large ones in Dublin, such as Fatima Mansions, St Michael's Estate, Dolphin House, O'Devaney Gardens, St Theresa's Gardens, Dominick Street and Charlemont Street. One developer that got three of these deals was the aforementioned Bernard McNamara. Almost 2,000 households were involved, a quarter of Dublin City Council's entire social housing stock at the time. They were in locations that provided homes and communities to social housing tenants. But unfortunately for them the State had given up on them and on social housing, and the value of the land they were living on had escalated in the Celtic Tiger. The sites were perfect for private developers to make big profits from building high-rise and commercial development. The government and Dublin City Council claimed they were getting new social housing built for 'free' and the developers got to cash in.

In this bizarre measure, Dublin City Council was selling its land, and it would not build social housing in areas that already had social housing, due to the 'social mix' and 'not building ghettos' ideologies. A similar activity was taking place in Ballymun, where private apartments were being developed as part of the 'regeneration game', but no new additional social housing was being built. So those in need of social housing were forced into taking private rental subsidies in the new private rental apartments.

So we had the perverse situation that in areas where housing need was greatest the State was doing the least to respond to the need. Noel Ahern explained the government's ideology: 'I hope the days of building vast tracts of one-class housing estates are gone because we can all see the problems, inefficiencies and fractured communities that type of thing created in the past.'

This anti-social housing bias ignored the reality that it wasn't the *building* of social housing estates that was the problem. The cause of disadvantage was the residualization of social housing to those most in housing need, combined with poor estate management and lack of play and community facilities, and lack of funding for local authorities in the 1980s. Most of all, it was caused by the inequality and poverty of the 1980s and 1990s that led to a crisis in some of these social housing estates. The truth was that most council housing estates functioned well, with very strong communities that provided essential networks of family and community support.

It shows how the underfunding of public housing, as with public health, becomes a virtuous cycle for the private developers and investors but a vicious cycle for those in need of housing. It is a self-fulfilling prophecy, policy and ideology that justifies further underfunding and outsourcing to the private sector. It was quintessential privatization: the sale of a public good and asset that is then profited from by the private sector. It was because the government had given up on the idea of housing as a public good – the idea of social housing itself – and was abandoning those in need of the public good to the market.

So the narrative of the Celtic Tiger being down to us 'all partying' is far from the true story. As we have seen already, land-owners and developers kept increasing land and house prices, just like the landlords and investor funds are pushing up rents now. House prices and rents don't just rise magically, somebody decides to increase them. And it is because they are maximizing their profits. We don't talk enough about the rise in house prices being because developers and sellers keep increasing house prices (and banks kept expanding lending to developers and home buyers to pay ever increasing prices). This was because we handed housing delivery completely over to the private market. But a major reason why house prices increased so much was because people were buying a property not as a home, but to rent as an investment asset. And the banks were lending massively for this. This is the untold story of the Celtic Tiger – how homes were turned into property investment assets. A buy-to-let boom added fuel to the fire and started squeezing households into becoming Ireland's first Generation Rent.

How investor landlords fuelled the boom and created Generation Rent

Financialization is when housing is turned into a financial asset. The first phase of financialization in Ireland was the expansion of credit (lending) for mortgaged home ownership. A lot of the credit came through global financial markets – hedge funds – that invested through the Irish banks and mortgage securitization. These were essentially how mortgages were bundled together, sold to investors and traded on the stock market.

But the other aspect of this first wave of financialization of housing in Ireland was the expansion of lending for the purchase of housing as a property investment – to rent out. Individual landlords – who came to be termed 'mom and pop' landlords – bought property using buy-to-let mortgages. The banks, the government, financial advisers, and media commentators, who make their money from this investment, all advised them to invest their money in property. They were incentivized by government through tax measures and 'cheap' credit. The volume of mortgage lending for buy-to-let investments in Ireland increased by a phenomenal 400 per cent between 2003 and 2008, from €10bn to €50bn.

Irish people were encouraged, as part of 'asset-based' welfare, to invest in buying a second home, to rent out, as their future pension. The house could be liquidated if required to meet costs such as elder care or healthcare. Therefore, this could be used rather than the government having to guarantee a good pension or public healthcare for the elderly. The government again reneged on its responsibility for social provision and handed it over to the individual and the market to invest, accumulate and speculate.

This, of course, was simply transferring the cost of the pension to future generations by turning them into renters. Boomers' pensions created Generation Rent. This has become a driving issue of inequality and financialization of housing not just in Ireland, but internationally, as massive pension funds globally seek to maximize their return – investing in rental housing (with rents paid for by Generation Rent) as a key area with a high return.

So the Celtic Tiger story – where house prices continued to rise despite the increase in supply – is not just about excessive lending to home buyers. It is also about excessive lending to homeowners and investors who were buying up properties to become landlords as part of the 'buy-to-let' phenomenon.

Shockingly, it wasn't until 2007 that the Irish Central Bank actually investigated the role of this form of property investment, termed 'investor demand', in creating house price inflation, putting the economy at risk and crowding first-time home buyers out of the housing market.

The proportion of mortgages held by residential landlords increased from 16 per cent in 2003 to over a quarter of all mortgages in 2008, while the proportion held by homeowners fell from 84 per cent to 71 per cent. This residential investment letting, or buy-to-let purchasing, had increased their share of new loans at the expense of home buyers since 2005. The value of new buy-to-let mortgages rose by 83 per cent between Q1 2005 and Q4 2006. First-time buyers (FTBs) were squeezed out, and in Q4 2006 there was a fall of over 20 per cent in the number of loans attributable to FTBs.

Wait for this. The Central Bank suggests that a half of all new homes bought in 2006 and 2007 were bought by investor purchasers. That means that in the region of 80,000 homes in just two years were bought to rent out. Some were being bought and just left vacant. The share of vacant dwellings in total housing increased from 10.5 per cent in 1996 to 16.7 per cent in 2006. They were being bought as investments, not homes.

It is unsurprising then to see that between 2002 and 2006 the numbers renting privately increased by 39 per cent, from 141,000 to just under 200,000. Something profound was taking place in these years in Irish housing. A tremor that turned into an earthquake happened to our housing system at this point in the second half of the Celtic Tiger. This would have ramifications for the coming generations. Unsurprisingly, as private rental investors bought more new homes, the proportion of housing comprising private rental increased and, for the first time in 60 years in Ireland, rates of home ownership began to fall as a new generation of potential home buyers were pushed out by investors buying homes to rent and pushing up house prices. And we see, for the first time since the 1950s, an increase in the number of tenants in the private rental sector and the re-emergence in the Irish economy, in significant numbers, of the private for-profit landlord.

The generational divide was opening up, as prices rose dramatically and home ownership was pushed out of the reach of many people, including those who were on good salaries. Many who were excluded didn't qualify for social housing either, so their only option was renting in the private rental sector. And private rental investors were now buying up more of the new homes, limiting what was available for home buyers, and therefore pushing them out of the home purchase market, which added to rental inflation and the emergence of Generation Rent from 2003 onwards. In their early twenties in 2004, they are now in their late thirties and early forties. They might spend twenty years in the private rental sector, and still have no prospect of a secure forever home.

What made the investment in the private rental sector so profitable? It was fundamentally the shift in state policy of not building social and affordable housing but relying on the private market – and increasingly the private rental sector – for social housing. From a supply side, this supported increased investment in private rental as it made it attractive as an investment asset. Landlord investors knew there was a guaranteed rental return into perpetuity. State use of the private rental market for social housing was a form of de-risking investment. If you know the State – which always pays – will pay the rent, you can find a tenant who will pay. This underwrites the risk of banks' lending and for you as property investor.

The rent supplement system as a form of social housing policy put an upward pressure on rents as it meant an increased demand for private rental accommodation, and it acted as a price floor under the market, as landlords knew they would definitely get this rent from the State. So social housing policy turned the private rental sector into an investment opportunity. This further increased the purchase of homes as private rental property, thus making it more likely that future generations would have to go into the private rental sector also.

The lack of social housing also meant that there was greater demand for private rental homes. Those who would have got social housing in the past were forced to find housing in the private rental sector. As the State stopped building social and affordable housing, it created a new market of unfulfilled housing demand (and need). This was creating an investment opportunity for the private sector. By reducing its supply, the State gave landlords as property investors a clear path of future investment return. This was the start of Generation Rent – people were being turned into an investment asset.

We can see this today as well.

All this meant that the market careened out of control. People had no alternative but to try to pay what they could to buy from the market. If there had been a supply of social and affordable housing there would not have been the same demand pressure on the market. Prices and rents would not have risen and then of course developers', banks' and estate agents' profits would not have been as high. What is clear is that the more for-profit private rental homes in the housing system, the more commodified, financialized and unaffordable housing becomes. So we need to reduce the proportion of for-profit private rental in our housing system.

Just imagine how affordable house prices would have been – and consequently how high the levels of home ownership, and how low the levels of private rental – if homes had been restricted to purchase by home buyers, not by investors, in those years of the Celtic Tiger, and if the State had continued to build social and affordable housing like it did in the 1960s. It would have avoided a lost decade of economic and social catastrophe. We would not have the housing crisis of today.

The Celtic Tiger was game, set and match to the private developers, banks and landlords. It handed a monopoly of control over housing to the private sector. But free market economics is supposed to be against monopolies because they can control supply and prices and become inefficient. Wasn't that the argument against the state monopolies? But then perhaps it's just a problem when it's a government monopoly.

A deep personal value shift also took place among the Irish people through this market takeover of housing. Through these years, there was a cultural shift in our attitude to home. People were encouraged, by the media, by government, by financial analysts, banks, advisers and economists, to think of housing as an investment asset. Housing became property – real estate. It was no longer home.

In 2006, Noel Ahern was asked in the Dáil about the massive rise in house prices. He replied:

Despite increased house prices, affordability has remained relatively favourable . . . The level of output by the industry has hugely increased. Under any law of economics, supply should sooner or later equal demand, which should bring a bit of sense to the situation. There is a tendency to get carried away with the average house price.

But a few months later, in early 2007, house prices started to fall, and the Irish economy was about to experience an unprecedented crash and economic recession.

Chapter 4
How did Housing get Unaffordable Again?

Between 2008 and 2020, key government decisions made housing unaffordable again. After falling to affordable levels in 2012 and 2013, government policy resulted in rents and house prices increasing exponentially over the following years. It abandoned a generation stuck in the private rental market, invited real estate vulture funds into Ireland, gave subsidies and public land to private developers and their obsession with resuscitating the private market all but wiped out social housing. It is a terrifying timeline, but a revealing one.

2008

House price: €295,000 (-15%)[*]
Rent in Dublin: €1,149 (-8%)
Rent outside Dublin: €750 (-6%)[*]

On 15 September 2008, the collapse of the multi-billion-dollar financial company Lehman Brothers caused the largest bankruptcy in US history. It sent a shockwave through the global financial system and markets crashed as they realized their investments were made up of 'subprime' mortgages that people couldn't afford to pay back. House prices were plunging. Two weeks later, on 29 September, the Irish

[*]Average prices. Per cent change refers to the change on price from the previous year.

Minister for Finance, Brian Lenihan, stood up in the Dáil and announced a blanket state guarantee for all the Irish banks. The banks had lent out billions to developers for property investments that were collapsing in value. The property industry shuddered to a halt. Construction of new homes fell from 51,000 in 2008 to 26,420 in 2009 to 14,000 in 2010, and then to 7,000 in 2011.

The Fianna Fáil–Green Party coalition government would go on to bail out the banks and developers with €63bn of taxpayers' money. This cost was then placed on the shoulders of the Irish people and future generations, through a series of 'austerity' budgets. Remember how austerity in 1987 led to devasting impacts on social housing delivery? Well, history was about to repeat itself. Austerity Round 2 from 2009 to 2014 would have just as devastating an impact. Public services and welfare were cut while taxes were raised. Vital supports to the most vulnerable in society were cut, such as lone parent and disability welfare supports, community development funding and social welfare for the under-25s. And, reflecting the governments' anti-social housing ideology, the social housing budget was decimated. This was a major contribution to the housing and homelessness crisis that was to emerge over the coming decade. Those who had nothing to do with causing the crash – working people, the marginalized, the young, and future generations – would pay for the bailouts, first through cuts, then through the next housing crisis.

2009

House price: €213,183 (-19%)
Rent in Dublin: €991 (-14%)
Rent outside Dublin: €644 (-14%)

In September 2009, as unemployment rose and people's livelihoods were being destroyed across the country, Brian Lenihan stood up in the Dáil again. This time he announced the setting up of the National Asset Management Agency (NAMA). It is hard to overstate how fundamental this decision was in creating the future housing and affordability crisis in Ireland. NAMA was set up to save the banks, by giving them €54bn of taxpayers' money in return for taking off the banks' balance sheets the 'toxic' loans of developers and property investors that had gone pear-shaped due to the property market crash. These were the loans given to developers to speculate in building shopping centres, buying up land and building housing developments. Lenihan explained that NAMA was being set up to 'facilitate the speedy removal' from the banks of 'higher-risk property-related assets which are clogging up the banks' balance sheets.' He said it straight. This was all about saving the banks, not society.

The government wanted to take the bad loans from the Irish banks so that the financial system could get back to 'business as usual'. NAMA was created to get the banks and the property market up and running again, i.e. to get them back into profitability. In the coming months the Government (using the money of the Irish people) bailed out Anglo Irish Bank at a cost of €34.7bn, Allied Irish Banks (AIB) with €20.7bn (it effectively became owned by the Irish State), and in total put up €62.8bn to bail out all the banks.

As the crisis deepened, the government implemented more harsh austerity cuts, and a massive mortgage arrears crisis emerged. By the end of 2009, 28,000 households could not afford their monthly mortgage payments. This shows what happens when a housing bubble bursts and when house prices that had risen to unaffordable levels crash. Home buyers who had been forced to take on debt beyond their capacity to pay simply could not afford to pay it back. This is the problem with increasing mortgage debt to pay for higher house prices. And it is happening again in 2022.

2010

House price: €191,776 (-8.9%)
Rent in Dublin: €979 (-1%)
Rent outside Dublin: €626 (-3%)

In 2010, house prices fell by 8.9 per cent to an average price of €191,776 nationally, and €237,000 in Dublin. Just 14,000 homes were built. The austerity budgets between 2009 and 2010 cut almost €11bn in state spending, and increased taxes. Child benefit was cut. Wages were cut across the public and private sectors. In the public sector, newly hired teachers, doctors and gardaí were put on a lower pay scale than existing employees. This led to the 'pay inequality' affecting a generation of newly (mainly younger) recruited staff doing the same work for less pay across the public sector. To cut costs the public and private sector shifted away from permanent contracts to short-term and lower-paid contracts, and the precarious and gig economy emerged, again hitting younger people hardest. Jobseeker's benefit for the under-20s was halved to €100 a week. The younger generations were made to pay; and the reductions in wages and welfare would also impact on their ability to pay for housing in the coming years. Collapsing incomes and unemployment meant more and more households were forced into mortgage arrears, the number rising from 28,000 in 2009 to 44,000 in December 2010.

People did not take this lying down. There were massive protests against austerity. One of the largest ever protests held in Ireland was organized by the Irish Congress of Trade Unions (ICTU) in November 2010, with over 100,000 marching in Dublin. Students marched against increases in student registration fees, cuts to the grant and increasing unemployment and emigration. In December 2010, the Irish Government was forced into taking a bailout from the International Monetary Fund (IMF) and the European Central Bank (ECB).

2011

House price: €165,000 (-12.9%)
Rents in Dublin: €985 (+0.1%)
Rents outside Dublin: €612 (-2%)

In February 2011, the wave of public anger over the crisis and austerity resulted in Fianna Fáil suffering an election wipeout. The new government, made up of Fine Gael and the Labour Party, and headed by Taoiseach Enda Kenny, promised major change. Sitting at the cabinet table was a new Minister for Finance, Fine Gael TD Michael Noonan; Fine Gael TD Leo Varadkar was Minister for Transport; and Fine Gael TD Simon Coveney Minister for Agriculture. The new Minister of State with responsibility for housing was Labour TD Willie Penrose.

In 2011, house prices fell a further 13 per cent to €165,000 nationally and to €198,260 in Dublin. Rents were static in Dublin and fell 2 per cent outside Dublin. Just 494 social housing units were built by local authorities in 2011, a reduction of 85 per cent on the 3,362 built in 2009.

The Fine Gael–Labour government did not deliver on its promises. It did not take the opportunity to start a new direction for Ireland's economy and society with the delivery of affordable housing at its heart. It saw the collapse in house prices as a major problem for the banks, the developers, and their high net wealth, home-owning voters. It did not see the opportunity to make housing permanently affordable for future generations in Ireland. Rather than accepting that the private property market model had devastated the country, and changing back to the approach that had worked in the 1960s, when the State was central to delivering affordable and social housing, it continued many of the same failed policies of the Celtic Tiger, and through NAMA it made the situation even worse by bringing in the real estate investment trusts (REITs).

It was unwilling to provide affordable or social housing through the State, so it decided that the future for new households and people in need of housing would be as private renters. Most people would no longer own their home or occupy social housing; they would instead get their housing from the private rental market. This would provide a demand of renters to the increasing numbers of buy-to-let landlords who were in arrears on their mortgages, and vulture investor funds interested in buying property from NAMA, and thus help the landlords and the banks.

Minister Willie Penrose launched a new national housing policy in June 2011. This made the shift to pushing people into the private rental sector actual policy. It shut down local authorities' role in building social housing. It closed the programmes of affordable housing delivery, stating that there was 'no longer any rationale for delivery of affordable housing'. It turned to the private landlords, developers and financial investors to deliver social housing by buying it from them and renting it; and introduced 'leasing' schemes, where the State would pay 90 per cent of market rent to the property owner for a 25-year lease of the property to house social housing tenants. Social housing turned into private market housing. As the Department of Housing explained, it was implementing a 'reorientation of housing policy from construction to acquisition and leasing' and 'housing sections within local authorities' were to be 'reconfigured' by 'sourcing social housing units from the private sector through RAS and long-term leasing.'

This essentially turned social housing into an investment asset, upending its purpose of being an additional supply to the market.

The policy shift to private rental was justified by blaming excessive levels of home ownership for the 2008 crash. But this was a complete misdiagnosis. It was the withdrawal of the State from building social and affordable housing that led to people having no choice but to try to buy their home from the private market. This led to a massive demand for house purchase from the market, and thus the rise in house prices during the Celtic Tiger, which necessitated ever-higher borrowing and thus unsustainable indebtedness of home buyers. Added to this was the increased speculative purchase of housing by individual buy-to-let landlords. Yet now, in 2011, housing policy was continuing the very measures that led to the 2008 crash. The government ignored these lessons. But this 'new' approach also justified austerity cuts to social house building, which was a policy choice. Government prioritized the needs of landlords and banks over funding local authorities to build social housing. The social housing capital investment budget (the budget for building new social housing stock) suffered the second-highest proportionate budget cut of any area during this period. It was reduced by 88 per cent from €1.46bn in 2008 to €167m in 2014. This policy had massive repercussions, as it removed the key staff and capacity of local authorities to build social housing over the coming years.

2012

House price: €157,000 (-5%)
Rent in Dublin: €1,017 (+3.2%)
Rent outside Dublin: €608 (-0.1%)

Average house prices fell to €157,000 in 2012. This was an affordable level for those on average salaries, requiring just over three times the average income to buy a house. However, given the lack of lending by banks and the income cuts and job losses among younger households, most were unable to buy a home in this time. In the second half of 2012, rents in Dublin also increased for the first time since 2007, eating up renters' savings and potential deposits. From 2007 to 2012 house prices fell by close to 50 per cent, while market rents fell by 22 per cent.

In 2012, youth unemployment reached a high point of the crisis – 31 per cent, up from 13 per cent in 2008. The government told young people who were out of work to take up unpaid internships through the JobBridge scheme, where they would get €50 on top of their welfare payments. In this year, 40,000 young Irish people were forced to emigrate because of the lack of jobs. The Minister of Finance, Michael Noonan, angered the public when he said that many were emigrating 'as a lifestyle choice' to go and see the world. Between 2010 and 2015 a quarter of a million young people – people in their twenties, thirties and forties – were forced to emigrate. That is the combined population of the cities of Waterford, Cork and Limerick. It resulted in huge pain and loss, in the break-up of families and communities. GAA clubs couldn't field teams, and parents died without seeing their children or grandchildren. Almost 70,000 construction workers emigrated over these years, a huge loss that would impact the housing crisis in future years. A generation and Ireland's future capacity to build housing was sacrificed for austerity to save the banks and re-inflate the property market.

The mortgage arrears crisis also worsened significantly in 2012, increasing to 94,000 households in arrears, while the number of landlords with buy-to-let mortgages for rental properties in arrears also increased massively to 28,421. One in five landlords with rental property mortgages were in arrears. This was a much higher proportion than home buyers, one in ten of whom were in mortgage arrears.

In October 2012, the head of NAMA made a presentation to the Oireachtas on its work, explaining that NAMA was 'increasingly shifting its attention towards attracting international investors'. It was looking to sell off the toxic loans and property to global vulture and real estate funds. NAMA asked the government to create new legislation for REITs in Ireland. These REITs were a new type of property investment fund that was growing internationally. Setting up REITs in Ireland would help international investment funds, NAMA explained, to 'bid for, and purchase, Irish property assets' from NAMA. These funds would enable them to pay little, if any, tax.

NAMA said that it had 10,000 apartments and houses in its 'portfolio' that were being rented on an annual rent roll of €100m. Rather than selling these as affordable homes to home buyers or to social housing bodies, it was going to undertake 'the sale of entire blocks of apartments to equity firms which have teamed with property management specialists, and which are interested in purchasing apartments on a bulk basis'. So the bulk sale of Irish homes to investor funds by an Irish state agency under direction from the Irish government started here. NAMA went on to explain that this sale of housing and land to vulture funds would help with 'the resuscitation of the residential property market'. What it meant was the resuscitation of house prices and rents, i.e. raising rents and house prices back to unaffordable levels, and the resuscitation of the zombie private market of developers and investors.

The vulture funds and REITs had come knocking at the government and NAMA's door, and they were welcomed with open arms. In December 2012, the Irish Government duly obliged NAMA and the vulture funds and introduced legislation to support the creation of REITs in Ireland. In contrast to its consistent refusal to deliver rent controls or build social and affordable homes for ordinary citizens, when the global vulture and as I call them, 'vampire funds', asked the government to jump, it responded 'How high?' The Minister for Finance provided 'for the establishment of real estate investment trusts, REITs, which allow for investors to finance property investment'. The introduction of REITs, he explained in his budget, was intended to help NAMA sell off its loan portfolio and 'allow it to bring more ... activity to ... residential property markets'. The new REIT measure and the real estate investment trust tax relief mechanism was on top of other existing tax avoidance and reduction loopholes available to investor funds. This meant that the investors could buy up Irish homes, and profit from rising rents, and the flipping of property and land, essentially tax-free. This was a huge enticement to invest. And who influenced these policies? It was not a coincidence that the government had been meeting regularly with investor fund representatives, including US real estate investors.

2013

House price: €171,000 (+6.4%)
Rent in Dublin: €1,102 (+8%)
Rent outside Dublin: €608 (no change)

In 2013, a new housing crisis began in Ireland. In many ways, it was just another phase of a crisis that had been ongoing since the housing bubble of the 2000s. Ireland was in fact entering its second decade of a housing crisis. And it would be even worse than the first.

In 2013, house prices stopped falling and increased for the first time since 2007, and rents in Dublin rose by 8 per cent. It might seem illogical to consider that rising house prices is a bad thing. An annual increase of 1–2 per cent could be reasonable. The problem is that when house prices increase by 5 or 6 or 10 per cent a year, we end up with another housing bubble. Those who can sell, yes, they might profit; but if they are buying elsewhere, they have to pay the higher price. But the ones who really suffer are those who are trying to access the market.

By 2013 average house prices were €171,000. The average home in Dublin City in 2013 was €185,265; in Kildare it was €177,040; in Galway €159,000; in Wicklow €225,674. By the end of 2021, these house prices would have increased by 114 per cent nationally, and by 119 per cent in Dublin.

And when it comes to rents, increases of 5–10 per cent a year are utterly devastating as they eat up renters' savings and income, severely threatening any prospect they might have of getting a secure home of their own. The national average rent would increase by 76 per cent between 2013 and 2021, rising from €793 in 2013 to €1,397 in 2021. In Dublin, the average rent would increase from €963 in 2012 to €1,916 in 2021.

Local authorities built just 293 social housing units in 2013, while the number of households in need of social housing reached 90,000. The mortgage arrears crisis for home buyers reached its high point of 104,000 in December 2013; and the mortgage arrears crisis of buy-to-let landlords continued to worsen. The number of buy-to-let mortgages in arrears reached 39,250, close to a third of these mortgages.

Unemployment dropped to 13 per cent, and Ireland exited the IMF/ECB bailout programme in December 2013.

NAMA made its biggest sale of Irish loans and assets so far, in the form of a packaged 'portfolio' to international investors. It sold Project Aspen for €200m to US investment fund Starwood Capital Group, Key Capital and UK-based Catalyst Capital. The portfolio included commercial sites and offices in Dublin.

2014

House price: €188,000 (+16.3%)
Rent in Dublin: €1,220 (+11%)
Rent outside Dublin: €635 (+4.4%)

Through 2014, as rents and house prices increased rapidly, NAMA accelerated its sale of assets to, as it explained, 'tap into the increased international – and increasingly domestic – investor interest in Irish real estate'. State agency, NAMA, under direction from the government of the time, had provided the asset sales to start what was to become an avalanche of investor landlords and vulture funds in Ireland. NAMA was the key driver of sales of portfolios of loans to global investors in Ireland in this period. The Irish banks also sold loan portfolios; for example, Ulster Bank and AIB sold mortgage loans to Goldman Sachs and Beltany Property Finance. Ninety per cent of assets sold by NAMA went to US equity and vulture funds. It explicitly stated that 'assets were sold early in the cycle to drive market recovery and to attract international capital willing to invest in Ireland.'

Ireland's first REIT, courtesy of NAMA

Using the new REIT legislation introduced by the government, in April 2014 a new real estate investment trust focused on Irish residential property was formed, the Irish Residential Properties Real

Estate Investment Trust (IRES REIT). It was largely funded by a Canadian REIT, CAPREIT (Canadian Apartment Properties REIT), and floated on the Irish stock market. IRES REIT is explicit about how NAMA, by providing it with residential assets, enabled it to become Ireland's largest private rental sector landlord. NAMA sold its Orange portfolio (including 761 residential apartments in the greater Dublin area) to IRES for €211m: 'With the closing of this transaction, our property portfolio will grow to a total of 1,202 apartment suites, transforming IRES into Ireland's largest non-governmental residential landlord.'

NAMA was selling off loans, land and property to foreign vulture funds that then evicted tenants and raised rents to unaffordable levels. It sold the portfolios of residential property on the basis of continued rising residential rents into the future. Selling to investors that expected a high rate of return placed huge upward pressure on rents for these apartments and the wider market.

NAMA was also getting involved in financing and developing commercial office and luxury residential apartments, in partnership with US investor funds such as Los Angeles private equity fund Oaktree and Kennedy Wilson, and developing new expensive homes for sale by Irish developers. These were the most profitable forms of property development at the time. Delivering affordable housing wasn't given a look-in.

In 2014, NAMA entered into a joint venture with Kennedy Wilson in which adjoining sites on Sir John Rogerson's Quay were combined and created an investment fund. The fund submitted a planning application to develop 313,000 square feet of office space and 204 apartments. This would become the infamous 23-storey Capital Dock development.

The cherry on top for the vultures was NAMA's Project Cherry portfolio, which it sold to the US real estate giant Hines and another American fund, King Street Capital Management, for €270m. This portfolio included a juicy cherry for Hines – the largest development site in south County Dublin, the 166-hectare Cherrywood site. In a joint venture with Dutch pension investor APG Asset Management, Hines then developed plans for 1,221 build-to-rent apartments in

Cherrywood. Hines and King Street also sold 47 hectares of the development land in Cherrywood to US vulture fund Lone Star for a reported €140m. This shows how real estate vulture investors were making hundreds of millions in profits (which were paid for through rising house prices and rents) from the Irish housing market by flipping land and properties, facilitated by the Irish State by acquiring the assets at discount from NAMA.

Property industry control over NAMA

There is often not enough consideration given to the skills of those employed in the housing market. NAMA's staff were mainly 'real estate' industry specialists: property, finance, banking and legal professionals. They had little knowledge of, or interest in, social or affordable housing. Senior staff working for NAMA then went to work for the real estate funds in various areas of asset and portfolio management. The real estate industry was benefiting from the 'resuscitation' of the property market. NAMA also kept many of the developers who had crashed the economy on its payroll. In 2014, NAMA was paying €11m in 'allowances' to 134 developers; three of them were receiving more than €200,000. It was a real failure of government to stop the real estate and developer industry essentially dictating what NAMA did, by driving their own interests. The government should have hired social and affordable housing professionals who would have brought NAMA in a very different direction. But that wasn't the direction government and the property industry wanted NAMA to go.

Social housing as a bailout for landlords and investors

Another nail was driven into the coffin of social housing with the development of the Housing Assistance Payment (HAP) scheme. In July 2014, Alan Kelly, the Labour Party TD for Tipperary, was appointed Minister for the Environment, with overall responsibility for housing and local government. He described the implementation of HAP as 'a key Government priority and a major pillar of the Social Housing Strategy 2020'. HAP was a new payment to private landlords to house social housing tenants. The minister explained that one of the key reasons for introducing it was to 'provide certainty for landlords as regards their rental income'. So rather than investing in building social housing, the government wanted to ensure that private landlords (whose mortgage arrears crisis was worsening – which was a problem for the banks) were guaranteed rents. Local authorities built just 102 homes in the entire country in 2014. The decision to continue austerity in cutting social housing and handing it over to the market to deliver and not building any affordable housing resulted in higher housing need and forced more people into the private rental market, pushing rents up further. This added to the attractiveness of the rental market for investor funds and kept the buy-to-let landlords in business. In 2014, the number of buy-to-let landlords in arrears reached 35,000, or 25 per cent of such mortgages. This remained a much higher proportion than that of homeowners, of whom 14.5 per cent were in arrears.

The real estate funds knew if they bought up property in Ireland, and even if they couldn't find private renters who could afford their rent, the State would pay to rent it out or lease it. It was another way housing policy enticed in these investors.

2015

House price: €204,000 (+ 6.9%)
Rent in Dublin: €1,319 (+16%)
Rent outside Dublin: €704 (+11%)

In 2015, the number of people in employment grew by 70,000. For the first year since 2009, there was positive net migration growth of 6 per cent into Ireland. Yet a quarter of the population and a third of all children in the country were experiencing deprivation. Forty-two thousand Irish nationals emigrated. The population had increased by 130,000 since 2010 to reach 4.7 million. Yet in 2015 the government built the lowest number of social housing since the foundation of the State – just 75 local authority houses. This lack of social housing was contributing to a new growing homelessness crisis.

NAMA stokes house price rises

Despite the evidence that we were back in another upward cycle of rising prices, NAMA argued that house prices needed to rise further in order to provide sufficient return and profit to attract international investor funds to buy up NAMA property and loans. NAMA stated that 'many of those who are interested in buying development land in the Dublin area at the moment will have rate of return targets of 15–20 per cent and realistically those targets are unlikely to be met unless market prices rise significantly from current levels.' The government supported NAMA's approach.

NAMA continued with the sale of property and land to global funds. It sold a property portfolio, aptly named Project Plum, that included 568 apartments in Dublin for €120m to Marathon Asset Management, a large US-based property fund. Marathon would go on to sell the apartments to IRES REIT in 2019. Bidders for the portfolio were told that they could take advantage of the rental shortage and increase rental income from €14.7m to €17.7m per annum, a 20 per cent increase in rents. Marathon is likely to have made a plum profit in the millions from this flipping of apartments.

NAMA also sold a further 442 apartments in Tallaght to IRES REIT. Ulster Bank sold loans worth €5bn to Lone Star; they included 687 hectares of prime development land across Dublin.

Limits to lending for home buyers

While there was no limit on how much investor funds could spend on purchasing housing, new borrowing limits for home buyers were introduced by the Central Bank. This meant that someone could only borrow 3.5 times their annual income when buying a home. So, for example, if you earned €40,000 a year, you could borrow a maximum of €140,000. But each year, 20 per cent of mortgages for first-time buyers, and 10 per cent of loans for second-time and subsequent buyers, could be above this cap. Also, a deposit rule was brought in where first-time buyers had to provide 10 per cent of the value of the property upfront as a deposit, and second and subsequent buyers had to find 20 per cent. So if you were a first-time buyer and you wanted to buy a house for €300,000 you'd need a minimum deposit of €30,000 before you could be lent the remaining €270,000.

Rents rise but government puts landlords first

Rents were rising dramatically. In Dublin, rents rose by 16 per cent in 2015. In Galway, rents had risen by 50 per cent since 2011. In one case, the rent for a three-bed semi-detached house increased from €800 per month in 2011 to €1,300 in 2015. In the Dáil, the opposition made a proposal to Minister Alan Kelly to link rent increases to inflation. Inflation was running at close to zero at the time. This would have effectively frozen rents at that point. But the government refused, explaining that, in its view, the increase in rents was being caused by 'a mismatch between levels of supply and demand for rental accommodation'. It was true that there was a growing demand for rental homes (caused by government policy) and a lack of supply. But the actual reason rents were increasing was because landlords were hiking up the rents. If the government was being honest about its policy, it should have said 'Landlords are taking advantage of the lack of supply to increase rents. And landlords are also able to increase rents as they see fit because we will not cap them.' Rents increase because landlords demand tenants pay more – they don't just magically rise. Minister Kelly went on to explain that the government wanted to allow rents to continue to rise to encourage investor funds to buy up property and build new rentals, thus providing the new 'supply'.

We saw this market theory argument from governments during the Celtic Tiger: the market needs to be incentivized and allowed to do its work, and through the 'invisible hand of the market it will efficiently allocate resources' and deliver a 'supply' to meet housing 'demand'. At that future point (that in reality never comes) house prices and rents will become affordable. But supply rose massively in the Celtic Tiger period and house prices didn't fall, while rents kept rising. Over the years 2008 to 2016, housing need grew hugely, yet the market didn't supply housing. The market theory of housing has been repeated over and over by politicians and property economists since the 1990s. But it hasn't worked in practice. It is, after all, just a belief, an ideal of economic theory, of how 'perfect' housing markets work. But it's not the reality.

This is not how real housing markets operate. There is a significant monopoly control over major parts of the housing system by private speculative interests who hold large amounts of land, control the building process and own large numbers of buildings. They hoard land, which results in asset price appreciation, and they fix prices, so that even with 'incentives' they do not necessarily build and increase supply, while the 'supply' they do provide is always aimed at profit maximizing, not provision of affordable housing. We can see this in the private construction industry's 'strike' in Ireland in relation to house building from 2013 onwards, when it clearly became profitable/viable to invest in, and build, housing, yet they did not build. This led to further increases in the price of land, houses and rents. There has been an issue for private developers and builders in getting finance to fund their building developments in this period, as the traditional source of funding, the Irish banks, were unwilling and unable to lend. The private developers as a result turned to global investment funds and equity to finance them. This is an issue in which the government should also have intervened, but it let the market 'work' here too.

Yet the market theory of housing is treated like a quasi-religious belief among government, policymakers and property market economists. It is used as a justification for the State not delivering social and affordable housing itself and regulating the market. It shows the strong ideological belief that has driven housing policy – a failed market theory of housing.

At this point we see a shift in emphasis from government. Added to the argument that investor funds were needed to buy up the toxic loans from NAMA, now there was a new rationale to justify them. The global real estate investor funds, the new institutional landlords, would provide a supply of rental housing. The Irish property development industry – the private market – was not delivering, so the investor funds would solve the supply problem. There were just 7,219 new homes built in 2015. Of those, 3,200 were individual one-off homes, so the private developer/investor market built under 4,000 homes (including 670 apartments) in 2015.

And because government was unwilling to take on the challenge and responsibility to deliver social and affordable housing, these new REIT investors and international global property funds would be given the major role in addressing the 'supply' crisis.

But the problem with that approach was that this particular type of global real estate investors were only interested in building rental property with high returns – which required high rents and no homes for purchase. This meant that they did not view policies to keep rent affordable, such as rent regulation, or the delivery by government of affordable homes to purchase, favourably. And so government neither controlled rents nor built affordable homes.

Government refuses rent caps

In the run-up to the 2015 Budget, as rents continued to rise, it was reported that there was a possibility the government might introduce rent regulation (such as linking rent increases to inflation). However, following intense lobbying, including by US real estate investors, the government instead introduced a two-year rent setting mechanism, which just postponed rent increases and did little to stem rising rents.

In a letter to Minister Noonan dated 30 September 2015, and later published by the *Irish Examiner*, US real estate investment company Kennedy Wilson Europe wrote: 'Investors and their funding banks will see the new proposed regime (some form of rent certainty) negatively. This will certainly limit and, potentially, eliminate future investment.'

It should be very clear what was determining housing policy at this point. It certainly was not the interests of renters, those in need of social housing or potential home buyers.

2016

House price: €227,000 (+8.5%)
Rent in Dublin: €1,461 (+11%)
Rent outside Dublin: €769 (+9%)

April 2016 saw the hundredth anniversary of the Easter Rising and the signing of the Proclamation of the Irish Republic, which aimed to create a nation that would 'cherish all children of the nation equally'. Erica Fleming, a young mother who had been stuck in homelessness emergency accommodation for almost ten months, stood with her nine-year-old daughter, Emily, in a dignified protest while officials attended the 1916 commemoration. Erica said she was 'ashamed' of what she and her daughter were going through after they were made homeless. In the protest she wanted to highlight that in 2016 'over two thousand children are homeless, anxious and upset . . . denied a chance to have a normal, happy childhood, free from worry and discrimination . . . denied a basic human right.'

The Dublin Simon Community warned that 'the number of people stuck in emergency accommodation in Dublin is increasing at an alarming rate'. It called on the government to 'tackle the homeless and housing crisis before it gets even worse'. The number of individuals experiencing homelessness in Dublin had grown from 1,975 in February 2015 to 2,692 in February 2016, a 36 per cent increase over 12 months. The number of children experiencing homelessness with their families in Dublin grew at a shocking rate – from 803 in February 2015 to 1,616 in February 2016.

A general election was held in February 2016, and a new 'minority' Fine Gael government was elected, with Fianna Fáil supporting it from opposition. Simon Coveney was made the new Minister for Environment and Housing, but unfortunately policy remained on the same path and the housing and homelessness crisis continued to worsen.

NAMA continued its sales, for example selling two portfolios, Project Emerald and Project Ruby, to Los Angeles private equity firm Oaktree. There was no hiding from the fact that NAMA was giving precious jewels to the vulture funds. They included almost 1,000 apartments in blocks across Dublin. Oaktree invested in them through a new Irish fund, Targeted Investment Opportunities. Tenants of some apartments were given eviction notices so that NAMA could sell them with vacant possession. NAMA also sold a site for 935 student accommodation units on Dublin's northside to another US fund, Blackrock. At this stage, a fifth of all the homes built using NAMA funding had been sold to corporate investors and 40 per cent of NAMA homes were sold for over €400,000.

The vultures become vampires
These big vulture investors were making major profits from Ireland's housing crisis and becoming Ireland's new corporate landlords. For example, Kennedy Wilson started investing in Ireland after the crash and by 2016 had €2bn of assets in Ireland. A representative of the company told the *Irish Times* in 2016 that 'Dublin is the most attractive property market in Europe.' Kennedy Wilson had become one of Ireland's biggest landlords with over 1,000 rental units.

IRES REIT generated net income of €5.5m between July and the end of September 2016, an increase of 53 per cent on 2015. It told the *Irish Times* that the current housing crisis, with a 'deep imbalance between demand and supply on Dublin's housing market', meant their profit outlook was 'very positive'.

From the government's perspective, its policy was working. It was attracting the big vulture real estate investors by making investing in housing in Ireland very profitable.

Minister for Finance Michael Noonan spoke candidly to a special committee set up by the Oireachtas to develop solutions to the housing and homeless crisis in April 2016. The minister explained that he 'introduced the Real Estate Investment Trusts tax regime in the Finance

Act 2013. This intervention has been successful in encouraging large scale investment into the commercial and residential property markets.' He gave examples of this 'positive' impact by highlighting that in Dublin in the previous few months, 'the largest property developer in the world out of Texas, Hines, has bought Cherrywood where there is potential for approximately 4,800 units.' He also gave the example of Cairn Homes, which along with Lone Star had bought Project Clear, a portfolio of loans off Ulster Bank with 1,700 acres of prime residential land stretching from west Dublin to Portmarnock, with the potential for 20,000 homes.

Cairn Homes was set up by Michael Stanley and Alan McIntosh in 2014 and floated on the London stock exchange in 2015, where it raised €440m in equity. Michael Stanley's 'pay' at Cairn Homes PLC in 2020 was €966,000. Cushman & Wakefield stated that Cairn Homes was the largest purchaser of development land in Ireland in 2016, making up 34 per cent of transactions, after dominating 2015 with purchases in partnership with Lone Star. Cairn bought the 164.4-acre Argentum portfolio for €105.6m. This deal saw Cairn acquire six prime Dublin suburban and commuter sites (including what would become Griffith Wood). According to Goodbody Stockbrokers, 'Growing house prices also supports higher development land residual values.' It is important to understand the link between land and house prices. Higher house prices mean land values rise, as bidders pay more for land based on higher future house prices. Higher land prices then feed into higher house prices. Those selling the land make big money as the market goes up. Developers and investors who own land can then control the housing market as they control the supply of land and supply of housing. By maintaining housing supply at a relatively low level, they can keep prices and rents, and their own profits, higher.

But back to the Oireachtas Committee. Minister Noonan said that what this all meant was that 'The market is correcting itself.' The market certainly was correcting itself. Putting itself back in the 'correct' position to make huge profits for investors and developers through higher house prices and rents.

Rebuilding Ireland

In July 2016, the government made a big splash with the launch of a new national housing plan – Rebuilding Ireland. The plan was based on the assumption that most of the younger generation would become lifetime renters:

> [T]he incomes of many households are such that aspiration to home ownership in the communities in which they came from and work is unlikely to be realizable: this is despite the fact that in the recent past households in similar relative economic positions may well have bought houses in those communities.

So the government was telling a new generation they would have to give up on the aspiration of owning their own home, but the government would continue to help investor funds and REITs realize their aspirations of converting the would-have-been homeowners into a generation of permanent renters from the REITs. As Rebuilding Ireland stated:

> It is envisaged that Real Estate Investment Trusts (REITS) and other institutional investors which have been successful at raising development finance and investing in the commercial office sector, have the potential to begin significant investment in build-to-rent projects.

In reality it was a developers' and investors' plan. It was made for them to reboot the property market. The role of the government was simply to subsidize the market. There was a growing demand for housing and a real growing housing need, but the developers and investors weren't making enough profit, so they were still not building. So much for market theory of demand and supply. Just under 10,000 homes were built in 2016. Of these, just 5,078 were developer-delivered 'scheme' homes, 1,177 were apartments, and 3,660 were one-off single dwellings.

Through the Rebuilding Ireland plan, and various policies in the coming years, the Irish Government introduced measures to make house and apartment building 'viable', i.e. even more profitable for developers and investor funds to woo them into building new homes: by allowing house prices to increase, by reducing apartment standards and sizes, by allowing the tax breaks to continue, and by delivering new social housing through leasing and rental as an investment asset for vulture funds. It was all focused on 'correcting' and 'resuscitating' the market instead of using the resources and tools government had – the huge NAMA land banks and finance – to build social and affordable housing. The government allowed an artificial scarcity of housing to emerge. The private sector was not building as it wanted prices to rise further, so that was creating a scarcity. The State added to that scarcity by not building social or affordable housing, even though land and finance were available to build homes. Neither the State nor the private market built. And not only did the government not build, it worsened the crisis by adding demand pressure to the rental and house-buying market by renting social housing and buying it from the private market. Through Rebuilding Ireland, the government made it clear that private rental was the way forward for housing in Ireland. It claimed it was the younger generation's lifestyle 'choice' to rent, ignoring the reality that most people were being forced into private renting in Ireland because of the lack of affordable homes to buy or any real secure social housing.

Social housing 'solutions' are not homes

Rebuilding Ireland misled the public as to the level of actual new-build social housing it was going to provide. It stated that 134,000 social housing 'solutions' (note, not new-*build* homes) would be provided over the lifetime of the plan. There would be in the region of 25,000 per year. It sounds really impressive. But the overwhelming majority of these social housing 'solutions', a whopping two-thirds, were to come from private sector supply, through 83,000 households in the private rental sector where the landlord is paid HAP subsidies. A further 11,000 were to be bought from the private market and 10,000 were to be leased from the market. A tiny proportion, just 15 per cent of the new social housing 'solutions', were to be new builds by local authorities and housing associations. This flawed approach essentially handed the delivery of social housing to the market and investors. This way of delivering social housing would take a huge proportion of supply away from an already overheated market, adding to price and rent inflation.

If the government had spent the same amount of money on direct building by local authorities and housing associations as it did in paying the money to HAP and leasing to private landlords and investors, it could have built 55,000 social housing units over a ten-year period and 165,000 units over thirty years.

But Rebuilding Ireland was explicit about the real purpose of new social housing. The new leasing scheme was 'to facilitate larger levels of private investment in social housing'. Property owners would be paid up to 95 per cent of the market rent for 25-year lease agreements with the State (up from 80 per cent in the last scheme) and the asset (property) would be retained by the private sector, with the State left with no asset at the end of the lease.

Investor funds and developers lobbied government heavily for the development of these social housing schemes. They provided a market for housing when home buyers were constrained in what they could borrow. These new social housing schemes were developed in the long-term interest, not of the Irish State and Irish taxpayers, but of the profitability requirements of private global investors, landlords and developers.

In 2016, local authorities built just 320 social housing units, while social housing associations built 340, but there were 16,000 social housing tenants housed in the private rental sector via HAP to private landlords. We can really see in 2016, then, the huge increase in HAP tenants, and this added significant pressure to an already undersupplied rental market. Almost a third of the private rental sector was some form of state-funded housing. There were 50,000 tenants in receipt of rent allowance, 16,000 HAP recipients and 20,000 RAS recipients.

The Rebuilding Ireland plan also showed that local authorities and various state bodies had a massive amount of land in their ownership on which they could build homes, with the potential for over 50,000 new homes. It identified 700 sites owned by local authorities and the Housing Agency (totalling some 1,700 hectares), and 30 sites (200 hectares) owned by state or semi-state bodies in the greater Dublin area and other major urban centres. The obvious response would have been to build social and affordable homes on these sites. But no. The government put them up for sale and opened new PPP developments to developers and investors. Property sections of national newspapers carried advertisements by Dublin local authorities of a lands initiative offering public land to developers as 'development opportunities . . . in prime locations'. This was to involve public land being handed over into the private ownership of private developers, with 70 per cent of the housing being developed as private units for sale or rent and only 30 per cent as social housing.

These developments were part of the government's macro-level approach to housing and economic policy, based on the market theory, which focused on providing an array of policy measures including private market 'incentives' and 'demand-led' policies in the hope of increasing the profitability of house building for private finance and developers and thus expecting to increase housing 'supply'. An array of government policies promoted increased property and rent prices: reduced development levies; a €220m infrastructure fund (helping to put in water supplies, clear sites, etc.) to make private developments 'viable' on already zoned land; halving the Part V requirement from 20 per cent to 10 per cent of developments in 2015; reduced apartment standard guidelines; delaying the implementation of a vacant site tax.

Because these policies provided incentives for financializing housing as an investment asset and subsidized the property industry, they fuelled another property bubble and created the latest housing crisis.

Rebuilding Ireland did not approach the provision of housing as a human right and a social need. It did not even mention the human right to housing.

Landlords increased rents by 11 per cent in Dublin, and 9 per cent outside Dublin in 2016. They had increased rents in Dublin by 50 per cent in the four years since 2012. Investor funds were also actively doing this. When the investor funds bought properties, they sometimes evicted existing tenants to get in higher-paying ones. NAMA-appointed receivers were likely to be doing the same. This made it more attractive to the funds as they could then rent at higher rates to new tenants. For example, by 2016 IRES REIT had amassed a portfolio of 2,300 apartments in Dublin. In 2016, the Irish Times reported that it increased rents in its properties at rates of up to 16 per cent.

In June 2016, the Minister for Environment and Housing Simon Coveney again refused a proposal to cap rents to inflation, because, he said, a 'properly functioning rental market needs to offer something for landlords as well as tenants'. He looked at the housing crisis from the landlords' and investors' perspective. Rent controls were seen as a 'disincentive' to invest. And housing and economic policy had been made completely dependent on their supply. But in reality they were not dependent on these vulture and vampire investors. State and housing bodies could have been delivering affordable rental and purchase homes.

The Minister for Finance also explained that he saw rent controls as 'counterproductive'. He explained that 'intervening in the market can be quite tricky' and 'One needs to be very careful . . . It is very easy to say we want to have rent certainty and not allow rents to rise but who will get involved in investing in rental property in that case?' He explained that landlords' income was a key concern of government: 'Unless a landlord in the private sector can generate an income from investing in a block of apartments, or a house which he converts into two apartments, he will not do it.' So, according to the minister, 'If one interferes with the market to the extent that normal commercial activity does not proceed, one will not fix it; it actually causes the problem.'

The refusal to consider an alternative housing system, one where the State plays a key role in delivering housing, was evident when he said:

One has to be very careful because most of the housing market is supplied by the private sector. Affordable houses are supplied by private vendors and rental accommodation is provided by private landlords.

So it was back to relying on the private market for supply, and therefore any intervention that might potentially impact on that privately provided supply – even if it protected tenants from higher rents or evictions into homelessness – was not possible because the government had made policy based on the private market.

PPPs return

O'Devaney Gardens had housed almost three hundred social housing flats for almost fifty years. It had been put forward for regeneration during the years of the Celtic Tiger. When those plans collapsed with the crash, its community had been dispossessed of their homes and by 2015 it was largely gone. New plans were developed by the council to hand the public land to a developer to build mainly private market homes on it. In July 2016, Dublin City councillors approved a motion put forward by Workers' Party councillor Éilis Ryan that the site should be redeveloped with 100 per cent public, mixed-income housing. The public housing proposal suggested that 50 per cent of homes would be for social housing tenants and 50 per cent for those above the social housing limits but in need of affordable housing, those struggling in the private rented sector. But Minister for Housing Simon Coveney made it clear that there would be no central government funding for such a plan. The plan was hardly radical – the State would fund the building of a complete affordable housing development built on public land for a range of income earners in the middle of a housing crisis. The minister insisted that it should be just 30 per cent social housing, 20 per cent affordable-to-buy and 50 per cent private market price.

Investor funds lobby for housing policy

The *Irish Times* reported that a number of the big investor funds lobbied government in the summer of 2016 in the run-up to the budget. The funds were concerned about potential new rules that might affect their level of tax and rents. Kennedy Wilson, for example, warned Minister Coveney just a week before the October Budget that such changes would 'have a very negative impact on the perception of Ireland as being a stable and reliable market in which to invest'. Oaktree wrote to the government warning that any changes would 'give a clear message' to international investors that Ireland's business rules are 'unpredictable'. Oaktree's executives and lawyers actually met with Department of Finance officials on 25 November 2016.

Their lobbying was successful. Late in 2016, under huge public pressure to act on the rental crisis, the government introduced Rent Pressure Zones (RPZs). They portrayed these as a major intervention to control runaway rental inflation. But far from freezing rents or linking them to inflation, they allowed an incredible 4 per cent annual increase on rents – with no evidence to justify such a high annual increase. Media reports cited 4 per cent as the level of return sought by institutional investors, so the new rent measures were set to ensure that investor funds had the 'stable investment environment' to get the profits they wanted.

RPZs were mainly restricted to Dublin, and huge parts of the country were left with no rent controls. Also, the new rent control legislation contained exemptions that helped the investor landlords in their strategy of evicting tenants to get in higher-paying ones. Exemptions included properties that had undergone substantial refurbishment, properties not let in the previous two years, and, significantly, the first setting of a rent price in a newly built property or a property which had never previously been let. This provided a clear continued incentive for investor landlords to buy up and develop build-to-rent property.

In his last year as Minister for Finance (Paschal Donohoe would take over in 2017), Michael Noonan made it clear that bringing the vulture funds to Ireland was no accident. It was government policy, and the government considered it a huge success. He explained that if NAMA had not sold property at a discount to the vulture funds, the market would not have recovered. That was the fundamental purpose of the government's intervention – to reboot the Irish property market, despite its proven failure to deliver affordable homes. He said:

> There are various arguments about property being given away and I was asked why I did not wait and so on but unless somebody sells cheap and there is somebody to buy cheap, there is no market. It is from then on that the market builds. There is a viable market now for commercial property in Dublin but that is on the back of these initial sales which recreated the market.

He then went on to say something that really laid bare the government's view that vulture funds played a 'natural' role in cleaning up the mess of the economic crash. His quote went viral:

> The TD criticized me for not intervening with what she described as vulture funds. The investment companies in question may be colloquially known as vulture funds but it was, in the first instance, a compliment when they were so dubbed in the United States where vultures provide a very good service in the ecology through cleaning up dead animals that are littered across the landscape, especially in the prairie provinces.

Who were the dead animals the vultures fed off? It was us.

Some people decided they had had enough. A group of about a hundred activists, trade unionists and musicians occupied the empty NAMA-controlled office building of Apollo House in December 2016 to provide shelter for the growing number of homeless people on the streets of Dublin and to highlight that, for some, the housing crisis had become unbearable. And for many citizens it had become utterly unacceptable, and they wanted to change it.

2017

House price: €240,000 (+11.7%)
Rent in Dublin: €1,579 (+8%)
Rent outside Dublin: €836 (+9%)

In 2017, NAMA sold over 1,300 residential rental units to Kennedy Wilson. Global wealth funds from across the world were looking at Ireland, and Dublin's property in particular, as a 'hot' site for investment. The PWC Europe 2017 report quoted one US investor describing the attractiveness of investing in the private rental sector in Dublin: 'The private rented sector in Dublin is a home run.'

In June 2017, Leo Varadkar became Taoiseach. He was voted in with the support of independents and by Fianna Fáil abstaining from the vote. Paschal Donohoe was appointed Minister for Finance and Eoghan Murphy Minister for Housing. They were all new in their positions, but nothing new was developed in housing policy. It was 'business as usual'.

In 2017, the government said it provided 25,000 social housing 'solutions'. As previously highlighted, these 'solutions' do not actually mean new-build social housing as you and I would think of it. There were in fact just 400 new builds by local authorities. But there were an incredible 18,000 private rental properties taken up as HAP, and 2,200 social housing units bought in the private housing market.

Rents and homelessness rose further. But again, the investor 'supply' was the priority for government. In January 2017, while still Minister for Housing, Simon Coveney said in the Dail that he understood there was a need 'to find a mechanism to slow down dramatic rental inflation and protect against landlords taking advantage of the fact that there is a significant supply shortage in certain areas'. At least he admitted that was what was going on – landlords were causing rent inflation by increasing rents and taking advantage of the supply shortage. But he also knew there was a mechanism to slow down rent inflation – legislation to control rents, and building of social and affordable housing by local authorities and housing associations. But the government was unwilling to do either because its focus was the profitability requirements of investors, developers and landlords. 'What we are trying to do is to ensure that the viability of residential investment is significantly improved.' Coveney said that the policy of allowing 'extraordinary increases in rents' was working, as there was now a growing 'appetite' for investors to build. The incentive was the lack of rent controls, which meant that tenants were paying ever-higher rents, and a government policy that wouldn't build social or affordable housing, thus leaving people with no option but to get housing in the private rental sector from the investor funds. So the government created Generation Rent as an incentive for investor fund landlords.

The word 'appetite' is really striking here. The minister understood that these investor funds have an appetite for rents and profit. Like vultures and vampires, they need to be fed. And the government provided Generation Rent on a plate, to feed the funds. As Minister Coveney outlined:

> We are starting to see an appetite for risk and investment in residential property in Dublin. We have seen extraordinary increases in rent for residential properties which has changed that appetite. . . . We need to make sure the incentive remains in place to ensure that money is investing significantly in residential property.

In April 2017, the Central Statistics Office (CSO) released data from the national census of 2016. It showed that, while a housing and homelessness crisis was raging, of the two million houses and apartments in the State a whopping 183,312 were vacant: 140,120 were vacant houses and 43,192 were vacant apartments. This shows the failure of the housing market and market theory in allocating housing to meet needs. A market doesn't allocate according to need, but according to the profit motives of owners of commodities. Owners of vacant property had no interest in and faced no penalty for leaving their private property vacant. And so we had, and continue to have, a sufficient 'supply' of housing in the country. It's just that housing is allowed to be treated as a private asset, and is not allocated to those who need it. The fact that the government knew there were 180,000 vacant homes in 2017 and yet put no vacant homes tax in place and made no serious attempt to address this high level of vacancy and dereliction is also a reason why the housing crisis persisted. There was a potential supply of housing there – in vacant and derelict buildings – but tackling that would not have profited property owners, investor funds and developers, and so they were left vacant and derelict while the housing shortage continued.

The census showed that total housing stock grew by just 8,800 (0.4 per cent) between 2011 and 2016, but population growth was 3.8 per cent, up from 4.58 million in 2011 to 4.76 million in 2016. It also showed that there was, for the first time since 1966, an increase in overcrowding in Irish housing. One in ten households were over-crowded, with 95,013 households with more persons than rooms, a 28 per cent rise on 2011. It also showed the collapse in home ownership to 67.6 per cent, the lowest rate of home ownership since 1971. The age at which most people were able to buy a home had increased from 28 to 41. The point at which two-thirds of house-holders owned their own homes (with or without a loan) occurred at age 41 in 2016, while in 1991 the equivalent age for that milestone was 28 years.

Land hoarding

It was also revealed in 2017 that most of the land that NAMA was selling to investors was not being built on. It was being hoarded as investors watched land prices (and their future profits) rise. Between 2010 and 2015 NAMA sold development land (sites) to investors that had the potential for up to 20,000 housing units. However, just 5 per cent of the land bought from NAMA was developed by 2016. The speculative purchase of land by these investors also enabled them to exert considerable control over the production and prices of housing.

The issue of land banking and its ownership and control has been central to the housing affordability crisis since the Celtic Tiger days. During the Celtic Tiger it was estimated that 90 per cent of the development land in the greater Dublin area was controlled by a dozen developers. Then a lot of that land was bought by global investor funds or Irish developer funds backed by global equity.

The government announced a vacant sites tax to tackle this, but it was only at 3 per cent of the value of the land, which, as the minister for finance admitted, 'does not incentivize anybody at the moment' and in any case it was not due to be introduced until 2018. There were also huge exemptions to it. The minister explained that part of the reason for this was the strong property rights in the Constitution. This meant the government needed to give a long lead-in time to avoid a legal challenge from land and property owners:

> The 3 per cent levy was guided by that. Given the strong property rights, it had to impose the levy that was proportionate. It would be open to challenge if it had imposed a higher levy... the problem was in that space and that was the reason it landed there.

The concentration of land ownership, and the speculative purchase of development land, is another example of how private housing and property markets contain significant monopoly elements, where investors and developers seek to maximize their land ownership, and will hoard that land, giving them significant power over the supply and thus increasing prices and their profits. It shows how applying the economics theory that markets are efficient allocators of resources and that they ensure supply will meet demand simply does not work when it comes to housing.

2018

House price: €254,000 (+7.3%)
Rent in Dublin: €1,699 (+7.6%)
Rent outside Dublin: €896 (+7%)

In January 2018, Taoiseach Leo Varadkar was questioned in the Dáil on the housing crisis, and confronted by how hopeless it was for Generation Rent to get the deposit together to buy a home when faced with exorbitant rents. He responded by ignoring the particular difficulties of today's generations struggling for housing and the Central Bank requirements for deposits, unlike the Celtic Tiger days when he bought his home. He said that people should emigrate, move back in with their parents or go get money off the 'bank of mum and dad'.

It's always been the case that a person needs to raise a deposit to buy a house. People do it in many different ways. Sometimes people go abroad for a period and earn money. Others get money from their parents. Lots of us did. Others get money through other loans. Sometimes people stay at home for a period and raise a deposit in that way.

His comments provoked an angry backlash from the public.

In March 2018, Minister for Housing Eoghan Murphy issued new design standard guidelines for build-to-rent apartments, under which planning applications could bypass the local planning processes and submit development plans to the national planning agency, An Bord Pleanála, for 'fast-track planning'. Build-to-rent could also have reduced unit sizes below minimum guideline size and 'flexibility' on internal storage and could be entirely for rental. This promoted the development of co-living-type housing, providing en-suite bedrooms for tenants with shared communal living areas. Bartra Capital Property Group, a privately owned international property company founded by property developer Richard Barrett, was an early developer of these new forms of 'living'. Barrett set up investment fund management companies to give Chinese and global real estate investors access to property in major international cities, including Dublin.

Bartra quickly proceeded with build-to-rent developments and announced that it was planning Ireland's first co-living developments, dubbed 'niche living', including 222 co-living units in Tallaght, 208 in Dún Laoghaire and 100 in Rathmines. On its website (www.nicheliving.ie), Bartra explained the important role of the new guidelines in developing co-living projects:

> Following the release of the Sustainable Urban Housing: Design Standards for New Apartments residential guidelines in Ireland, March 2018, Bartra are now able to introduce a fresh and innovative concept, delivering the first purpose-designed individual shared living suites in Ireland.

In 2018, NAMA sold €300m of loans in Cork to Deutsche Bank as part of the Project Lee portfolio, including a mixed-use development in Cork City centre, offices, the Mahon Point Retail Park, and apartments close to University College Cork.

In October, housing activists occupied Airbnb's Dublin offices in protest at the way in which many longer-term rental homes were being turned into short-term tourist rentals. Landlords could make even higher incomes from renting out to tourists than from the already exorbitant rents paid by longer-term tenants. It was also a way to circumvent new rent legislation and get existing tenants out.

Later in the month, the Raise the Roof coalition of civil society groups including trade unions, the National Women's Council of Ireland and the Union of Students of Ireland organized a protest of over 15,000 at the Dáil to coincide with a motion put forward by the opposition. Raise the Roof called for a major increase in government spending on building public housing – social and affordable homes on public land. It also called for a rent freeze; the cessation of tenants being evicted; ending homelessness; formulating policy to treat housing as a human right and a public good, such as education and healthcare had; and for the government to hold a referendum to establish a right to housing.

Speaking at the protest, Sheila Nunan, president of ICTU, told the crowd:

> It is an emergency when students cannot afford to go to college or families cannot afford their rent. It is an emergency when rent is no longer payable and too many people are dispossessed and homeless. Ten thousand homeless people is too many and it is a scandal when thousands of children are living in hotels, hostels and bed and breakfast. Housing is a basic human right. Too many of our citizens are affected.

Inside the Dáil, the government again refused to deliver a referendum to make housing a human right in the Constitution. And in November of that year, the Minister for Finance made it very clear whose policies the government was prioritizing.

The Minister for Finance, Kennedy Wilson, and Capital Dock
There is a photograph on Kennedy Wilson's website of the launch of its Capital Dock build-to-rent development. In the picture, smiling broadly as he cuts the ribbon, is the Minister for Finance, Paschal Donohoe, standing alongside senior Kennedy Wilson executives. The press release accompanying the launch says that the Capital Dock development at Sir John Rogerson's Quay in Dublin's South Docklands includes 190 units for rent. The 'five-star' development offers 'a concierge team alongside its signature exclusive five-star resident amenities to include a dedicated on-site management team, resident lounges, cinema, professional gym, chef's kitchen and dining, business suites and external terraces'.

At the launch, Peter Collins, president of Kennedy Wilson Europe, outlined its ambitious growth plans for Ireland, describing Capital

Dock as a 'cornerstone development', and laid out the company's target of owning 5,000 units over the coming years.

Two-bedroom apartments in Capital Dock are being advertised to rent at between at €3,500 and €4,600 a month. The *Business Post* reported that some of the apartments have been left vacant. This was the housing that NAMA and the government prioritized and provided. No wonder the housing crisis continued to worsen.

2019

House price: €156,286 (+0.9%)
Rent in Dublin: €1,744 (+2.6%)
Rent outside Dublin: €942 (+5%)

In 2019, the number of homeless people in Ireland climbed to its highest ever number: 9,968. According to the homeless charity Focus Ireland, 3,811 of those were children, and, shockingly, one child became homeless every four hours in Dublin in 2019.

While there was an increase in the supply of new housing to 21,000 in 2019, a lot of it was being bought up by investor funds. Institutional property funds bought 95 per cent of all new apartments built in 2019.

In March 2019, the United Nations wrote to the Irish Government expressing its 'concern' with the 'government's practice of adopting laws and policies which treat housing as a commodity and undermine the enjoyment of housing as a human right'. It was concerned about 'laws and policies which have allowed unprecedented amounts of global capital to be invested in housing as security for financial instruments that are traded on global markets, and as a means of accumulating wealth'. This expanding role and unprecedented dominance of unregulated financial markets and corporations in the housing sector is now generally referred to as the 'financialization of housing' and it is having devastating consequences for tenants. The UN Rapporteur for Adequate Housing Leilani Farha told the government, 'Contrary to international human rights obligations', investment in housing in the Republic of Ireland 'has disconnected housing from its core social purpose of providing people with a place to live in with security and dignity'. The letter was ignored.

In July, Bartra applied to An Bord Pleanála for permission to build one of the first co-living developments under Eoghan Murphy's new design standards. It was a 208 'single occupancy bedspace' development, with an estimated 42 people per kitchen. The Minister for Housing said co-living blocks offered an 'exciting' choice to young workers and people should be 'excited' about a future of co-living where they will have 'less space for less rent'. However, the housing charity Threshold called the co-living development '21st-century bedsits with a glossy makeover'.

Speaking on Newstalk Radio, Minister Murphy said co-living was something he had seen in other cities, 'where you have your own private room, ensuite, but you also then have shared community spaces, a gym, a movie room, a games room, potentially, a kitchen, a living room'. The presenter Kieran Cuddihy at this point compared what Murphy was describing to a prison. But Murphy replied: 'Sorry, no, not at all like a prison, I mean if you've been in one of these places it's not at all, it's more like a very trendy, kind of, boutique hotel, type place, right.'

Bartra Capital's proposal for another major co-living development in Cookstown, Tallaght, was rejected by An Bord Pleanála because it would 'fail to provide an acceptable living environment'.

In September 2019, it emerged that Dublin City Council had chosen Barta as the developer of the public land of O'Devaney Gardens. Of the 824 homes on the site – 768 to be built by Bartra – 50 per cent (411) would be private dwellings for sale at market price by Bartra, just 165 would be affordable-to-buy and 248 would be social housing. The council also said the 'affordable' units would be €250,000 for a one-bedroom apartment and €320,000 for a two-bedroom apartment. There was outrage at the idea that these were somehow actually affordable. Minister Murphy told Dublin City councillors that unless they backed the deal there would be a five-year delay to the project.

2020

House price: €269,000 (+0.7%)
Rent in Dublin: €1,783 (+2%)
Rent outside Dublin: €992 (+5%)

In the February 2020 general election, housing and health were the main issues concerning voters. A majority of 25- to 34-year-olds said housing should be the priority for the new government. The housing 'youth-quake' delivered a very clear message to government. Both Fianna Fáil and Fine Gael lost seats in the election, receiving their lowest combined vote – a mere 43 per cent of the total. Sinn Féin had the largest support of any of the parties, largely because of their commitment to change housing policies.

But a month later, it was the world that changed. The global Covid pandemic emerged, and the massive public expression for a transformational change in housing along with the growing housing protests and advocacy dissipated in the context of the emergency responses to Covid. Understandably housing was put on the back burner as media, politics and the public tackled an unprecedented health and social crisis. But the global pandemic didn't stop the investor funds continuing their takeover of Irish housing. And government policy didn't stop their support of them either. As Gordon Gekko said in the movie *Wall Street*, 'Money never sleeps.'

Investor funds continued to flood into Ireland, doubling their purchase of property from 6,266 a year in 2016 to 12,378 in 2020.

In 2020, NAMA sold one of the real jewels of prime development land in Dublin – the 37-acre former Irish Glass Bottle site in Ringsend, Dublin 4. It's just a twenty-minute walk from the city centre, beside Dublin Port, looking out over Dublin Bay. It had incredible potential to be developed as a sustainable mixed-income community. Instead, the government sold it to a private developer, backed by a US real estate fund. The Ronan Group Real Estate investment firm – founded by Johnny Ronan, a familiar name from the Celtic Tiger era – and US investment firm Oaktree bought an 80 per cent stake in the site. NAMA retains 20 per cent. It is the largest vacant plot in the capital and is expected to deliver up to 3,800 homes. But just 25 per cent of these will be social and affordable housing.

We are back full circle to the Celtic Tiger, with multi-million developers profiteering from a housing crisis, except now it's multi-billion, and global real estate funds are leading the game.

In 2020, the State was paying close to €1bn to private landlords on various rent subsidy schemes to house social housing tenants. There were 60,000 private rental HAP tenants. In total, some 100,000 households, a third of the private rented sector, needed income support to pay their rent. The State was now bankrolling a third of private landlords, including real estate funds – the new institutional property landlords.

A glimpse of something different

Yet in 2020 and 2021, we also got a glimpse of a very different housing system, one based on housing needs, that would be possible if a different policy approach was taken. In response to the Covid pandemic crisis, the government did what it said it couldn't do all the way through the last decade of the crisis – it froze rents and put a ban on evictions. The number of evictions in the private rental sector collapsed. Renters described feeling, for the first time, a sense of security in their homes. Their constant low- (and not-so-low) level anxiety was lifted temporarily. Homelessness fell dramatically. The collapse of tourism meant that thousands of properties that had been rented out on short-term lets were suddenly available for renters, and for housing the homeless. Unfortunately, it took a global pandemic to show what was possible to solve the housing crisis. Even more sadly, the measures were just temporary, and as soon as the pandemic receded, so too did the emergency housing policies that had given some relief to those hardest hit by the crisis.

2021

Houseprice: €290,998 (+11%)
Rent in Dublin: €1,916 (+7.4%)
Rent outside Dublin: €1,114 (+12%)

The expectation was that Covid, with the shift to remote working, and the controlling of rents, would see an easing of the housing crisis. But that is not how it turned out. The pandemic led to a further restriction in supply as sites closed for months, and heightened purchase and development of homes by investors. Increased savings meant some people had more to spend on buying housing which, given the limited supply, further increased house prices. The ongoing failure to deliver social and affordable homes meant that people were still forced to try to find private rental homes, adding to further unprecedented rental inflation.

The ban on rent increases and evictions was lifted as soon as the government got the chance, in April 2021. Rents rose a further 7.4 per cent in 2021 to €1,916 in Dublin. This meant that rents in Dublin had risen by 99 per cent since their low of mid-2012 and were 47 per cent higher than the Celtic Tiger high rent in mid-2007. Rents rose outside of Dublin by 12 per cent as people relocating from Dublin sought homes to buy or rent in a tight market.

While many suffered income losses during the Covid crisis, for home builders and Properties, investors and REITs, it was boom time. Margaret Sweeney, head of IRES REIT, took home €1m in salary, up 42 per cent on 2019. CEO of Cairn, Michael Stanley, took home €960,000 in 2021, while Stephen Garvey of Glenveagh Properties took home €750,000. Glenveagh Properties' revenue rose to €476m in 2021. It was also appointed by the State to two partnership developments on public lands – for the Oscar Traynor site in Dublin City and the Donabate development in north Dublin. This particular deal highlighted the ongoing issue of the State handing public land over to private Properties and failing to build housing on a scale that might challenge the market and reduce house prices. The Donabate deal involved Fingal Council handing over 28 hectares of publicly owned land to Glenveagh in return for the developer building 20 per cent social housing and 20 per cent affordable housing. But the developer would get to sell – and profit from – 60 per cent (720) of the homes at market prices. On top of this, the council agreed that the houses would only be drip-fed on to the market over ten years, so as not to flood the local housing market. The council said the ten-year development timeframe was to take 'account of the number of houses the local market can absorb at any one time'. So again, the government created an artificial scarcity of housing as it delayed the building of homes in case it might flood the market and lead to lower prices. You couldn't make it up.

Meanwhile, the head of Lone Star, John Grayken, an American-born Irish billionaire who is now an Irish citizen for tax purposes, increased his worth to $8.7bn (according to the 2021 Bloomberg Billionaires Index). Irish property developers Luke and Brian Comer also joined the list of Irish billionaires.

In May 2021, the *Business Post* revealed that Round Hill Capital, a global real estate investment firm and one of the largest private landlords across Europe, was buying up most of the 174 houses in a newly built suburban estate in Maynooth, County Kildare. It caused a wave of anger across Ireland. For individuals and families who thought new homes being built across the country would be available for them to purchase, it was the last straw.

Crisis heaped upon crisis

By July 2022, house prices reached close to Celtic Tiger levels, and rents are breaking all records. We are repeating the mistakes of the not-so-distant past. It's in a different way now, though. The new bubble is being inflated by a lost decade of delivery of social and affordable housing and the pressure of investor funds out-bidding home buyers and providing the only new supply as hugely expensive rentals. As we stare down the barrel of another property crash, we are still, a decade later, dealing with the effects of the last property crash. The previous crisis is part of today's housing crisis. It is crisis heaped upon crisis.

It should be clear by now that the government does not actually want you to be able to buy or rent an affordable home. It created an unaffordable housing system that is focused on delivering housing as an investment asset, not a home.

In 2013, house prices had crashed, and rents were half of what they are today. Our housing system at that point was actually relatively affordable. But in the following years government policy made many homes completely unaffordable. As the economy began to recover, and rents and house prices started rising, the government was called on to implement rent controls and to build social and affordable homes. But it refused over and over to do this.

The government's 'affordable' housing measures were demand-side ones that added pressure to house prices, not providing a supply of affordable homes that would reduce prices. For example, the help to buy scheme (introduced in 2016) provided first-time home buyers with their deposit, while the shared equity scheme (introduced in 2022) enabled borrowers to take on more mortgage debt beyond the Central Bank rules.

But in the absence of an increased supply of affordable homes, this extra credit fuels house prices. Even more important, it gives home buyers little additional chance of competing with investor purchasers who face no limits on what they can borrow and invest in housing. Investor funds and Irish developers can borrow limitless amounts from global equity funds. And Irish landlords, property investors or Airbnb investors can borrow from banks and funds with buy-to-let mortgages, use equity in their homes or other property they have, or use their deposits and investments.

There is, therefore, a huge inequality between investors and home buyers in regard to lending and spending limits on housing, and thus between who can buy housing and who can't. There's also a fundamental flaw in the Central Bank rules, which were put in place to stop rising house price inflation. The Central Bank rules control lending to home buyers, but there are no limits on what investor funds and Irish property investors can spend on housing – which helps explain how house prices have continued to rise, while credit lending to home buyers has been constrained.

Furthermore, there are those who can draw on the bank of mum and dad, who have parents who can give their children the deposit, or large cash amounts on top of the mortgage, to outbid others and push up prices. Another inequality of access to housing. This additional spending also fuels rising house prices.

A large number of homes in Ireland are being bought as second homes, as investments for retirement, as an investment to bring in income as an Airbnb. There is still a fundamental conflict and inequality between the purchase of housing as an investment asset by those with money and wealth in Ireland, and those on low and average incomes who are trying to buy or rent that housing as their home.

Not only did government policy do nothing to address these issues over the last decade, it also compounded the inequalities between those who are trying to buy or rent a home, and those who are buying housing as an investment.

The solution is not to expand what home buyers can borrow to try to compete with investors – that would just push up their debt further, and it would not be sustainable, leaving us with more mortgage arrears. Nor is the solution for first-time buyers to hold back or go on strike, as some economists suggest – the investors would just step in and hoover up even more homes. The solution is to restrict housing purchase to those buying their home – as their primary residence – and focus on supplying homes, not investment assets.

We can see that the overall aim of policy was not to provide affordable housing but to facilitate and support rising housing prices and rents, so that property would be an attractive investment to global investors, to buy up all the toxic loans from NAMA, and to provide rising values for banks balance sheets, and recoup more value when they repossess and sell homes in mortgage arrears. For over a decade, policy has prioritized the interests of property, finance, developers, investors and landlords over those who are looking to get an affordable home.

Hikes in house prices have dramatically outstripped wage increases. Over the last eight years, wages grew by just 9 per cent while the cost of a home soared by 68 per cent. The national median price of a dwelling – which includes apartments and houses – stood at €157,500 in March 2013. By March 2019 it had risen to €264,544, a 68 per cent rise. A full-time worker's average earnings were €44,709 a year in 2013, rising to €48,946 by 2019 – an increase of 9.5 per cent. The generational issue hit incomes too. The under-40s were worst hit by rising rent and house prices and lower wages, insecure contracts and pay inequality. The low-wage gig economy and cuts to welfare further restricted younger generations' ability to afford a home.

Making house prices and rents more unaffordable has been an accepted consequence of Irish economic and housing policy over the last decade. The evictions of families and children into home-lessness has been an accepted consequence of government economic and housing policy. The reality is that the interests of real estate investors, developers and banks dominate housing policy and thinking. There is a reluctance on the part of government to do anything significant that would disturb or disrupt the market and make house prices and rents actually affordable. This is because they have hitched their wagon of housing supply to the REITs, and ulti-mately the State ideologically still does not want to take responsibility for housing provision – which it should; rather, it wants to leave it with the market and investors. The underlying reason for their failure to provide affordable homes is the ideological opposition to social and affordable housing and their capture by investor interests. The market and investor ideology did not believe that the State should do this. It saw the private market as the main way to deliver housing, and so, rather than having a vision that would see the State and not-for-profits play a huge role in delivering housing, all policy was focused on resuscitating the market.

Noam Chomsky described the military–industrial complex as the elite group who really ran foreign policy in the USA. The wars of the future would arise not from conflict but because the military–industrial complex need to make money from weapons, and therefore they need wars. You can draw a direct analogy with our housing crisis. It's not an accident or a policy mistake. The crisis has emerged from policy designed to meet the needs of the property–investor–landlord–bankers complex that does not want to solve housing crises, but wants them to continue, without end.

Government policies resulted in a lost decade of housing from 2010 to 2020 and the creation of Generation Rent, Generation Locked-out and Generation Emigration. We are in this crisis because of the policies pursued over the last decade, not because of anything millennials did. Governments were willing to sacrifice a generation and housing for future generations for short-term political gain and to protect the property values and wealth interests of those they represented and valued in society.

Governments also wanted house prices to rise so that the older generation of home-owning voters would get their property values back up. They had a narrow view of that particular interest, with no concern for the longer-term impact on future generations. They wanted to protect the value of the assets held by the privileged groups in Irish society, the political party funders, and lobbyists, and ignore the generations coming after them.

After the Celtic Tiger, we were at a point where we could have completely reshaped our housing system. The State had enough land and finance to provide an affordable housing supply for the next twenty years, but governments between 2009 and 2022 decided not to do that. Instead, they chose to get the property interests back up and running again. They removed the availability and access to affordable housing that essentially sacrificed future generations and their ability to get affordable housing. They should be held accountable for those decisions. They handed the housing future of generations to vulture funds and REITs, to extract rent from them for the rest of their lives, setting up a permanent drip from the veins of Generation Rent into the mouths of the vampire investor funds. The government resurrected a zombie Celtic Tiger model of housing and replaced buy-to-let Irish landlords with build-to-rent global investor landlords.

Generation Austerity – the homeowners who went into arrears, the tenants who were evicted – Generation Rent and Generation Locked-out are the carcass that the vulture funds fed from. And our government enabled this feast. NAMA was the pallbearer that took the carcass to the mountain top for the vultures to feed from. Our government stood at the bottom of the mountain urging NAMA to get on with the job so that it could get back to business as usual.

And the government sheds its crocodile tears about the decline in home ownership, rising homelessness and renters stuck facing high rents. How could you claim to care about a carcass – a generation – when 250,000 were forced to emigrate, when 15,000 children were forced to become homeless? Generation Rent was the collateral damage, the accepted price of 'recovery'.

But this isn't new. Emigration has been a safety valve for the Irish political establishment for generations. It has been willing to accept the social devastation of parts of the population – generations-long emigration, or the institutionalization of poor lone-parent mothers and their children – in order to keep the privileged interests in place and the system ticking along. We can trace it back to the colonized days, when a section of middle- and upper-class Irish professionals worked as administrators for the Empire. They had to turn away and ignore the suffering they were colluding with. It goes back to the Famine, and the humanity that had to be suppressed by the wealthy landlords evicting starving families from their hovels. Irish society must no longer tolerate this acceptance of human suffering.

The biggest failure of governments in this period was the failure to build affordable housing. Not one affordable home was built by the Irish Government – local authorities or any state body – from 2008 to 2021. And what did the investor funds say was the biggest threat to their continued investment in Ireland? The State building affordable homes. Because that would have removed the vampire funds' market and reduced their ability to turn Generation Rent into a permanent investment for them.

We have created a situation in housing that is absurdly dysfunctional in meeting the basic human need of shelter and home.

We can understand this better by making a comparison with the provision of primary school education.

Think about it like this: all the children in a local area are due to start junior infants in the local primary school. There are usually thirty places in a class, and there might be two or three junior infant classes in areas of higher population. The parents who want their children to attend the school enrol them, turn up on 1 September, and their kids get an education for the next fourteen years, delivered by excellent teachers, paid for and provided by the State, guaranteed as a right under our Constitution. Of course, there are exceptions and exclusions and sometimes a lack of spaces, but in the main, that's how it works.

Now, if access to primary education were delivered like housing is in Ireland, this is how it would look.

The parents of children due to start in junior infants in September go to enrol their kids in the local school but are told the local school was bought up by an investor fund. The fund rebuilt it as a fantastic giant new building for sixty kids. But to get a place in it, you have to pay €10,000 a year. So only ten kids from the wealthiest families in the area can afford to attend it. Most of it lies empty. The next nearest school is a one-hour drive away. But, as most primary education is now delivered (as housing is) through the market by private for-profit education providers, that school is run by an Irish private education developer. It has thirty places available. But it costs €5,000 to get your kid in for the year. Five of the thirty places are paid for by the State to be made available to low-income families as part of the government's obligation to deliver 'education for all'. The private education developer has given an education agent the role of selling the other 25 places to interested families. The agent sells them to the parents who make the highest bid. The higher the price, the higher the agent's commission, so they have a few tricks that keeps the bidding going as high as possible. The families end up in bidding wars and have to pay between €5,000 and €10,000 to get a place. You are outbid and your child can't get an education.

They're stuck at home, with you trying to home-school them. And remember how impossible and pointless that was during the lockdowns!

It seems an outrageous way to deliver public education and access to the fundamental right of primary education. But we are doing the same with access to, and allocation of, the fundamental human right of housing.

Chapter 5
Home as Haven:
The True Value and Meaning of Home

We need a complete rethink and reappraisal of how we view and understand housing. Our conversations are too often about housing as 'property' and investment 'units', not as a home. We talk about the property ladder, the rise and rise of property prices, how much our house is 'worth', how we can get an increased 'supply' to meet 'demand'. But in all this, the true meaning, purpose and value of housing to us – as a home – is missing.

What is home? We say to a welcome guest, 'Take your shoes off, put your feet up, make yourself at home.' Home is our sanctuary, our haven. It shelters us from the storms of weather and the storms of life. It is the first place we live in, the place we are born into. It is where our children grow and develop, and where we hopefully grow old and age in peace, surrounded by familiarity and comfort.

A home is essential to our wellbeing, our physical and mental health. It is central to our sense of self and our identity as individuals, families, communities and as a society. It is a place with deep emotional meaning for us that we create through our daily living. Home is the place where we dream, make memories, create ideas and the future. It is, as French philosopher Gaston Bachelard described it, 'the shelter of the imagination'.

From the moment you are born, your housing shapes and forms you. It is fundamental to child development – by providing a secure base and a protected space to grow. A home is not just where we live; it enables us to develop and thrive. During the Covid pandemic this became crystal clear: our homes became not only our space for living, but also crèches, schools, offices, gyms . . .

These are the true values, functions and meanings of home. What matters to us in relation to our homes is not its status as property, wealth, economic commodity investment, but the emotional meaning and wellbeing it gives us.

But not all housing provides a home. Is it a home if you just have a temporary lease, or if you live in fear of eviction, or where there is mould or damp, or you are in a cramped hotel room or Family Hub? How can we create our own identity and meaning in a home if we cannot paint the walls, hang a picture, or if it isn't ours but our parents' home?

Home as shelter

Your home is your health, more than it is your wealth. Good housing means you are more likely to have better health. The psychologist Abraham Maslow's well-known theory of human need explains how fundamental housing is to our health and wellbeing. His theory involves a hierarchy of five levels of human need, often presented in a pyramid diagram, with basic needs at the bottom and higher-level ones at the top. We need to have the basic physiological needs met or we will suffer from ill-health, but we also need these needs met to achieve the higher needs such as a job, creativity and self-actualization. Shelter, as in housing, is one of the basic physiological needs identified in Maslow's hierarchy. So, as humans, we cannot function or realize any of our other needs without shelter.

This makes complete sense. Public health experts describe housing as one of the key 'social determinants' of a person's health. Substandard housing makes us ill. Damp, and associated mould, are linked with respiratory illnesses, asthma, headaches, diarrhoea, fever and creating general susceptibility to poor health. Cold homes have been linked to raised blood pressure and cholesterol, as well as excess winter mortality. Not to mention the negative mental health impacts of poor housing conditions.

Bachelard, who was chair of the Philosophy Department at the Sorbonne in the 1960s, took a particular interest in the role of home as shelter. He described how severe weather, such as storms, reveals the true meaning and purpose of home. A storm makes sense of shelter, he wrote, because it is when we are inside a comfortable home in a storm (think of the howling winds and persistent torrential rain we get in Ireland) that we realize we could not survive without our home. Our home really becomes shelter during a storm. We listen to the rain against the window, and there is a beauty and power in it that makes us realize that home is protecting us from it, and even enabling us to enjoy it from a place of safety. It serves as a stark reminder of the central human necessity of shelter and how those living on the streets are exposed to weather and stripped of one of their basic needs for survival. The owners of homes affected by mica, which are literally crumbling, describe how recent storms have left them terrified that their house will fall down around them, as they listen to the walls cracking apart.

Home meets our human needs

We need housing to meet not only our shelter needs, but all our needs across the five levels of Maslow's hierarchy. We need a home to meet the basic physiological needs of food, water, rest, clothing, overall health and reproduction. We need housing for physical and mental health. We cannot rest properly if we do not have our own space, our own bed and room, in our own home. And it doesn't get any more basic than the reproduction of the species – you need your own secure stable home to have and raise children. And you need it before you even get to that point – to make and hold the relationships required to start a family, and then provide the secure base for children. The home is where most of us eat our food, where we store food and prepare meals. We get our drinking water and water for sanitation at home.

At the second level of Maslow's hierarchy are 'safety needs', which include protection from violence and theft, emotional stability and wellbeing, health security and financial security. A home is essential to all of these. It is the shelter we need to withstand, navigate and survive the multiple vulnerabilities and increasing precariousness of the human life journey. By providing a secure base, housing provides a deep sense of psychological safety and stability, known as 'ontological' security.

Ontological security is fundamental to our sense of ourselves, our self-identity and our feelings of security about the reliability of life. It enables us to trust the world around us, have confidence in other people, in the social order and in our place in society. It enables a belief that our self-actualization can be achieved. Our home provides the secure base to enable this sense of ontological security.

We can use the attachment theory of psychologist John Bowlby to help explain this fundamental human need for a secure base. Bowlby explained that for a child to grow and develop emotionally and cognitively they need a secure base of attachment with a caregiver who meets their needs, and to whom they can turn as a safe haven when upset or anxious. When children develop trust in the availability and reliability of this relationship, their anxiety is reduced, and they can explore and enjoy their world, safe in the knowledge that they can return to their secure base for help. This lets them grow through each of the stages of development and forge healthy attachments with others throughout their lives. A securely attached child feels safe to explore, developing curiosity, confidence, competence and resilience.

Our home provides us with such a secure base. With the security of home, we are confident to go and live our lives – to get an education, to form relationships, to be creative. We can create new worlds, through art, music, and new life in children. Bowlby explains that 'All of us, from the cradle to the grave, are happiest when life is organized as a series of excursions, long or short, from the secure base provided by our [home].' (To paraphrase Bowlby, replacing his term 'attachment giver' with 'home', as I think this quotation is an excellent description of the vital psychological role of home in our lives.)

A home, therefore, should be a place of constancy and reliability in our ever-changing lives. Now more than ever, in a world of heightened social risks, inequality, precarious work and climate change, we need a stable home. As Bachelard put it so eloquently, without a home we 'would be a dispersed being'. Home, he wrote, maintains us 'through the storms of the heavens and through those of life. It is body and soul. It is the human being's first world.'

The philosopher Martin Heidegger's concept of 'dwelling' also expands our understanding of home from shelter to a space of restoration where we can relax, rest and recuperate. Heidegger explained that 'to dwell' is to be able to come home to one's existence; to be, to gather yourself together, with your possessions, your thoughts, your feelings, your important others, with what matters to you, with what belongs. Lindsay Graham, a psychologist at the University of California's Centre for the Built Environment, beautifully describes home as 'holding who we are. Where we can truly be ourselves. It's meant to be a place of restoration. We can completely let go and be our true selves.'

To 'feel at home is', of course, an emotion itself. Home is somewhere we can control the boundaries. And within this boundaried place we have the necessary privacy and safety to rest. Here we can be the gatekeepers of our own life.

But the more uncertain and unpredictable our lives are, the more we feel insecure the more energy we expend in dealing with anxiety and uncertainty and the less we devote to developing our potential in other ways. Not having a protected, secure space and base of a home from which we can pursue our own goals leads to a deterioration in our sense of self and our self-esteem. It worsens our own ontological insecurity, and it adds to a collective anxiety about social cohesion. This is why renters want to get out of the insecurity of the private rental sector in Ireland

and either own their own home or get secure social housing. Private rental housing in Ireland does not give you or your children a secure base where you can fully live.

A home is about giving us the space and place to deal with the suffering, pain and existential vicissitudes of life. A dwelling, a home, is therefore a core dimension of, and necessity for, human wellbeing, especially in the modern world. To be, we need to have a home.

I asked people on social media to describe what home meant to them. There were some incredible answers that captured the real meaning of home. I provide some of these throughout this chapter.

A home is putting roots down for you and your family. The walls around you can be changed, painted, you can hang family photos. Leave the marks of your children's growth spurts on the door and know they're there for as long as you want them to be. Fill an attic to the brim and let the dust begin. Have that place your family can always feel safe and you can sleep a full night without the fear of it being pulled from under you with no next lease. Have comfort that as the world changes around you it's the one solid that remains.

Home, then, is essential for the higher-level needs in Maslow's hierarchy. These are our need for human interaction – friendships and family bonds, physical and emotional intimacy; our esteem needs, including self-respect (the belief that we are valuable and deserving of dignity), and self-esteem (confidence in our potential for personal growth and accomplishments); and self-actualization needs, which include education, skill development, achieving talents, caring for others, and life goals.

Self-esteem, our positive sense of self in how we view ourselves in relation to others, is an important component of wellbeing. But this can be threatened by a sense of shame, which can happen when a person does not live up to their ideal self and thus becomes less sure of their place in the world. If home represents who we are and how we would like the world to see us, and how we see ourselves in the world, then clearly being locked out of housing, in insecure housing, living in poor housing conditions, impacts on our self-identity and our mental health. This can lead to feelings of shame, stigma and status anxiety. The phrase 'house proud' has been replaced by the opposite feeling of 'housing shame'. A whole generation is being made to feel a sense of personal shame and stigma for not having a secure home of their own. This can have psychological impacts, as people internalize their inability to get a house as a personal failure, and are restricted from achieving their higher-level needs.

Another central human need and component of wellbeing is having autonomy and control over your life. Autonomy is the freedom to express yourself without the need to have your actions approved by others or to conform to others' expectations. Control is a feeling of having agency over ourselves, our finances and our decisions about how and where we live. Such agency could be affected by how high our rent or mortgage is, or the extent to which renovations to accommodate the needs of people living in the home are permitted. Control is the extent to which we can decide what happens to and in our home.

Having control over your home, as an individual, or in partnership and cooperation with others, is essential for this sense of autonomy, of feeling in control of your life.

Insecure renting reduces the sense of autonomy over our living space and the ability to personalize our home or to feel settled because of the lack of tenure security. This insecurity impacts on younger people's decisions to form families because of the potential costs of continuously moving between homes and the impacts of such moves on children in terms of accessing crèche spaces, childcare arrangements (often with grandparents and other family), friendships and family support.

Having control also extends to our human need for relationships and intimacy with animals – our pets. Pets play a deeply important role in human life, providing companionship, connection and meaning for many people. Being able to decide to have or not have a pet is an important aspect of how home can inhibit or promote wellbeing.

Being able to make and modify, alter, and adapt - 'do up'- our homes is another key aspect of having autonomy and control. As a renter explained:

> For me home means freedom – to own a pet, to hang up a painting, to repaint the walls or change the wallpaper. But also freedom to listen to whatever music I like, to wear pyjamas all day, to cook anything I want without negotiating with a room-mate or parents.

Architects and planners highlight that people should be able to design and create their environment to make it 'their' home. People need to be able to alter the physical building to suit their needs, to reflect their desires and to express their personality.

But how can you achieve this without privacy in, and control over, your own home? How do people living in their parents' home experience control or autonomy or self-actualization in their housing? Or if you are house sharing in your thirties? Lack of privacy was highlighted as a major issue by 76 per cent of adult females living at home with their parents. A home without control, without personal autonomy, does not fulfil human needs and wellbeing. A young person explains that, for them, a home is:

> Somewhere I can securely start my life. I'm 26 living at home with my parents. I need somewhere that's mine where I can properly begin my life with my partner without being on the poverty line.

The Danes know about the true meaning of home and its role in happiness. They are the second happiest nation in the world. The Danish word *hygge* is about making your home cosy and comfortable, nurturing an inner sense of contentment, wellbeing and connection with others. The Danish Happiness Institute undertook research in which they asked people across Europe the impact their homes had on their overall happiness and wellbeing. They found control was one of the five core factors that influence how happy our home makes us, along with pride, identity, comfort and safety. Happiness within the home was closely linked to many other states, such as feeling at ease, feeling safe, feeling connected with ourselves, and feeling in control. They found that having control, having a home that can be adapted to future needs and having a home that feels spacious are among the most important conditions for a happy home. Because our lives are ever-changing, a happy home is a lifetime project that we need to be able to adapt: we have children, we need more space, we get divorced, our kids move out, our elderly parents move in, we grow old. They found that owning your home does not necessarily make you happier, and renters can be as happy with their homes if they feel in control of their home, of housing costs, tenure security, home improvements and where they are living.

Your home is not a property asset or investment. It is your gaff. It is a place where you can have people over, where you can do the things you want to do, where you feel warm, safe, secure.

At the third level of Maslow's hierarchy are the human needs for love, belonging and connection. These are fundamental psychological needs. Having a secure sense of belonging and attachment to a place, a home, is necessary for wellbeing. This means feeling a connection to and sense of ownership over our surrounding living environment. Our attachment to our chosen place, how we take root, day after day, in our corner of the world, is a psychological phenomenon. Having our own place, our home, gives us an emotional bond, a rootedness, a connection to the world around us, to our neighbourhood, community, town, city, rural area, our country and society. It is central to constructing our identity. We belong to the society where our home is. Without a home we don't belong.

In understanding a person's connection with their home and their place, we need to understand that our bond to our home also comes from the emotional memory in the building. Doctor Craig Gurney, a lecturer in housing studies at the University of Glasgow, gave a fascinating TEDx talk called 'The Meaning of Home: More than Bricks and Mortar?' He describes home as 'an emotional warehouse wherein grief, anger, love, regret and guilt are experienced as powerfully real and, at the same time, deposited, stored and sorted to create a powerful domestic [space]'.

When we don't belong to a place, we suffer from 'placelessness', a 'root-shock'. This can be felt as a physical sensation of unsteadiness and restlessness and experienced as a traumatic stress reaction.

The drive to short-term, precarious contracts in the gig economy, and to flexibility and mobility in modern neoliberal capitalism ignores our connection to place and home the essential human need to belong. We are expected to up sticks and move to another part of the city or to another country to find a place to rent or for a job. The resulting sense of emptiness and placelessness creates mental distress and alienation. People then try to fill this void other things, like consumerism. This is the business plan of corporate capitalism. People who have a secure home and connection to the people and community around them are less needy of consumption and social media. That is not what big corporations and social media giants want. A home can provide people with an economic and individual independence to pursue their own goals and interests, not just be driven by corporate profit agendas.

Our attachment to home is also intimately connected to, and affected by, the communities within which they are located. Neighbours and family members living in an area provide essential support. They comprise people's close networks and relationships.

Of course, people move home, and do so all time. But it is said that one of the most stressful things in life is moving house. That is because home has such deep psychological and emotional importance and meaning. So do the relationships and networks of trust we build around our home – with neighbours, with family, with the local community, the local shopkeeper, the familiar faces we say hello to as we walk to school, get the bus, play with our children or walk our dog in the park. Our neighbours keep our spare set of keys. They feed the cat when have to go down the country to visit relatives. We mind each other's kids, we check in on our elderly neighbours or those who need support. This gives us all, and especially those more vulnerable and marginalized in our communities, a sense of security, joy, belonging. At times, it's a lifeline. We had an elderly neighbour living next door, and we would always hear her moving around in her house. One evening there was silence, so we called in and found she had fallen down the stairs. We rang the ambulance and got her help. This is priceless human connection and support.

Such close relationships of trust and dependency with neighbours and other people in the community take years to build. The family connections in areas are irreplaceable. They create long intergenerational roots that hold communities together and give individuals and families deep bonds and commitment to a place. Forced moves from these areas are extremely distressing as they result in a disruption to, and in some cases diminution and even destruction of those bonds, networks of support and relationships.

A core dimension of home, then, is the ability to feel secure, which then allows you to foster connections without fear of them being ripped away. It provides the ability to get to know your neighbours. If people are unable to create their own place, to make a home within their 'place', if they are in insecure housing, forced to leave their community, or unable to get a home of their own, they feel less attachment to their place, to their community and to society. This has both individual and societal implications. It weakens a sense of connection and responsibility to their neighbourhood, community and wider society. It weakens the social contract between the individual, society and government.

As housing has become an economic product, a commodity, controlled by the wealthy, investors, REITs and Airbnb, the human needs within housing are reduced, deprioritized and replaced. Homes become 'boutique hotels' or 'co-living spaces', new transitory 'experiences' of living. The essential aspects of control, autonomy, connection to place and bonds to community are removed. We suffer alienation from our living space, from our home, from our society, from our surroundings, from ourselves.

We need to ask, then, not just how many units of housing supply are we building, but how are we ensuring that everyone has a home that enables them to be secure and therefore to grow, develop relationships, contribute to society, to their families, their neighbourhood, their community?

The ability to contribute bolsters our self-esteem which then strengthens feelings of belonging, approval and sense of success. This is not just an individual sense of self, but a sense of the individual within society. The individual and societal experiences of self-esteem are interlinked and interdependent. And so it is with home.

To have your own home, your own place, is not just to have a building; it is to have a place in the world. You are recognized as legitimate, as a full person, when you have 'your place'. From a practical point of view, you need a place, an address, to get social welfare, apply for a job, apply for a loan. From an inter-personal point of view, in developing a relationship, one of you needs your own home. You feel inadequate, immature if you don't have 'your place', your own gaff, to live in. Home gives us an actual position, existence and meaning in the world. To be requires a place to 'be'.

Child wellbeing and housing

Home is a place where my children can feel safe. Where we can make memories in peace without fear. Where we can put our mark that says this is our space, our place, the place where we rest our heads and can be entirely ourselves.

Home has a particularly fundamental role in child wellbeing. Home is the nursery where babies and children need to feel safe to grow physically, cognitively and emotionally. It is the cocoon where newborn babies are cradled for the first precious months, when they need warmth, attention and caregiving. As children grow it is the place where they learn to play. Home is the place they can be themselves. They gather the 'stuff' of childhood and life – their toys, trinkets, shells from the beach, their favourite toy dinosaur that they play with for hours and then bring to bed with them, or the Paw Patrol or Peppa Pig doctor set, or the figurines they set up in a playhouse. Their bedroom is a sacred place. My daughter has a shrine of teddies and notebooks, posters and pictures around her bed and on her wall. When I look at her in her bed with her meaningful life possessions providing a blanket of protective familiarity, I think how difficult and traumatic it must be to have to gather these together, or in some cases choose just a few favourites – an impossible task for a child – and put them in a bag to take to homeless accommodation, or to a new, strange rented place. A child's bedroom in their home is their little universe, it is their sacred corner of the world within their parents' corner of the world, where they should be able to feel safe and secure – physically and psychologically – to rest, and dream, and be a child. Yet housing insecurity, homelessness, substandard housing, deprivation and housing stress can remove all that, leaving major psychological scars, potentially lifelong scars, on children and young people.

American psychologist Urie Bronfenbrenner explained that children's experiences and perceptions of their environments are fundamental to their wellbeing. They shape who they are and affect lifelong health and learning. The foundations for virtually every aspect of human development – physical, intellectual and emotional – are laid in early childhood. What happens during these early years (starting in the womb) has permanent effects on many aspects of health and wellbeing, from obesity, heart disease and mental health to educational achievement and economic status. Early childhood and early adolescence are particularly vulnerable times when stress and insecurity can negatively impact development.

To develop to their full potential, children need safe and secure housing. Housing deprivation can increase the risk of severe ill-health or disability during childhood and early adulthood by up to 25 per cent. In 2019, the faculties of Public Health Medicine and Paediatrics at the Royal College of Physicians of Ireland published a paper on the impact of homelessness and inadequate housing on the health of children. They found that homeless children in Ireland are 'more likely to have higher rates of developmental, emotional and behavioural problems', with 38 per cent suffering disorders of 'clinical significance'. Teachers report visible mental health issues, including high levels of anxiety, stigma, embarrassment, and low levels of self-esteem among pupils experiencing homelessness. Homeless children themselves express 'feelings of sadness, confusion and anger'.

A study into the physical effects of inadequate housing in Sweden found that children living in homes where there were three or more signs of dampness were nearly three times more likely to experience recurrent wheezing compared to those living in dry conditions. Poor-quality housing and overcrowded conditions are also associated with an increased incidence of injuries in children.

Child development experts explain that the lack of an adequate home (substandard or insecure housing) can have detrimental impacts on children's physical, cognitive and emotional development. Take emergency accommodation or severely overcrowded housing where space is limited, for example. This can have a detrimental impact on babies, as lack of space impedes their natural curiosity for exploration and thus delays or inhibits them from meeting developmental milestones such as crawling. It can also affect toddlers and schoolchildren who have no suitable place to play or complete homework, as well as older children who have no privacy for sleeping or study. In such circumstances, members of a family unit have no place to come together after a day at school or work, even for the most basic aspects of family life such as a shared meal. Children are unable to have their friends over for play dates or birthday parties.

In primary schools, whole strands of the curriculum deal with the child and the home as a recurring theme for lessons. Just imagine what such lessons are like for a child living in emergency accommodation, the shame that child must feel trying to cover up their circumstances when their peers are talking about the colour of their bedroom walls, their toys, how many rooms they have in their house, the colour of their front door, or what games they play in their garden. You can see how a simple maths question, 'How many steps are there from your front door to your back door?', can leave a homeless child feeling excluded and distressed. A child needs a place to go where they have personal belongings that give them comfort and enjoyment and where they can develop a self-identity. In emergency accommodation settings, children's capacity to express themselves and be themselves is limited. They are unable to bring with them their treasured belongings and must curtail their personal expression and development. There is also a trauma in losing their home, or having to move multiple times between rental homes.

The seriousness of the impact of the experience of evictions, housing loss, homelessness and housing insecurity on a child's life can be appreciated when viewed through the lens of the trauma-informed theory of adverse childhood experiences (ACEs). A child who has experienced homelessness is significantly more likely to experience negative outcomes in adulthood, including mental health difficulties, unemployment, substance abuse and so on. The concept of ACEs is logical: if you experience significant trauma/adverse experiences in the formative years of childhood, your health and wellbeing are likely to be adversely affected for the rest of your life. Significant childhood trauma affects cognitive, social and emotional development at a stage when a child is developing an internal model of themselves and the world they live in.

Chronic housing stress related to housing affordability issues, the loss of a home through evictions in the private rental sector, forced housing mobility and substandard housing conditions are also traumatic experiences that impact on children. The stress faced by parents trying to find a home or in fear of the loss of their home, or in an insecure or unaffordable housing situation, can become all-consuming. Housing stress can lead to relationship problems; people feel angry, which can cause arguments or make it hard to discuss housing issues. It can lead to the breakdown of relationships, such as with a partner or parent, further worsening housing stress and general wellbeing. A mother explains what a home should provide:

> Security and a safe place for you and your children to grow together and meet your full potential. You can't reach your full potential if every day your brain is occupied with the worry of not having a home or are we going to lose our home.

The massive increase in the number of children being raised in the private rental sector, with associated changes in their housing experiences, means that understanding the influence of housing on children's wellbeing is important. In contrast to just a decade ago, hundreds of thousands of children are now growing up in the insecure, unaffordable and substandard conditions of the private rental sector. Many are exposed to housing stress and deprivation. Rising housing unaffordability, because of rising rents for example, can add to parental stress and worries about finance and even about maintaining the home.

Parents under stress are less likely to be engaged and more likely to be irritable and distant with their children. Particularly in the early years, positive bonding experiences and interactions between parent and child are fundamental to building competencies that support growth and development. Parental negativity and over-reactivity can impact emotional and behavioural development in children. Toxic patterns of significant persistent stress in the parent–child relationship during infancy and childhood can be associated with subsequent mental health problems.

Such stress also causes physical ill-health. Housing stress and related stressful events, such as housing insecurity and evictions or forced relocation, experienced by the child themselves or by their parents or guardians are linked to an increased risk of respiratory problems. Stress is directly associated with impaired immune system function, but it also affects children's health indirectly as parents experiencing high levels of stress are not able to adequately attend to children's health needs.

Parental self-esteem and confidence, as well as feelings of self-efficacy, can also be impacted by chronic, intractable housing problems. Situations of overcrowding or families forced into situations of house sharing can lead to reduced privacy and issues of surveillance of parenting. Parents with inadequate privacy may be less able or willing to socially engage with their children and may feel judged in relation to their parenting, leading to further stress and anxiety. Families living 'doubled up' either in rental house shares or in multi-generational households, increasingly the situation in Ireland due to the housing crisis, can lead to emotional and behavioural problems among children. In these situations, children restrict themselves as they are not free to play and just be themselves in someone else's home. As a parent of a child with additional needs explains, this is why a home for families must be:

A place where we won't have to pack up from one day to another. Where I can make adjustments to the house so it's more suited to my kids' additional needs, where they have a retreat from all the external demands put on them and can just be themselves without anybody judging them.

Children living in homes that suffer from damp or mould are at a high risk of developing asthma. During my time as a Community Regeneration Worker in the social housing estate of Dolphin House, we found there were major problems of mould, damp and waste-water discharge inside people's homes, that high levels of housing-related illness also impacted on children's education because they missed school more often, compounding issues of educational inequality.

Research has found that better housing affordability is associated with better health, behaviour and school engagement for children aged 12–17. This points to the particular impacts of housing stress and deprivation on children in the teenage years, a time of already potential heightened stress and anxiety. Frequent house moves, particularly ones that are forced or related to housing stress, have been found to 'take a toll on children's social–emotional wellbeing'.

High housing costs also push families into poverty and deprivation, taking from spending on other essentials, including food, social and educational resources, with major implications for children. An additional 100,000 children are left in poverty in Ireland after housing costs are paid for by families, meaning that a quarter of all children in the country are in poverty after their family has paid the rent or mortgage. Renters are hardest hit. A third of renters who do not receive any state supports are in poverty after they pay their rent. Sixty per cent of renters who receive state supports toward their rent (HAP, RAS) are in poverty after they pay their rent.

Residential instability, insecurity and forced mobility is a clear example of where housing exacerbates existing disadvantage and inequalities. Frequent moving is more common among lower-income disadvantaged groups, and it is often the children of these disadvantaged groups who have the worst outcomes when experiencing forced mobility.

It can also have specific impacts on older children, who are more connected to their local area, with school ties and established friendship groups. They suffer major loss when they move out of their area. Being forced to leave friends, school, the familiar surroundings of your home and neighbourhood is a massively disruptive event for children. It is a loss of part of their base and affects their ontological security. In a sample of 11–12-year-old Canadian children, there was evidence of increased behavioural problems among those who had moved three or more times.

Overcrowding also has particular impacts on children's, especially teenagers', educational, behavioural and health outcomes relating to issues of privacy, reduced ability to study, disturbed sleep and personal space.

Finally, lack of access to outdoor space can undermine children's wellbeing, particularly in relation to play but also in terms of general health, development and cognitive functioning.

Chronic housing stress

Chronic stress – high levels of stress lasting for long stretches of time – has been shown to have major health implications. Housing can be a cause of chronic stress for people going through persistent and extended periods of housing insecurity (living in the private rental sector for months under an eviction notice, for example, with little prospect of finding somewhere else), or housing anxiety related to living in your parents' home with no hope of getting a home of your own. Such stress and anxiety can lead to illness. Ongoing housing affordability problems and insecurity cause significant and measurable decreases in mental health as well. Research published in the *Journal of Epidemiology and Community Health* in 2019 showed higher levels of the biomarker C-reactive protein (CRP), a marker of inflammation associated with infection and stress, in private renters. This points to the physiological effects of stress associated with unaffordable, poor housing conditions and insecure housing. As the authors of the paper point out, 'Where control is low, ontological security is reduced, which may affect health through chronic stress responses.'

It has been shown that chronic stress is linked to macroscopic changes in areas of the brain – volume variations and physical modifications of neuronal networks. Chronic stress is associated with depressive disorders. Persistent exposure to housing stress is a 'chronic psychosocial strain'.

Psychological and chronic stress can impact on the immune system, inducing the acute phase response commonly associated with infections and tissue damage, and increasing the levels of circulating cytokines and of various biomarkers of inflammation. Diseases whose development has been linked to both stress and inflammation include cardiovascular dysfunctions, diabetes, cancer, autoimmune syndromes, and mental illnesses such as depression and anxiety disorders.

The extent to which stress impacts on our physiological health also depends on our perception of how much we can control the source of the stress. The most detrimental forms of stress are ones where people have little control over the cause of the stress, such as in situations of poverty and inequality. Housing is an area where people experience a low level of control. For example, renters have little control over the stability and security of their home. They are dependent on whether the landlord increases the rents, whether the landlord decides to sell up and evict them, and then whether there is anywhere else to rent. Someone who's hoping to buy a home cannot control rising house prices, or are outbid by investor purchasers, or don't know whether or not the bank will lend to them. These are all hugely anxiety- and stress-inducing events that are largely out of the control of those renters or prospective home buyers, leading such would-be renters/buyers to internalize feelings of blame for housing 'failure' and causing feelings of anxiety, defeat and shame.

Housing stress and anxiety can also be caused by issues of structural problems of maintenance in the home – broken windows, mould, damp, leaking roof or pipes, broken cookers – that the landlord, whether private or social, fails to fix. This can leave a tenant worrying and suffering for months, even years.

Homes with structural problems due to poor building regulation is a major issue in Ireland. The mica and pyrite scandal affects thousands of homes in Ireland, particularly in the north-west. Homes that were once safe, warm and secure are cracking, crumbling and falling apart. A survey of families living in homes affected by mica found that 70 per cent were suffering from anxiety, 65 per cent had difficulty sleeping, 46 per cent were affected by low mood and 25 per cent by depression. They described it as 'a constant source of dread every day, a dark place where you cannot escape from the fear of what is to come'. They no longer feel secure in their home and 'feel trapped'.

The UK mental health charity Mind outlines that living with mental health problems can also make it harder to cope with housing difficulties. Thus, poor mental health can be exacerbated by housing issues.

It feels like life without a secure home is the same as being in a constant storm. All the time unsure of what will happen.

Ireland's housing crisis and increased number of families and people living longer in the private rental sector is exposing hundreds of thousands of families and children to chronic toxic housing stress. They are financially insecure and housing insecure. This means they are more likely to be suffering from various forms of ill health, from depression to cancer, because of their housing situation, which results from a failure of government policy. Ensuring secure, affordable homes for all is surely a key response to mental health issues caused by the housing crisis.

Housing and inequality

Authors of *The Spirit Level: Why More Equal Societies Almost Always Do Better,* Richard Wilkinson and Kate Pickett, highlight that countries with higher inequality also have more social problems. They found that part of the reason is the anxiety and stress caused by status inequalities. This is related to shame and low self-esteem, which has a strong link to mental ill-health and depression. Inferior social comparison is a 'psychosocial risk factor' for ill health (for example heart disease) and a partial explanation for health inequalities.

What we perceive others think of our situation is important, and in more unequal countries there is greater amounts of status shame and anxiety as people feel relatively worse in comparison to those who are very well off. In Ireland, inequalities in housing have risen dramatically in recent years. There are now multiple inequalities, particularly for people who are unable to buy a home and are stuck in housing situations such as private rental or living with their parents. The inequality between them and those who can afford to buy, or between them and previous generations leads to a sense of personal failure and shame. This has particularly negative impacts on people's physical and mental health.

If we are happy with our housing situation, our housing status and the place we live, we can draw a positive sense of esteem and value from it. Conversely, feeling shame and stigma about it results in a lower sense of value and self-esteem.

The Danish Happiness Institute found that in more equal countries where people's basic needs are met, for example the Netherlands, Germany and Denmark, levels of happiness and trust are higher and people are also happier with their homes. People in more equal societies have similar access to the necessary resources that make them happy with their homes. Greater trust in society also leads to more trustworthy neighbourhoods and communities, which, in turn, make people feel safer, more connected, happier with their homes and happier in general.

This is why it is so important to tackle housing inequalities. Not only are housing problems such as bad standards, unaffordability and the lack of tenure security negative in themselves, they cause additional anxiety and feelings of shame in those that have to live with and in them, which can lead to mental and physical illness.

Housing deprivation and inequalities also exacerbate income inequalities. Housing is an outward expression or manifestation of inequality – it is one we are judged on (or at least the one on which we judge ourselves relative to others). You cannot see someone's income, but you can see their home. That is why it is important that social and rental housing should be of equal standard to home ownership – because how our house looks, and the status of our housing situation impacts on our sense of self, our ontological security, and our self-esteem. Housing inequalities also affect wider society by causing reduced levels of trust, social cohesion and community, which has implications for the health of society as a whole.

The impact of housing design on mental health and wellbeing

Architects and planners know that the way a home is designed and laid out is essential for it to function well and promote wellbeing. Space, light and access to green and outdoor space really impact on wellbeing and help make a house a home. The Happiness Research Institute says that the importance of space is 'hard to overstate'. It found that access to green and outdoor space, even a balcony or a yard, is fundamental to our happiness, with access to a garden giving the highest happiness. The design of our homes and neighbourhoods can also impact on our ability to control our homes and gain social support from our surroundings.

We have a fundamental need to connect with nature. We have lived and thrived in the natural world for more than 300,000 years, and therefore it is the environment in which we have adapted to feel most comfortable. We have an emotional and cognitive need for a connection with nature where we can feel calm and satisfied. There is now very strong evidence that living in places that have plenty of trees, parks and green spaces is vitally important for people's mental and physical health. Even being able to see a tree or green space through a window can have a measurable beneficial effect on people's health. In addition, access to local green spaces has been shown to be particularly beneficial for sections of the population with the poorest health.

This also highlights the importance of access to green areas in the wider neighbourhood, and the importance of wider neighbourhood design with community and social facilities. The conditions of our neighbourhood deeply affect our experience of home because it provides opportunities for neighbours to get to know each other. There is a range of evidence that feeling lonely or isolated is bad for people's mental and physical health and wellbeing – and that, conversely, living in a strong community, with regular contact with neighbours and a sense of belonging supports good health and wellbeing. Well-designed neighbourhoods create opportunities for people to meet and socialize as part of their day-to-day lives, and this supports good health and wellbeing. Stable and secure housing, with a low incidence of people moving in and out of the area, is also key to developing strong and active communities that can support health and wellbeing.

Access to well-designed and well-maintained community facilities, streetscapes and green areas is therefore essential. Mid-rise developments (four or five storeys) provide healthier homes and communities than high-rise homes that can lead to social isolation. For all these reasons, planning rules and guidelines are important to set the standards for building so that what is being built as new supply of housing actually provides liveable healthy homes and neighbourhoods that foster healthy living and nurture community.

Fundamentally, environmental sustainability is central to home. Our homes are the front line in the battle to save our planet. We also need them to protect us from a changing climate. We must adapt our understanding and meaning of home to an ecologically sustainable and climate-resilient one that plays a role in a zero-carbon future.

Diversity of home

There are many different experiences of home. Our experience of home is most influenced by who we are at home with and the quality and nature of our relationships with those we live with, and our neighbours and wider community. For too many people, home is a place of abuse and fear. For some, particularly women and children, their home is not safe. They need access to a home where they can be safe. This is part of the housing crisis now, where the lack of social and affordable housing means a particularly gendered inequality of risk. Some women (and some men) feel unable to leave situations of domestic violence because of the lack of an alternative home. The housing crisis is exacerbating gender-based violence. Rather than having a supply of affordable and social housing dedicated for those fleeing domestic violence, the current crisis is resulting in people being locked into domestic violence. In these cases, a sufficient supply of dedicated homes for those subjected to domestic violence could provide them with at least the potential for a more secure, stable and eventually flourishing life for them and their children.

There is a long-standing gendered dimension to home. The conservative view in Irish society has been that 'a woman's place is in the home'. That nonsense is actually still in our Constitution, which refers to a mother's 'duties in the home'.

Women still face the unequal burden of care responsibilities in the home in modern Ireland. Women provide the overwhelming majority of care to children, the elderly, those with a disability requiring care, those who are ill, or children being fostered. All this care takes place in the home. So the provision of homes, and their quality, their size, design and layout and suitability has a disproportionate impact on women.

Yet in the construction industry, most housing policy debates, economic analyses and the planning and delivery of homes are all dominated by men. Many men are aware of the central role of home in care responsibilities. But too many are not aware, and do not value or understand the central purpose of home as a place of care. A feminist understanding and approach to home, therefore, is important as it elevates this 'caring' role of home as its primary function – over its economic function as an investment commodity. This should lead to greater emphasis on designing and delivering homes that enable caring, sociality and liveability for everyone.

For people with disabilities, too, an accessible, adaptable and suitable home is essential for independent living. To live independently is a key part of being able to live a decent life. There are also major problems in inappropriate housing for children with autism, mobility needs, sensory needs, and for the elderly who have particular needs.

Housing should enable those with a disability to live independently and with dignity, to fulfil their potential and to flourish. Our housing crisis is compounding the exclusion of many people with disabilities. This highlights how essential it is to include in our provision of homes housing that is not just accessible but adaptable and liveable for those with a disability (i.e. that the person who lives in it can get into it, live in it and do what they need to do safely and comfortably). It should also be possible to access essential services by walking or public transport.

Not providing appropriate suitable homes comes at a larger economic cost to the country in terms of additional spending required to deal with poor and inadequate housing – such as higher health expenses where children and adults become ill due to dampness or chronic housing stress. The cost of institutionalizing or providing care facilities for people with disabilities is higher than housing them independently.

Irish Travellers are an indigenous nomadic ethnic group with a long-established past in Irish history dating back to the twelfth century. Traditionally, Travellers played a vital role in agrarian society as seasonal labourers, tinsmiths, and poets. They were nomadic for either part or all of the year and lived in extended family groups. Changes in Ireland in the 1960s arising from industrialization, mechanization and the cheap availability of plastic led to a reduced role, income and status for Irish Travellers. Travellers were identified by the Irish State as a 'problem' that would be solved by 'absorption' and settling the Traveller population in traditional houses. Since then, Travellers have suffered huge housing discrimination and inequalities. Travellers have organized and campaigned, as a key part of Traveller ethnicity, for Travellers to be able to live together in accommodation that respects their way of life. The Irish Traveller Movement explains that on the basis of their culture, many (but not all) Travellers prefer to live in what is called 'culturally appropriate' or 'Traveller-specific' accommodation – halting sites or group housing schemes, where large extended families live together based on their shared identity. While Travellers are more likely to talk about 'accommodation needs', Travellers and settled people alike have the same right to a home, regardless of what that home might be. From a Traveller perspective, it is a home that keeps their Traveller identity intact.

Housing as home

The value of housing in Ireland is mainly measured in property prices – the economic value shown on the Irish Central Bank's balance sheet. Yet the true value of housing is a deeply social and psychological one. We have our measurement of the value of housing all wrong. There is a growing consensus that we need to shift away from measuring country development through GDP figures on economic 'growth' – which is only related to the average wealth, products produced and financial transactions of an economy. Instead, countries like New Zealand are using wellbeing indicators, such as gender and social equality, the achievement of the sustainable development goals and human rights, and levels of health and happiness to measure progress. We need a similar shift in housing. We need to measure our housing policy and housing system, not just through crude measures of property 'value', build-to-rent planning permissions and units of supply, but through whether we are delivering homes that meet the housing needs of people, that deliver the human right to housing, and contribute to individual, community and societal well-being.

Housing is people's single most important 'asset', but resources such as wealth and housing assets are good only insofar as they promote human development. The role of housing must be centred on how it contributes to the unique value of the human person and for each person to function as fully as possible and so live a flourishing life.

How does housing contribute to flourishing? We flourish when we have autonomy and when we exercise this autonomy in positive relationships with others. We flourish when we have scope to use our imaginative and creative potential – knowing that our needs and interests change and develop over time. We have actual and potential capabilities that naturally seek outlets for expression in the service of others. We are social beings who flourish when we can help meet other people's needs. Housing can and should enable this flourishing.

Changing our treatment of housing as property instead to housing's primary function as home can be a way to overcome and move beyond the destructive dominant ideology of individual greed, competitive individualism and consumption, the market theory of individuals against the world – to instead see ourselves as being part of society, being part of a social contract. If people have a stable, secure, affordable home of their own, they are empowered to contribute to society, to enhance cohesion and trust.

For each person born on this planet, a secure, adequate home is a fundamental human need and requirement for them to live in safety and dignity, to develop and grow. A home is a universal human requirement. A home should provide a place of safety, a secure base in which to raise children, and to rest and sleep; it is vital for our physical, social and emotional health, and for participating in society, being part of a community and gaining employment and an education. Without a secure, healthy home all this is extremely difficult, if not impossible, to achieve. Human development is stalled, denied and impossible without a home. Article 25 of the Universal Declaration of Human Rights defines housing as a basic human right: 'Everyone has the right to a standard of living adequate for the health and wellbeing of himself [or herself] and his [or her] family, including . . . housing.'

In 1991, the UN Committee on Economic, Social and Cultural Rights set out in detail what should be in the Right to Adequate Housing. They defined it as 'the right to live somewhere in security, peace and dignity' with 'adequate privacy, adequate space, adequate security, adequate lighting and ventilation, adequate basic infra-structure and adequate location with regard to work and basic facilities – all at a reasonable cost.' Governments, states and city authorities are obliged, according to the UN Committee, to 'ensure security of tenure and that access is free of discrimination, and progressively work to eliminate homelessness'. This definition provides a clear vision for what ensuring the right to housing for all actually means, what states are responsible for, and what each person should have access to.

A safe, secure home, built to a decent standard, is central to our very existence, our physical health and psychological wellbeing. A gaff, a home, is central to the dignity of each and every person and is the foundation of every person's life. The importance of a home is shown most clearly by what happens to people when they don't have one. It is visible in the devastating physical and mental health impacts on those who are homeless, in particular on children. A social justice, human rights and psychological approach to housing emphasises and understands its primary function as meeting the fundamental need of shelter and the secure ontological base of a home.

Of course, home has wider meanings too. Those living abroad – emigrants – always talk of 'coming home'. So home has broader meanings, and we can make a home wherever we are, with the people who matter. But the bonds between us as human beings, the relation-ships, take time to build. We are not just individual islands of consumers – much as social media corporations and advertisers would like us to be. We are social beings who yearn for rootedness, connection and purpose. We saw this during Covid. Those who are happiest live in societies where people trust each other more, which are more equal societies – they are not alone, they are part of communities. A secure, decent-standard home is the foundation stone, the central pillar. Here individuals can belong, build communities of trust and social cohesion and create and nurture societies of trust and cooperation.

Home is the place where we see ourselves in the world, where we consider how society sees us, how we are valued. How valued by society does a young teenager feel growing up in an overcrowded, mouldy, damp private rental house, or, worse, in emergency homeless accommodation? What does that tell them about how society values them, about how included they are in society?

We most definitely know what a home is not. It is not a place where you live in fear and worry about the landlord will sell the property. A home is not somewhere that leaves you in a perpetual state of chronic stress and anxiety about being able to afford the rent.

In Ireland, the private rental sector does not allow you hang a painting or paint your home. If you can't paint your walls or make changes to a physical building to express yourself and personalize it, it isn't your home.

A lot of social housing – housing delivered by local authorities and housing associations – does provide a home for people. People get lifetime security of tenure and rents are affordable. Neighborhoods are built and nurtured. Unfortunately, issues around standards and maintenance and control, the ability to exercise autonomy over their home and alter it, can diminish those other important wellbeing aspects.

That means, then, for social and private rental housing to be a home, it should be lifetime secure, with the ability to alter and upgrade it yourself; and you should not be at risk of eviction for 'no fault' reasons. But also, for home ownership to be home, it must be affordable, not requiring massive mortgages and unsustainable debt, and available in places where people want to live and that nurture community and social cohesion.

This is why it is essential our housing system provides people with access to homes that provide shelter, and lifetime – secure, affordable, decent-sized, quality homes, in neighbourhoods where people want to live.

In housing policy and debates about the supply of housing, we should consider, above all else, how is our housing system providing a home, as a human right, to everyone? Yes, a gaff is a basic human right. Are we designing healthy, adaptable homes, in communities connected with nature and meeting climate targets? And how does our housing system provide homes that enable people to express themselves, to have as their own. Home should provide the secure building block and base for human flourishing in today's precarious world. Without a home, without a gaff of your own, there is constant fear. If having a home (more than just shelter) is essential to the human condition, housing policy and provision must deliver not just housing, but homes.

Chapter 6
Generation Rent

If you were to describe who lives in the private rental sector in Ireland you would probably say it's mostly students or young people spending a few years saving to buy and figuring out where they want to live before settling down and having a family. That was the case twenty years ago. But today the picture looks very different. The private rental sector is no longer a transitory place for young people before they buy a home on the 'property ladder'. The property ladder has been pulled up from Generation Rent, who are now stranded in the private rental sector.

In the space of just over a decade, the private rental sector has gone from providing a home to fewer than 10 per cent of households to housing over 20 per cent – one in five of all households in the country. In 2006, there were 145,000 households renting. Today, there are 300,000. These are mainly the millennial generation in their twenties and thirties, but there are also tens of thousands of renters in their forties and fifties. Seventy per cent of renters are aged 25–44 (43 per cent are aged 25–35; 27 per cent are 36–44). Would you believe that almost half of all private renters are families with children? And they are mostly young families, with children in primary school or younger. One in four of every child in this country is living in the insecure private rental sector. This is a massive social change with major social implications. Renters are no longer mainly the early twenties, young, mobile professionals. They are working in every job going, but more are working in lower-paid jobs. Many are parents; the nurses, bus drivers, teachers, crèche workers, civil servants, cleaners, shop workers, trying to raise their kids, with all the challenges of that – to find a crèche, to find a school. This is the group in society who need the most security and stability in their lives – to give children a secure base to grow up in. Instead, We have a generation of children growing up in the most insecure form of housing, which is too often also of very poor standard. They are facing the highest costs of living, like rent and childcare, while they are on the lower wages of younger generations, while trying to save to buy a home as well. They are the most stressed and yet they are the ones facing the worst housing insecurity.

A fifth of renters are couples without children. Many are trying to scrape together the money to get a secure home of their home and start a family. For others, their life's dream of having a family has been stolen from them as the lack of a secure home meant they just couldn't take the risk. It just got too late; the struggle for housing tore apart their dreams. What we would think of as typical renters – people sharing a house with others who are not family – now make up just a quarter of renters (24 per cent), and over one in ten (12 per cent) are 'living alone'. The typical renter has been living in rental accommodation for almost eight years, rising to ten years if you rent outside Dublin. They have been forced into renting for a much longer time. This is a generation who feel their lives are on hold, stalled indefinitely. They feel they are waiting in limbo, in a state of purgatory, paying for the sins and greed of the Celtic Tiger, the governments, the banks, the investor funds. They are just looking for a place to call home.

They face massive insecurity and constant churn by landlords evicting them to get in higher-paying tenants. Fifty-four per cent of renters have moved property within the last two years. In contrast, the stability offered by social housing and home ownership is shown by the fact that just 15 per cent in social housing and just 8 per cent of homeowners had moved within the last two years. And most private renters (75 per cent) had moved in the last five years, compared to just over a third of those in social housing and just 16 per cent of homeowners. Families describe moving seven times in five years. It is a transient life that does not allow people to be part of a community, to experience the sense of belonging that is such a fundamental human need.

Renters live in fear of every letter that comes in the door, and every email in their inbox, in case it's an eviction notice. They are frustrated, waiting for weeks and months to get basic things fixed by the landlord or estate agent.

They are also increasingly middle-aged and older, in their forties, fifties and sixties. One renter in every six (17 per cent) is over forty-five. They feel not just that their lives are on hold, but that their lives have been taken away from them, their dreams and hopes of a home of their own, of stability and growing into their mature years being able to relax, wind down, make their comforts in their own home. Instead, they are stuck in the private rental sector, living in fear of how they will pay the rent when they retire. The idea of getting old in rental accommodation that is damp, mouldy, energy-inefficient, with very high rental costs, terrifies them. They live in fear and anxiety of becoming a homeless pensioner. They are angry that this could be their 'end of years' after a lifetime of working and paying taxes. There are 58,000 people in their fifties who are renting in Ireland. It's a ticking social timebomb. Older renting couples will tell you they are very attached to their rental home, where they might have been living for a decade or more, but they will not be able to hold on to it when they go on the state pension, or if one of them gets sick and loses their job. They are the 'nearly homeless'. As one couple explained:

We are paying €1,200 a month for a one-bedroom apartment. So, we worry, a lot. It keeps us up at night. We know we are not in the worst of positions, that there are people worse off. But there are tens of thousands of us, the 'nearly homeless'.

Surveys show that of those renting, a large majority – 61 per cent – were born in Ireland, 21 per cent were born in the EU, and 18 per cent come from other parts of the world. But when you look at the proportion of the population, just 10 per cent of the Irish-born population is in the private rental sector, whereas almost 50 per cent of the non-Irish-born population is in private rental housing. So a much greater proportion of the new Irish are renting. And while it is true that many are from countries where renting is much more common, they also want to get out of the Irish private rental sector and get a secure home of their own.

Families and individuals who are looking to get a secure, affordable home have watched in horror as rents and house prices have risen massively. House prices have risen by twenty, thirty, fifty, even a hundred grand in a very short space of time. They worry about where their children will go to school, what school they will apply for, if they don't know where they will be living. They are being outbid on every house they try to buy. And they are often outbid by so-called 'cash buyers'. The rent they are paying is twice what they would pay for a mortgage. But they know that housing and apartments are being bought up by land-lords and investor funds that face no limits on what they can borrow or spend on property. The injustice is infuriating renters. None of the new apartments they are seeing being built are coming up for sale. Investment funds are renting them out at unaffordable prices. It is devastating. They feel they are being locked permanently into the Generation Rent trap. They feel hopeless, abandoned by the Irish Government, and increasingly they can't see a future for themselves in Ireland. As one renter explained:

> It is such a bleak situation. I love my job; I have an excellent income, but it seems I will have to emigrate (again) or hope to win the lotto to own a home. And to note, I have saved well over the deposit required and have no other debts.

This is the experience of thousands of people I have spoken to or who have contacted me who are desperate to get a home. It is the story of hundreds of thousands of people, and it needs to be told, and listened to, and, most important, changed.

The private rental sector is unaffordable

Rents are unaffordable in Ireland. Renters cannot save or have a decent standard of life in the private rental sector. Just look at the poverty levels of renters. They have worked, saved, paid rent and yet they still cannot seem to get by. For years renters had a cost of living crisis that nobody paid attention to. Now they have a new cost of living crisis heaped upon their permanent cost of living crisis.

If you are paying more than 30 per cent of your net income – your take-home pay – on housing costs, you are considered to have unaffordable housing costs (in some countries, they define paying more than 25 per cent of your net income as unaffordable). Yet half of renters are paying rents that are more than 30 per cent of their net income. In Fingal in north Dublin, two-thirds of renters are paying over 30 per cent of their net income on rent, a quarter are paying over 40 per cent, and a tenth are paying over half their net income on rent. In Dublin and Cork, even more renters – one in five – are paying over 50 per cent of their net income on rent. It is no wonder then that, as the cost of living crisis hit hard in late 2021, surveys showed that 60 per cent of private renters had 'some difficulty' in paying their monthly rent, almost double the rate of homeowners with a mortgage (34 per cent).

How can renters cover rising rents and pay rising electricity, gas and other basic bills too? Renters are going hungry, bills are going unpaid, arrears are building up. Average rents are €1,415 a month, up ten per cent in a year. If that increases another 10 per cent, then for some renters their rent will increase by €1,700 over the next year. That is an unbearable increase for most. Even in the Rent Pressure Zone (RPZ) areas where rents are supposed to be capped to 2 per cent, we are seeing increases by multiples of that limit.

Rents increased in RPZs by 11 per cent in Waterford and Dublin cities, and by 6 per cent in Cork City.

Another way of looking at how unaffordable rents are is by calculating what an affordable rent would be. For someone earning €30,000 a year, a rent based on 30 per cent of their take-home pay equates to €576 a month. For someone earning the average salary of €40,000 a year, an affordable rent is €750 a month. So the average rent takes up 53 per cent of the average salary. The average rent in Dublin is now only affordable (costs less than a third of net income) to the top 5 per cent of income earners (earning over €115,000 a year). If we want to provide affordable rents, the current rents need to fall by around 50 per cent.

The CSO has developed a new way of measuring the impact of rising rents and mortgage payments on inequalities and poverty. Its new calculation looks at the 'at risk of poverty' rate after people have paid for their rent and mortgage interest. What it revealed is the stark impact of housing costs. You are 'at risk of poverty' if your income is less than 60 per cent of the median disposable income in the country; in other words, if you have less than €14,205 a year to spend as your disposable income.

The CSO calculations show that almost one million people in Ireland are at risk of poverty after they have paid their rent or mortgage. There are 1.2 million children in the country under 18. Before taking housing costs into account, 202,000 of them are in families in poverty. But after housing costs have been paid, that figure increases by 50 per cent – to over 300,000 children in poverty. One in four children in this country are in poverty after their family has paid their housing costs. It is renters who are being hammered the hardest, to the point of being pushed into poverty. One in fourteen homeowners with a mortgage are in poverty after housing costs. But a staggering one in every three renters (who do not receive any state supports) are in poverty after they pay their rent.

For these renters, every month is a struggle to make ends meet. There is no leeway to pay an unexpected bill like a doctor or hospital visit, or a child's school trip. And it is usually the other costs that are cut back on – the children's social activities, the birthday present, the health costs, even food – but never the rent. The rent must always be paid.

The economy might have been roaring for some after Covid receded but during 2021 a total of just over 191,000 calls for help were made to the St Vincent de Paul Society across Ireland, the highest on record. Many were renters needing support to cover the rent. St Vincent de Paul commissioned the Red C polling company to check the financial impact on people post-pandemic. It found that a significant proportion of Irish society are facing 'a multitude of financial pressures' due to the pandemic and the rising cost of living. These include loss of income, increased household expenditure on basics, erosion of savings to meet ordinary living expenses, falling behind on bills and being forced to cut back on essentials like food, heating and electricity. They found that almost a third of those in employment were worried about meeting their housing costs. Shockingly, one in seven of those at work were worried about facing eviction or losing their home. One in every five of those unemployed were worried about losing their home. But again, it was renters who were hardest hit. Many of the lowest paid and most insecure workers who lost their job when the Covid pandemic hit were also renters. This has been a stressful time for those families and has set them back even further. The inequality grew between those who increased their savings during Covid and others who lost, who were more likely to be renters. So, some saved and can buy an additional property, while others lost income and saw their life's dreams further crumble into the rental dust. They are struggling to pay the inflated bills and the rent. And that was all before the latest cost of living crisis hit and was added to the cost of rent crisis that Generation Rent has been living with for years.

Over half of all private renters are worried about their ability to meet their rental costs in the next six months, much higher than the third of homeowners with a mortgage who are worried about housing costs (which is still very high).

An older renter describes feeling at the 'mercy of the rental market'. When you are living in rental accommodation, a large part of your income is going to cover the rent. It means that 'it's difficult to see anything else around you. Your life is so caught up in managing day to day that your focus is getting through the day.' At sixty-five, he is not looking to own a home, he just wants 'security of tenure'. He explains, 'the problem is that, in this country, ownership is about the only thing that gives security. If you can't get council housing, you are at the mercy of the rental market – and there is no mercy.'

The failure for two decades to build social or affordable housing on a serious level means that low-income households have nowhere to live except in the private rental sector. And because of the massive rise in rents, the government has had to provide rental subsidies for low-income renters. There are 105,000 households, close to a third of registered private rental households, in receipt of a state payment that is supposed to cover the rent. There are 13,000 in receipt of rent supplement, 62,000 in receipt of HAP and approximately 30,000 households in RAS and leasing schemes. In these schemes, the local authority pays the landlord the rent, and tenants then pay a smaller rent, called a 'differential rent', which is based on their income, to the local authority. It's the same rent level as local authority tenants pay. But while landlords have increased rents massively, the HAP and rent supplement payments have not been increased since 2016. So a gap has grown between what the State will pay as rental subsidy and the rents that are being charged. This means that to keep their home, tenants in receipt of state rental benefits must pay to their landlord a 'top-up' that covers the gap. These are families and individuals already struggling with the cost of living. Two-thirds are families with children, of which 43 per cent are lone parents with children, one of the groups already experiencing the highest poverty rates in the country. Most HAP recipients are working, but half earn less than €15,000 a year. The 'top-ups' mean that even those getting state housing benefits in the private rental sector are in poverty after paying their rent. Over 60 per cent of renters who get social housing supports are in poverty after they pay their rent.

The real scale of poverty among renters is shown when we add together the two groups of renters in poverty – those who get no state support towards their rent, and those who do get state support. There are around 33,400 households not in receipt of state subsidy in the private rental sector who are in poverty. After paying their rent, that jumps to 65,000 households in poverty. Then there are 23,835 households in receipt of state supports who are in poverty before their rent is paid. That jumps to 58,695 households after their rent (including 'top-ups') is paid. This means that there are 57,235 private rental households (or one in five) in poverty, but after they pay their rent that jumps by over 112 per cent to 123,000 – or 41 per cent of private renting households – who are in poverty after paying their rent. Four in ten private rental households in Ireland are in poverty.

The country of the arts where no artist can afford to live

This is a country of internationally influential arts and culture creators, poets, playwrights, musicians and artists. Our arts, music and culture are promoted as one of our unique attractions and attributes by the various Irish state bodies across the world. Ireland Inc. puts culture at the heart of the advertising of 'Ireland'. We are known globally for our culture, from Yeats to Patrick Kavanagh, JM Synge, Phil Lynott, U2, and many, many more. Our artists, musicians, writers and poets express the spirit and soul of Ireland. Yet our artists can no longer afford to live in this country. Artists, cultural workers and creators of all kinds are badly affected by the housing crisis. As workers with often insecure, low incomes they are reliant on the rental sector. Yet as renters they cannot afford to live in Dublin, or Cork, or even Ballina or Carrick-on-Suir. The housing crisis is destroying their ability to be creative, to link with other creators. The soul of our nation is having its lifeline cut off. Are we going to force another generation of our youth, our artists, our future to emigrate? The satirist, musician and podcaster Blindboy explained this very well:

So many people are unable to pursue a sense of meaning in their life – whether it is their career, their hobbies, their life – because of the housing crisis. There are people in the career they don't want to be in because if they changed it that would mean taking a risk with rent and they can't take that risk of not being able to afford the rent. So, there's a load of people who can't live the life they would like to live because everything is dominated by 'can I pay the rent each month'. So, people will accept anything that just lets them not have to worry about this rent. But you can't focus on who you are, on finding out about who the fuck you are, if all you are thinking about is making that extortionate rent every month. You can't take risks – you can't go back to college. Someone in their thirties who goes, 'I've been an accountant since I was 23 and I'd like to pursue the arts and go back to college.' No one is doing that. There is too much risk. Where are you going to get the money to pay rent to go back to college – you can't take a risk anymore. To think of that human potential of so many people – going back to education.... What would you be doing if you didn't have to worry about rent – if rent wasn't the only thing you were worried about?

You can't just 'shop around' for lower rents!

Given the lack of supply and, more important, the absence of an affordable supply, renters can't just, as one government TD advised in relation to the cost of living crisis, 'shop around'. Just a scan through what is available on the rental site Daft.ie will quickly reveal the extent of this crazy broken rental market. You can 'choose' to rent an investor fund apartment like one in Griffith Wood in Dublin where a three-bed will cost you €3,600 a month or take your pick from overpriced substandard housing.

There's a studio in Dublin 2 advertised for a thousand a month – for a place that looks like a small kitchen. And in the kitchen is, wait for it, the shower. Which is about two feet away from the sockets that plug in the kettle and toaster at the sink. There is a microwave, though. But it appears to take up half the only table available, which has two chairs at it. Although one chair is clearly blocking the door. So you can pay €1,000 to have a shower while you can watch the dinner cook. Clearly unsafe. Clearly in breach of regulations. But who enforces them?

Another property on Daft.ie was described as an 'excellent studio, newly refurbished to the highest standards. Wall bed to sleep two people. Viewing is a must.' But the picture of the place shows a hallway, which appears to have had a cooker unit installed in it and a cupboard that ingeniously folds down into a bed. So for €1,200 a month you can rent a hallway that sleeps two in a cupboard. Another great one, advertised for €1,450 a month, has a bathroom where the sink is being propped up by an old crutch. And it's not just Dublin; in Limerick, three-bedroomed houses are being advertised for €2,500 a month. That level of mortgage would buy a massive home in that county. Then there was the garden shed in a back garden advertised in Cork City for €1,200 a month to rent.

It is literally impossible to find anywhere to rent. You have probably seen the notices posted in shops, on lampposts and on bus and Luas shelters. One I saw read, 'We are a couple, in our mid-twenties, looking for a room or a house to rent. I'm Alejandra, I'm a support worker with a full-time job. I'm Adrian, I'm an economist with a full-time job. We are respectful, easy going and good-vibe people. Our budget is €1,000 for a room'. Isn't it awful? An economist and a support worker, both with full-time jobs and a large budget, unable to find a home. The housing system is truly broken. But it gets worse.

An investigation by the *Irish Examiner* revealed that women were facing 'sex for rent' demands when they tried to find rental housing. They found properties in Limerick and Dublin being offered for low or no rent in return for sex. The Dublin Rape Crisis Centre described it as 'an incredibly exploitative and enormously abusive tactic'. Immigrants who arrive in Ireland to take up new jobs or begin their studies and are trying to find a place to live are being exploited. One young Italian professional woman said that trying to find a room in Dublin 'is like falling in a dangerous hell' after her experience; she received offers that hinted at sex being required when replying to three separate advertisements online.

There are very few rental properties available that the state rental benefit will cover. Simon Communities research showed that in December 2021, there were just three properties in Cork available within the HAP limits, one in Limerick and one in Waterford. So just 4 per cent of the rental properties advertised in these three cities were within the HAP limits. Some landlords also refuse to accept HAP, and discriminate against one-parent families, Travellers and people with disabilities, even though this is illegal.

Lone-parent families face a particularly difficult challenge. A mother with two school-age children living in a small two-bedroom apartment quite a distance away from her children's school explains how hard it is. Her nine-year-old son sleeps in one bedroom and she shares the other bedroom with her five-year-old daughter. She needs to find a three-bedroomed home to rent so she and her children can have their own rooms, somewhere closer to the school. She has been looking for a place to rent for four years without success. She feels that because she is on HAP, she hasn't even been offered viewings. And the HAP limits are too low for the rents. Her daughter is, understandably, asking for her own bedroom, and the mom knows these requests will increase in the coming years. The mom has to explain to her daughter that she has no idea when they will get a house. Her son says that he is the only one in his class who does not live in the area, and she feels that as a result 'he is being excluded from socializing with his friends from school because we cannot invite people over for birthday parties because we simply have no space to accommodate people. The same applies to my daughter.' She describes the reality for Generation Rent:

> I feel like I am trapped in this apartment and there is no way out, but then I am grateful to have a roof over my head which other people don't have. I know a lot of people, my neighbours, friends

with two or three children living in small, two-bedroom apartments with no opportunity to move elsewhere because the rents are so high, and viewings are not even offered to people on social welfare. A few of my friends have depression and stress, which results in health issues.

This is what happens when governments don't build social or affordable housing, reduce housing standards to suit investors, allow housing to be treated like a commodity, and don't regulate the market. Investors buy up all the properties. The low-wage economy, rising rents and lack of social housing has created an unprecedented crisis of housing affordability for Generation Rent.

Rents clearly have a long way to fall before they become affordable. It will not be sufficient to just stabilize existing rents at 2 per cent a year growth. That is not sustainable.

Landlords hold all the cards

Along with being unaffordable, the other biggest issue affecting renters is the insecurity of their home. There are several reasons why landlords can get a tenant to leave – to evict them – even if the tenant has done nothing wrong. For example, the landlord might decide to sell the property, move a family member or themselves into the home, or undertake refurbishment. It really is incredible that a tenant living in their own home must uproot themselves, and the people they live with, even if they have always paid the rent and have never caused any problems, just because the landlord decides they want to do something with the property. We know that since rents started rising dramatically in 2014, landlords have evicted tenants in order to get in higher-paying tenants and take advantage of rising rents, and in some parts of the country not covered by Rent Pressure Zones, landlords take advantage of the lack of rent controls to increase rents significantly. Increasingly landlords are taking advantage of rising property prices to sell their property, and others are converting them into highly lucrative short-stay tourist accommodation.

The level of insecurity in the private rental sector is shown by a St Vincent de Paul poll that found that a third of renters are worried about facing eviction or losing their home. That is a three times higher level of insecurity than that experienced by those in local authority housing or homeowners with a mortgage.

As previously mentioned, a Rent Pressure Zone (RPZ) is a designated area where rents cannot be increased by more than 2 per cent per annum (it was 4 per cent up to 2021). This applies to existing tenancies and new tenancies in a property already being rented. RPZs are in parts of the country where rents are highest and rising and where households have the greatest difficulty finding affordable accommodation. But the RPZ system is not functioning. There are too many exemptions to the rules, which landlords are abusing. And the enforcement and penalties for landlords in breach of the rules is inadequate.

There are no rent control mechanisms for new tenancies in newly let properties. So new rental properties coming to the market are completely exempt from rent caps and are driving up rents. Many are expensive investor fund apartments. The government's position on renters is contradictory. They claim they want to get renters 'out of the rent trap', yet the new supply of homes leaves renters with little option but to be pushed further into the trap.

This means that if a new property is rented, or where the landlord sells on the property and a new investor owner buys it and rents out to new tenants, a new market rent will be charged. Landlords of properties that have been vacant for two years can also charge whatever rent they want. Some landlords are ignoring the rules and evicting tenants with the stated aim of selling the property or moving a family member in, but then don't do that and just get in new tenants on higher market rents or convert the property to an Airbnb. There is widespread breaching of the RPZ rules and regulations by landlords.

Added to this, many small towns and rural areas across the country are not part of RPZs, so they are still not covered by any rent caps.

Landlords in these areas have free rein to increase the rent as much as they want, which explains the incredible rent increases seen across the country in early 2022: up to 20 per cent in Mayo; 19 per cent in Sligo and Galway county; 15 per cent in Clare; 14 per cent in Kerry; 10 per cent in parts of Cork and Limerick.

The impact of evictions

In recent years most of the calls received by the renters' support charity Threshold have concerned evictions by landlords intending to sell the home. As we've seen, some landlords use this excuse to get rid of lower-paying tenants and get in higher-paying tenants. Such illegal evictions are a major problem. Between 2014 and 2019, there was a 75 per cent increase in the number of cases brought by tenants to the Residential Tenancies Board (RTB). In 2019 alone, the RTB registered 3,515 complaints against landlords. Of those, almost half related to illegal evictions. But because landlords hold the power in the Irish rental sector, and there is no real enforcement of laws, tenants are left vulnerable. The RTB process cannot stop an eviction taking place.

This means that renters are forced into a constant not-so-merry-go-round of being evicted from one rental property and having to try to find another one. But when they have to leave, because of rising rents they are looking in a more expensive rental market, and therefore end up paying higher rents. It has become a profitable game of musical chairs by, and for, landlords. It is a constant process of uprooting thousands of renters, moving them away from their family, friends, schools and work, and denying them housing that might be more suitable to meet their needs, or just a home they like. They must pack up their belongings and move to what is likely to be just another temporary home.

The instability caused by frequent housing moves puts additional stresses on people and causes psychological distress, particularly to families and children. Paul is a renter in his sixties. He lived in his home with his partner for ten years, but was served an eviction notice because the landlord was selling up. The loss of their home combined with the stress and anxiety of trying to find another one that they could afford has had a major impact on his mental health. He describes how in the months leading up to the eviction, his 'depression seems to be getting worse. Each day is a day closer to our eviction. I'm just getting more and more despondent. Where are we going to be? Where are we going to go? My life is being sucked out of me.' He spoke about the loss of the little things. He had made the house a home, built decking out the back, and collected a set of tools for doing DIY and the garden. But not knowing where he was going, if they might be homeless, he felt he had no choice but to try to sell the tools before they left. He explained:

> Today, I start emptying my tools from my shed, I'll be giving some away, some I'm hoping to sell. Ten years of tools and the enjoyment of using them soon to end! Eviction isn't only losing your home; it's about losing everything.

We can get a sense of the scale of evictions happening in the private rental sector from the data that the RTB provides. Where a tenancy is longer than six months, landlords must send a copy of the notice of termination to the RTB. (This has only been a requirement since 2019.) The figures show that 3,038 notices to quit (NTQs) were issued to private tenants in 2021. That was a 62 per cent increase on NTQs in 2020 (up from 1,902). Over 90 per cent of the evictions were for no fault of the tenant.

While the Minister for Housing Darragh O'Brien claimed new legislation addressed long-term security of tenure for renters, this was deeply misleading. He claimed that legislation providing for tenancies of unlimited duration 'enhanced security of tenure for renters'. But renters have no genuine long-term security of tenure when a tenant can be evicted by the landlord for 'no-fault' reasons.

Up and down the country there are towns with not one property available to rent (aside from Airbnbs). Renters in these towns live in utter fear of losing their homes as there is nowhere to go. One renter living in Tullamore described how there is just one property available to rent in the area, a two bed apartment for €900. They explained that if their landlord decided he wanted to sell their rental tomorrow, they are in dire straits. They had already moved five times in six years due to property sales, and rent had doubled in that time.

The insecure children of Generation Rent

Then there are the children of Generation Rent. Children who have no sense of long-term security in their home. Children without homes. Children who are uprooted every few years. Take Timmy, Leo and Aisling. They are six, seven and eight. They are all neighbours on the same street. They are all best friends. One of the families is from Poland, one from Mayo and one from Wicklow. Leo and Aisling don't see their cousins much as their wider families live the other side of the country or abroad; Timmy doesn't have cousins. So these kids are like family. They play together every weekend, they go to the same school, and Timmy and Aisling sit beside each other in class. Every day, one of them comes knocking for the others, and then they play together for hours, lost in their world of dinosaurs, make-believe, movies, bugs or jumping on the trampoline. Timmy gets upset if Leo or Aisling is sick even for a day. But Timmy and his family are renting their house, and they must move because the landlord is selling up. Timmy is heartbroken. His parents are worried they won't be able to find another place to rent in the area and they might have to move Timmy to another school. The three friends are torn apart by the housing crisis. Psychologists explain that a child can be deeply affected by the loss of a friend. It can make them more closed, less open.

One dad whose family was evicted describes how the rental insecurity is 'heartbreaking for families'. Their son was so distraught at having to leave their rented family home and his friends, and change schools, that his hair literally started to fall out and he was depressed for months. And, the dad asks, 'For what? Landlords' profit?' His story shows how the private rental system is operated for the landlord, and tenants are second-class citizens. They had been living in the same area for almost ten years and in the same apartment for five years. But then the estate agent emailed them to say the landlord would be raising the monthly rent by several hundred euros from the following month. The increase was well above the 4 per cent rent limit, so he pushed back and questioned the amount. Just a few hours later he had an email notifying him that the landlord had decided to sell. They had one month to find a new place. When he questioned whether this was correct, since they had been living there for five years without any issues, they got an extension to five months. But it was impossible to find a place they could afford in the same area. So they searched further and further away. Then they had to find a new school for their son. Many of their son's friends had left the area over the years, either going back to home countries or priced out of the rental market. Their son had handled that as it was happening over a period. But the twofold change of leaving their home and finding a new school was just too much for him to handle. His dad says:

> He is fine now but he still talks about missing the old home. As a parent you feel incredible guilt and question your own abilities for allowing this to happen. It's awful. I've been renting in Dublin since 2002 and as a single professional the regular moves to new homes wasn't too bad but as a family with schools, support circle and friends, each move is more traumatic than the last. We are hoping to move one last time and buy a house.

Families are also worried about their inability to provide a safety net of a secure home for their children who, as they become adults, might need to stay in or return to the family home. Increasingly, renters are leaving the private rental market and moving back with parents and extended family. This is part of Ireland's hidden housing and homelessness crisis.

Kate explains that she was lucky enough to be able to move back in with her mother and has a bedroom for her own child. But what was supposed to be a short stay is becoming long-term. She has now been living with her mother for two years. She has tried to get rental accommodation, but the competition is so intense. She doesn't want to live in the private rental sector because of the level of insecurity. She says:

> I want to give my child a stable home. She has additional needs, and my attention should be focused on her quality of life. I want to give her a garden with a swing and a dog where we know we can stay and just relax. My child is not getting the best from me because I'm always battling for something, housing, basic services, supports and therapies. I am lucky enough to have family and friends, an education and a decent job, but that is not enough to achieve basic security because housing has been commodified at the expense of workers, our children and our imagination. It's wrong and it's not our doing.

I wish I could take what Kate said and put it out on a loop on national radio and TV. It shows all that is wrong with the housing system.

Home should be about providing belonging and stability, networks, living near family (if you choose), being part of a community and a neighbourhood. Almost two-thirds of social renters and homeowners have family members living close by, compared to just a third of private renters. Most private renters have expressed their wish to live close to other family members. Only 16 per cent of private renters live in the area they grew up in, compared to 40 per cent of those in social housing. Just 8 per cent of private renters have lived in their home longer than ten years, compared to almost a half of those in social housing and three-quarters of homeowners. Private renters are denied the stability and security to set up roots, feel a sense of connectedness and belonging, and have a home of their own.

Airbnb

Landlords are also converting their property from long-term rentals into short-term stays for tourists, such as via Airbnb, in order to increase profit from their property. This is despite regulations that require homeowners in RPZs, such as Dublin, Cork and Limerick City, to apply to their local authority for planning permission to change the property use to short-term let, where such lets exceed ninety days a year. Many are ignoring the rules, while others in areas that are not covered by RPZ legislation don't have to abide by these rules. This is a major problem in many high-tourist areas of Ireland – and there are not many parts of Ireland that are not touristy areas. This means that renters across the entire country are at risk of being evicted to be replaced by tourists. Landlords can make multiples of what they earn from rent from short-term lets. They can make up to €50,000 a year, over double what they would get in rent. Renters in tourist-heavy counties like Kerry, Cork, Galway and Clare who are facing eviction explain there is literally nothing available but short-term lets. There is nothing to rent for people who are actually living and working in the area, just for tourists. This has major implications for the life of these areas, and for businesses that cannot find workers because they can't live in the area. For example, in the small town of Kinsale in County Cork, there are sixty Airbnb properties available, but just three to rent on Daft.ie. Threshold found that there were five times as many entire properties available as short-term tourist lets as there were properties available for long-term renting in the cities of Dublin, Limerick, Cork and Galway. They identified 4,000 homes that were available for short stays and just 757 entire properties available to rent long-term. Of these, only 164 properties cost below €1,500 per month to rent.

One landlord on a short-term letting platform was found to have a total of eighteen property listings. A landlord in Cork listed just under ten properties, with a short-term coastal two-bed apartment costing €302 for a two-night stay. The only two-bed apartment in the same area for long-term rent cost €1,650 per month. A Galway-based landlord offered over twenty properties in Galway City and suburbs, with a three-bed apartment near the city centre costing €735 for a three-night stay. In comparison, the nearest property to that location available for long-term rent is a one-bed apartment costing €1,430 per month. Therefore, the three-bed property only needs to be rented short-term for six days to yield the same income. In Galway, there are 972 full properties available on short-term lets, but just 45 as long-term lets.

The CEO of Threshold, John-Mark McCafferty, put it starkly:

It's troubling to see so many landlords advertising suitable long-term rental accommodation as short-term properties. We see a crisis situation, where current renters are frozen out of buying, and there is a major increase in termination notices – with tenants literally having almost no option of finding another home, which is causing the homelessness numbers to rise again. The lack of enforcement of the 2019 regulations, which restricts the use of long-term homes as holiday lets in the Rent Pressure Zones is not being enforced, from what we can see. This situation is certainly contributing even further to the major housing shortage across Ireland.

People are being evicted into homelessness, only for their home to be turned into tourist accommodation. Profit is again superseding housing needs. That is dysfunctional, unethical and bad social and economic policy.

But Airbnb wants to take this even further, and get more of the housing market turned into accommodation let out on a short-stay basis. The Airbnb CEO, Brian Chesky, posited that cities should think of their citizens as 'customers' who can make choices because they can work anywhere. And people are now 'living on Airbnb'. Chesky stated, 'The big change underway with Airbnb is that length of stay is going to increase and it's going to blur with living.' Nearly a quarter of Airbnb's global bookings are 'long term', or 28 days and longer. Millions of people are staying and living at Airbnb listings on a monthly basis. The CEO said, 'I think eventually in the future people will start paying for rent the way they pay for cable television, or for Netflix, you pay on a month-to-month basis.'

This is a terrifying prospect of even greater insecurity for renters, and further turns homes into financial commodities.

The private rental sector is bad for your health

The poor quality of rental accommodation is also a major issue for renters. Issues of mould and damp are constantly highlighted. One in six private rental homes have damp or leaks in their walls or roof – over double the proportion of homeowners affected by these issues. And we know how unhealthy that is, especially for cl   'n when their lungs are growing and bodies developing. One ir   rivate renters have difficulties keeping their house warm, a r   nigher proportion than homeowners. It is estimated that 55   ᵗ of private rented dwellings have a Building Energy Rating (BER) of D or lower, so in addition to poor health outcomes it costs these tenants more to heat their home. One renter who contacted me was living in the cold in a rental home in Galway. They are living with four others, and two of the housemates couldn't afford the energy bill. They were working from home all winter, so they needed the heat on during the day, and now can't afford to get a new tank of oil to heat the home. They are all working. As he explained, this was 'never something I thought I would be dealing with'.

There is also a major problem of local authorities failing to inspect private rental property to assess that it is up to standard. So tenants have been forced to accept substandard housing at a high rent, from landlords who do not maintain the home.

A gaff of your own?

Private renters do not have control over their own dwelling – their home. They can't do the things that give so many people joy in their gaff: DIY, retrofitting, painting the place, putting up a picture or a painting, gardening, even having a pet. They can't even leave their bikes or buggies at the front door or in the hall. They feel infantilized by being denied these basic choices and decisions. They have major difficulties in getting landlords and estate agents to carry out repairs. They have a fear of even asking the landlord to do things in case they will be served with a rent increase or eviction letter. And while most tenants describe their relationship with their landlord as positive, there is still a massively unequal power dynamic – the landlord or estate agent acting on their behalf can take your home away from you. A good relationship doesn't guarantee affordable or secure housing. It tends to be when a tenant raises issues such as maintenance that the relationship can deteriorate.

The power dynamic is profoundly unequal because the renter is dependent on the landlord for the most basic need of a home, and they have no real, substantial legal protections. The idea that tenants can challenge landlords is ridiculous. The level of ontological insecurity and vulnerability of tenants is so extreme and dependent on landlords that it leaves a massive power imbalance, which landlords exploit in multiple ways.

Renters just want a home where they are able to fix things themselves instead of, as one renter explained, 'waiting for the letting agency to fix a broken window for six months (and counting!)' and 'not having to hide my cats'. That one stopped me in my tracks. What? How can you hide a cat, and why would you have to? But it turns out that many renters cannot even have a pet. Pets are known to have a positive effect on mental health and wellbeing, particularly for those living alone. Their prohibition tells us a lot about the reality of a renter's life and the housing crisis in Ireland today. Landlords in Ireland not allowing pets is a manifestation of all that is wrong with the private rental sector. Even when they do allow them, it's now, farcically, common to charge extra for pets. So landlords up the rent because you got a kitten? Or if you got your kids a hamster, a budgie and a puppy, will the rent be increased for each pet? It's just one more inequality between homeowners and tenants and reason why people feel compelled to try to buy housing: they cannot make their private rented house or apartment their home as they are not allowed the basics such as having a pet.

You might think this is something minor – it is not. It goes to the heart of the absence of rights of tenants in Ireland. Landlords are all-powerful. Laws and culture are not strong enough to protect tenants. It goes back to the Constitution (which might seem a long way from pets): the protection of private property of landlords is enshrined in Article 43. But there is no right to housing in our Constitution.

The lack of control renters have over their home reaches its zenith in the experience of renters waking up in the morning to an electrician or the landlord unlocking their door. Landlords are entering tenants' homes, even their bedrooms, without warning and unannounced, even though this is against the law. The RTB outlines that though the landlord owns the property, 'while the tenant rents, it is their [the tenant's] home.' This means the landlord must respect the tenant's peace and privacy. This is called peaceful and exclusive use of the property. If the landlord needs to enter the property (for example, for an inspection or to carry out repairs), the tenant's consent is required to access the dwelling, and the landlord should give them reasonable notice. But that is ignored by landlords way too often. More worryingly, female tenants complain that they find the landlord or the 'handyman' fixing things in their bedrooms that were never broken to begin with.

Privacy is also a big issue for renters who share a house with unrelated housemates. More than half of renters in house shares – and 57 per cent of women – feel they don't have enough privacy. Despite sharing their home with others, a large proportion of renters in house shares report feeling lonely 'all or most of the time'; again, the rate is higher for women. Living in private rental housing where you don't have control over your home is bad enough without that control being further diminished by living in house-share situations. Disagreements about household chores and using and cleaning shared facilities are very common and impact significantly on renters' quality of life. More than half of renters in house shares have disagreements over excessive noise and over having people to visit. We know that control over your own living place and space is a fundamental human need. And so, continuing to rent a room and share communal spaces well into adulthood is not sustainable or desirable for many people.

You just cannot make a home in the Irish private rental sector.

Generation HAP trap

While a third of all private renters are in receipt of a state contribution towards their rent, they still pay significant rent – both to the local authority and as top-ups to private landlords. These renters are officially classed as being in social housing, with their housing needs 'met', and they are taken off local authority and national social housing waiting lists. But hang on a minute. How is that possible? How can the government consider that their housing needs are met when they are living in the private rental sector – unaffordable, of poor standard and, above all, insecure?

In genuine social housing provided by local authorities and housing associations, tenants have absolute security of tenure for life (aside from issues of antisocial behaviour and rent arrears in some cases). It is your home, your secure place. You have stability, you can set roots, have a family, be part of the community. You do not worry about being evicted. But in HAP, it's the private rental sector, where the landlord can evict you and tenancies are short. HAP tenants are even being evicted into homelessness. I can't see how something can be classed as social housing if you can be evicted from it into homelessness. Surely the raison d'être of social housing is the complete opposite?

Lisa, a lone parent with a sixteen-year-old daughter, told her story on my podcast, Reboot Republic, of her upset and worry as they face eviction from their Kerry home of twelve years. She described memories of her daughter coming down the stairs on Christmas mornings, and the strong bonds she has built up with neighbours, bonds that take years to form. Yet now she is being forced out of her home and away from the support of her community. She has state rental support, but a property owner bought her home and served her with an eviction notice. She believes her home will become a short-term tourist let.

In genuine social housing, the council or housing association allocates you a home. But in HAP you must find the rental property yourself, which is nigh-on impossible in a rental market which is unaffordable. Those who need HAP to cover their rent – the most vulnerable, such as lone-parent families, those fleeing domestic abuse, people with disabilities, refugees and asylum seekers, Travellers – face huge discrimination from landlords and do not have the income to cover top-ups.

As long as landlords can evict tenants for no-fault evictions, housing in the private rental sector does not provide a secure home, and HAP tenants should not be classed as being in social housing.

People just want a home

Given all the issues I have outlined here, it is no wonder that people do not want to live in the private rental sector. Just 15 per cent of renters want to keep renting in the private rental sector for the long term. Around 11 per cent are renting because they are waiting for social housing. Yet housing policy, the government, much of the economic and property commentators and of course the investor funds and REITs all promote private renting in Ireland as a new way of living, 'much like Europeans'.

They clearly have no understanding of the reality of the Irish private rental sector. It is nothing like the European secure, affordable, decent-sized, rental sector. There is a small group – of high-income earners, some internationally mobile – who see living in the private rental sector as a 'choice'. But even then, it is just while they are figuring out where they want to live, settle down and buy their home. Renting in the private rental sector in Ireland is a not a lifestyle choice for most renters, it is an imposed life sentence. Three-quarters of renters want to live in a home of their own, either one they own or in real social housing. But they can't buy and there is little social housing so they have no choice but to rent in the private sector.

The reason they are renting is not a lifestyle choice but because they can't buy a home. They can't get a mortgage, or find a house within their price range, or they can't save for a deposit while paying rent. Why would you choose to live with the enduring uncertainty and insecurity, the inability and lack of incentive to make your home nice, to buy furniture, to make your gaff a home? Why would you choose to spend all that 'dead money' on rent and have nothing to show for it when you can be turfed out at any time, no matter how much work you put into your home?

Renters aspire to live in a home of their own. Over two-thirds – 69 per cent – of renters want to purchase a property within ten years, and 50 per cent think they will actually own a home in that time. Most aspire to buy, but a half doubt that they will ever be able to afford to do so. That gap between aspiration and expectation is filled with a sense of hopelessness and unhappiness.

The private rental sector, particularly apartments, is not where people want to live. Just 2 per cent see themselves renting an apartment in ten years' time, while just 6 per cent see themselves buying an apartment. Most want to be living in a house. That is a real problem, given that most of the housing that has new planning permission is apartments, and investor funds are building mainly apartments. If people are offered the choice of a secure, affordable house or an expensive investor-fund apartment, they will choose the affordable house.

This really comes into focus when you look at renters by age group. You see that Generation Rent is really a generation locked out of being able to buy a home or access social housing. The figures are stark. A half of renters in their mid-twenties are renting by choice. Just a third in their mid-thirties are renting by choice. Of people in their mid-forties, just 20 per cent are renting by choice. This makes sense, because it is when you are in your thirties or forties, when (whether or not you have children) you are looking for stability and security, a home that you can make your own gaff. It is then that the insecurity, inappropriateness and lack of control and autonomy you have in the private rental sector really hits you. The inability of the private rental to provide a home really reveals itself. When people are renting in their mid-fifties, well, no one is there by choice. At that age, 60 per cent are renting because they cannot buy a home, and 40 per cent are renting because they cannot access social housing.

If this is people's aspiration – and we know it is better for their wellbeing, for society and the economy for people to own their own home, or to be in real social housing – why should we not just deliver that? Build social and affordable gaffs for people to give them the home we all need and have a right to. As long as that is denied them – while they see others on higher incomes or from families who can lend them the money to buy a home, or, even worse, while they see landlords and investor funds buying up homes everywhere – what does it mean for their mental health, their wellbeing, their sense of self? What does it mean for their commitment to citizenship, to society, for their desire to contribute, to engage in voting, with politics and community? How must they feel watching others buy homes and being able to live their full lives, while their lives feel stuck, on hold, and even ebbing away on a tide of never-ending rent and worry about having to move and find another rental? Locking people out of having their own home is corrosive, not only for them as individuals but also for our society.

This also explains why there is such intense lobbying and pressure by REITs to change the cultural narrative to 'We need more rental properties and apartments built' to help solve the housing crisis. And 'no one should object to high-rise build-to-rent developments'. But the reality is that the REITs want to foreclose, or remove, the possibilities and option for younger generations to access their own home – they don't want affordable houses or low-rise apartments available to buy or as social and affordable housing on a major scale. REITs need a housing crisis and shortage so that people are forced into living in REIT apartments, because the only reason people will rent them is because they don't have an alternative. REIT apartment living is not an 'exciting new way of living', it is a way of living that no one wants to live, but one that people are being forced and locked into because they have no other choice.

What should be done?

Private for-profit landlords do not provide proper homes in Ireland. This should make us think about the problematic nature of for-profit private landlordism as an entity of housing provision, and the dominant role it now plays in the Irish housing system. A private landlord is someone who has more housing than they need; they have an excess of housing. And because of the lack of social and affordable housing, they can charge those who don't have housing, who don't have the resources to buy housing, for their human need to have a home. And when the landlord charges them rent, the renter or person without housing is further excluded from the possibility of owning a home. And the private landlord gains more wealth from the renter, and so is in an even better position to buy more housing, which excludes more people from getting a home of their own. Instead, the renters now have to be permanent renters in the homes the landlord is buying up. It is a vicious cycle in which the rate of home ownership falls and the rate of private renting rises, to the benefit of the private landlords/investor landlords/REITs – exactly what is happening in Ireland today.

Let's be very clear. It is not renting per se that is the problem. It is the dominance of for-profit private rental and the type of private rental system we have in Ireland.

On top of the 300,000 households renting in the for-profit private rental sector, there are another 200,000 households renting in

Ireland. Those 200,000 are renting in real social housing – from local authorities and housing associations. This is a really good rental housing sector that we should support and build much more of. People living in this type of housing have a very different experience of rental than people renting from private for-profit landlords. The fundamental difference is that social housing landlords are not providing housing to make a profit; they are doing it to provide affordable, decent homes to their tenants. And an overwhelming majority of people living in social housing (despite all the media and social stigmatization) are happy where they are living. They have lifetime-secure homes with affordable rents. There are issues that could be improved, such as the conditions of some social housing, tenants having the choice to make changes to their own homes, and improving housing management and maintenance. But this is renting that actually works. That is the type of rental we should expand in Ireland.

The private for-profit rental sector is broken in this country. It is no longer fit for purpose. It does not provide affordable rents or stability and security for renters. It doesn't need to be 'patched up', which the government is currently looking at. It needs to be over-hauled and reconfigured so that it provides affordable, lifetime-secure, decent-quality homes. And it needs to be reduced as a form of housing provision and replaced by social and affordable lifetime-secure, decent homes.

If homeowners can have a forever home, why can't renters? Tenants are equal citizens, equally important, equally valuable, so why can't they have a place that they can call home? As a society it's time to rewrite the social contract for renters.

Why does no one ask the question about the economic justification of rising rents? Where is the evidence of an increase in costs of landlords to justify a 100 per cent increase in rents in a decade? There is a need for accountability of landlords' decisions. There's no rent fairy deciding what rents should be. Each landlord increasing rent does so as an individual (or company) decision. We need to question the justification for that decision.

The government and landlords need to realize that rental properties are people's homes. Renters are utterly dependent on their rented property for their fundamental need of shelter. A home is a human right, but renters in this country have no right to a home.

A significant minority of renters (around 45 per cent) would be happy to stay renting if it was affordable and they had security about staying as long as they wanted. Housing policy could achieve this relatively quickly, even more quickly than it can build homes. It could: (a) make private rental affordable by reducing rents by 25–50 per cent, and where that is not viable for a landlord the local authority should buy the property off the landlord; (b) immediately provide lifetime-secure tenancies, removing the ability of landlords to evict tenants for 'no-fault' reasons (this could be done tomorrow if the government wanted and it would provide massive relief to renters); (c) retrofit to improve the quality and standards of homes; and (d) provide a major funding grant to the RTB, local authorities and the tenants' union CATU (Community Action Tenants Union) to engage in a process of information and empowerment of tenants so that they know and assert their rights, and for the RTB and local authorities to have the resources to monitor and enforce legislation and rules on landlords in breach of them. Alongside these measures, given that a majority of renters want to leave the private rental sector because it is unaffordable, insecure and of poor quality, rather than expanding the private rental sector we should be aiming to reduce it over time and provide the majority currently in private rental with affordable home ownership, social housing and affordable, secure, cost-rental homes.

Chapter 7
Generation Stuck at Home

Locked out of buying or renting their own home by the housing crisis, Generation Stuck at Home are living in their parents' or relatives' home. They feel as if they are not real adults, their lives are on hold, their aspirations and dreams slipping away as they desperately try to get a home of their own. For some, if their house is big enough, and their family is small, it might be possible to have the space to develop independently in their own parents' home, but that is not the case for most.

The numbers are staggering. Ten per cent of our entire population – one person in every ten – is an adult living in their parents' home. That's half a million people – more than the number of households in the entire private rental sector. These are the unseen generation in the housing crisis. They are not teenagers – they are adults in their twenties, thirties, forties, and most are working. There are 350,000 young adults aged between twenty and thirty-five living at home with their parents. Moving out of the family home is a key life step to achieve independence, but it is being hugely delayed for them. The average age of leaving home has now risen to twenty-eight. Back in the early 1990s most people in Ireland aged twenty-eight owned their own home.

No one can deny the benefits to living at home. It can help with positive relationships between parents and children, and encourage intergenerational support and understanding. It can provide much-needed childcare support and family care. It can provide care and support for parents, and help with loneliness. It can even provide benefits for the climate – it is the most efficient use of buildings and housing to have multi-generations living under one roof. But it can be extremely stressful, with increased tension between parents and children, and between siblings. The bottom line is that it is not the life most adults want to be living. A survey found that 93 per cent of 21–30-year-olds living at home said they would 'prefer to be living separately' from their parents. There is no ambiguity in that statistic.

It makes sense. At home they are still treated like children. They cannot develop into a full adult with control over their life. More than half (52 per cent) of those living with their parents said their parents will not treat them like an adult until they move out; 70 per cent said they don't have enough independence, like being able to have friends around or even choosing what food to cook. Not having privacy is one of the basic things you need to feel comfortable, and to live a life of dignity in your home. Yet three-quarters of female adults living at home with their parents feel they do not have enough privacy.

Huge parts of people's lives are out of their control when they are living at home – how they live, who they live with, having relationships, staying out late, having friends over, even having kids of their own. It is a challenge to just be who you are and who you might want to be. The three basic psychological requirements for wellbeing are autonomy (feeling a sense of choice and control), competence (mastering one's environment) and relatedness (feeling connected to others). Being in your late twenties, thirties and even forties and living in a box room or sleeping in the living room clearly has negative consequences for your sense of control over your life, your sense of personal agency, and therefore your mental health and overall wellbeing. It can delay the transition to adulthood, impacting on independence, self-esteem and identity, and leading to anxiety about the future. For those in their mid-thirties and early forties, it can feel hopeless. They feel their lives have been stolen from them. Adult children feel infantilized. Those living at home feel a huge amount of shame. It has a real impact on their mental health as they worry about the future, how they will get a home of their own, how they can be independent.

Singles are hit particularly badly. They have just one income, yet nearly all the policies and talk of housing assume it's all about two-income couples. But why should they have to have a partner in order to be able to afford a home of their own? Why should they feel pressured into getting married or having a partner just to get a roof over their head? It is deeply damaging psychologically for people to feel that they are being forced into relationships that might not be suitable – that could even be abusive – just to have a home.

The silent crisis

We hear less about this experience than about renters because people stuck at home are reluctant to speak publicly, not only because they feel ashamed or embarrassed, but also because of concern for their parents. It's very difficult to speak out about their situation because they feel it makes them seem ungrateful, it could hurt their parents' feelings, or make their parents feel overly worried about them. It's much more challenging and complicated for them to highlight their plight than for tenants; at least tenants do not have the complicating factor of their landlord being their parents, people they have deep connection to and care for. So they remain silent, and largely hidden within the housing crisis.

This is a major problem, because their housing needs are not being adequately considered in public debates on the housing crisis or in government housing plans and policy. But this also means that they are internalizing feelings of blame for the crisis. They feel they cannot share to the same extent as others, such as renters, their difficulties and challenges or highlight the extent of the problem. This means then they are not reading or hearing about others in a similar situation and therefore they feel isolated and alone. I was really struck by this when I invited people to share their housing crisis stories anonymously. The response that surprised me most was the people who were adults and living at home with their parents who said they had felt so alone until they read the stories of other people in the same situation. Even for a short while, it lifted them out of their darkness and helped them to feel that they were not on their own. Shame is a deeply negative emotion, impacting on mental and physical health. People feel as if their housing situation is their fault, even though they are doing everything they can to save, to try to get a home of their own. Their emotions are complicated by the fact that they feel grateful, and thankful, and 'extremely lucky' to have a family who will allow them, and can facilitate them, to stay living at home into adulthood.

But that story needs to be changed. People have a right to complain, and to expect a home of their own. They have a right and a need to speak out about the challenges and difficulties of their housing crisis and for it to be given proper consideration in the media and in policy and politics.

There is also an unseen precariousness and insecurity in this situation. People are dependent on the kindness and goodwill of their parents and family, and on the maintenance of those relationships, for a home. So they too are living a precarious life. If that relationship breaks down, they are potentially homeless.

There are many who do not even have the option of the safety net of a family home. There are those whose parents are not around, who might not have a positive relationship with them, whose parents were abusive to them, or whose parents simply do not have the capacity, financially or space-wise, to support them.

Overcrowding and multi-generational living

When you think of a young adult living at home, you might conjure up an image of someone in their mid-twenties knocking around a three-bed semi-d with an older parent or two. But many young adults living at home with their parents are in situations of over-crowding. They might be in households with multiple young and older adults living at home, or several generations living under one roof, with grandparents, parents and children, and siblings of parents with their children. There are parents in their twenties and thirties with young children, who, because of rents or being evicted or the lack of social housing, have had to move back in with their older parents. But the house or apartment might not have enough rooms, there might be other siblings still living at home. The adult children end up having to share a bedroom with their young kids in the grandparents' house. This generation are the parents of another generation not growing up in their own home. They feel a failure as parents.

Trying to raise two, or even three, different families under one roof affects the stress and mental health of everyone. Rooms are being subdivided, in some cases in unsafe ways. Living rooms are being converted into makeshift bedrooms, bedrooms being subdi-vided, living space is becoming cramped and reduced, overcrowding is increasing. Young families are living in sheds in their parents' gardens. This overcrowding causes huge stress and strain. These are the 'hidden homeless'.

The housing crisis exacerbates inequalities. In 2020, 43 per cent of the lowest income decile experienced two or more types of depri-vation, while just 2 per cent of the top 20 per cent experienced deprivation. It's no surprise, then, that overcrowding is higher among lower-income families. The bank of mum and dad is much larger in higher-income households.

Covid also added stress for adults living at home with older parents who might be vulnerable, with concerns about going out to work, coming back to their parents and putting them at risk. In what would normally have been a time of social interaction, young adults still living at home were restricting their lives to ensure that their parents were safe. Covid rates were higher in overcrowded households, high-lighting the increased public health risks of overcrowding and the additional downside of adult children living at home.

'It's not my home'

Rob is thirty-five, and his story captures the experience of Generation Stuck at Home. He told his story on my podcast, Reboot Republic. He explains he is still living at home with his parents in Kilkenny. He feels fortunate to have parents who support him to live at home. He feels bad for them as he thinks they should have their own space and time in retirement, rather than dealing with him living there. This is an important point. Time and quality of life is being taken away from the older generation – they are losing out too. Most love having their kids around, but 50 per cent would prefer their adult kids to be living separately, so there are a lot of parents of adult children who are frustrated also.

Rob explains that despite working his entire life – he has had his own business – and he doesn't drink, has no major spending, he has 'fully accepted the fact that I will never own my own home in Ireland'. He says, 'This is not right. I've done everything I should have, I've done everything I'm supposed to do in this society, and yet I can't buy my own home.' He explains that the cost of housing in Kilkenny and Waterford is just so high that he as a single person cannot afford to buy.

It is ridiculous that people like Rob, who have worked all their adult lives, cannot buy or rent a home of their own. It's terrible that they are resigning themselves to not owning, or being able to rent, their own home. They shouldn't have to accept this. They have a right to aspire to own or rent an affordable, lifetime-secure home, and for that aspiration to become a reality.

They feel they cannot get on and live their lives when they are still living at home with their parents, because it is not their home. Rob says it pervades every aspect of his life. It affects the most basic of things. For example, when 'you come home after a day's work and you are wrecked, you can't just throw everything on the floor and just pan out – you have to be aware your parents are there.' He explains, 'It's not my house – I would always be conscious that it's their house.'

The parent–child dynamic is always there too. You are always their child, they are always your parents. The adult–parent relationship is a very different one from the teenage–parent relationship. It can be hugely stressful, even when adults move out and live their own life. There can be a lot of tension, even though most families get on well. But past a certain age the impacts just get bigger. As one person in their late twenties explained, 'There are massive personal implications, in terms of your own development, the relationships that you can have in your life, just your sense of self and identity'. They summed it up when they said, 'Being told you need to brush your teeth at the end of the day at age twenty-seven is just not where you want to be in life.' How long can young adults be expected to put up with questions, however well intended or innocent. such as, 'Where were you last night?', 'What time did you come home?', 'Will you be out late?', 'Did you brush your teeth?'

There is a sense of shame and embarrassment, even though there shouldn't be. It is not the fault of the person stuck at home; it is the fault of government policy. But government has spun a narrative that it is their fault. And we don't talk about it enough as a society or in the media, so parents are sometimes wondering whether their adult children could be doing more to save or work to get a house. Some parents think there must be something their children are doing wrong. But Generation Stuck at Home are doing everything they can and they still can't get a gaff because housing is unaffordable and unavailable. They can't do any more. Yet you still hear the nonsensical financial advice – borrow your parents' Netflix password, avoid socializing, stop spending money on food – this is what you can do to save and become a homeowner. People are doing it all but it is still not enough. They have multiple jobs to try to progress and save and get a mortgage so that they can finally have a home of their own.

There is also the personal shame when they meet other people, such as potential partners, when they tell them where they live. There is a stigma when your answer to 'Where do you live?' is 'At home with my parents.'

Alongside the rents and unaffordable house prices, another cause of a generation being stuck at home is the lack of social housing built by government. This has resulted in lone parents, single people, people with disabilities, those on lower incomes and multiple families in overcrowding being left stuck at home as adults.

People are getting extremely frustrated because they physically and mentally cannot do any more than what they are doing – and still they haven't a hope.

They are not counted in relation to housing need. In fact, very few of this Generation Stuck at Home are counted in terms of housing need in official statistics or national housing plans, or anywhere.

Having romantic relationships while living at home with your parents is a real challenge. Many young people in long-term relationships want to be able to live together but cannot because of the housing crisis. At least when you are renting you have the possibility of developing and having relationships. Forming and maintaining romantic relationships can be incredibly difficult and complex at the best of times, and you need the space and time to develop yourself and develop together. This is a problem with being at home in your twenties, when you are becoming an adult yet still living at home with your parents. The development of romantic relationships often begins in adolescence or early adulthood, and young adulthood is commonly a time of exploration, moving between transient romantic encounters and devoted relationships. But when you don't have your own gaff, a space to call your own, to craft in your own way, it's harder to develop relationships. How can you when you are under the watchful eye of your parents at an age when you are supposed to be branching out and discovering yourself? It puts people off having relationships at all because they feel they just could not bring someone home; they don't have their own personal space to share with a partner. So their life is stilted, reduced in possibility and expression.

There is even the issue of staying over in someone else's house after a night out. Those living at home will be thinking, 'Oh, I need to ring or text my parents' because they will be wondering why they didn't come home and where they are. If you're a parent, you worry; your kids know that, no matter how old they are. At times, though, your parents' worry becomes claustrophobic and life-limiting for you. So your social and romantic life is oriented not around what you as a young adult want and need to do, such as how you want to explore and express yourself, but by what won't put your parents out, what won't upset, embarrass, or worry them.

And where do couples have sex? If both are living at home with their parents, figuring out how to cultivate the physical side of a relationship becomes a logistical nightmare. That question was asked on one of the online boards. One respondent said, 'What do you do if you are on Tinder? Say I'm available, but dependent on when my mother goes out to Tesco for the weekly shop.' Another said, 'I'm 25 and yes the struggle is real. Especially if you have fairly old parents like I do . . . my mum would be getting the holy water out.' Other suggestions included booking a hotel, renting a car for a few hours, or telling your mother you're watching Netflix and the movie will be quite loud so she might be happier reading in the garden. Another suggested making sure to use a downstairs room, as it's safer for an escape if you need to jump out of the window!

Who knew the housing crisis would be stopping a generation from having sex? Ireland is one of the most progressive countries in the world, and our young people are the most open generation Ireland has ever had. But their basic ability to have sex is restricted by the housing crisis. They can only express that sexual liberation if they have a place of their own to do it.

Lives on hold

Beyond the fundamental human need and desire for sexual rela-tionships, it also has pretty obvious demographic consequences for the future of the country. Younger people who want children but don't feel secure in their living arrangements are either delaying having children, or won't have them at all. This will lead to a fall in the birth rate and lower rates of new household formation.

For example, one couple who were sharing an apartment before the pandemic were paying €2,000 a month in rent. They are in their mid-thirties, and just want their own space to live their own lives. They felt they had no option but to move back to each other's respective parents' homes. They now have a 'hopeless feeling' about their housing situation, and are delaying a family that they 'so desperately want' because they can't find a home. For them, moving back with their parents 'feels like regression'. They see each other only at weekends, after being in a relationship together for five years.

The Growing Up in Ireland study of twenty-year-old Irish people asked them to rate how concerned they were about a range of social and political issues including terrorism, climate change, racism and gender inequality. Access to housing was ranked as their greatest concern. The research found that there is 'an upper limit on how long parents and their adult children are content' with living at home. It pointed out that 'there will be increased pressure on young adults to find independent accommodation' at some point, and wondered what the consequences for everyone will be 'if they cannot find something suitable or affordable'. It found that a substantial proportion of young adults who were currently in an exclusive relationship expected to be cohabiting with a partner by the time they were twenty-five. This suggests that many people in their mid-twenties – possibly moving out of the parental home for the first time – will be looking for accommodation that is suitable for couples rather than single-person apartments or sharing with roommates.

That's an important point given the current emphasis on accommodation for single people. Having children requires having more than one bedroom and it requires a long-term secure home. The Irish rental system doesn't give that. Younger people who don't feel secure in their living arrangements are delaying having children, or won't have them at all.

Crisis within a crisis for people with disabilities

There is another group of adults stuck at home who face a sometimes even more difficult and hidden housing crisis within a crisis.
The lack of affordable and suitable housing for adults with disabilities in Ireland means that many are unable to lead independent
lives. The Irish Wheelchair Association describes the housing needs
of people with a disability as being 'the most invisible, hidden and
unmet housing need within the Irish State.' One in eight people in
Ireland, 643,131 people, have a disability. But people with disabilities struggle with housing issues all the time. From a younger person
living with ageing carers, to a working person looking to buy or
rent wheelchair-accessible housing, to a person who acquires a disability and has to reorganize all aspects of their life, to the parents
of a child with a disability, securing accessible, suitable and high-
quality housing is extremely challenging. They also face barriers
accessing social housing. The State requires them to navigate multiple
layers of bureaucracy to prove their disability and entitlement to
support. And it is their families, many of them ageing carers, who
are supporting them at home.

An increasing number of adults with intellectual and physical
disabilities are still living with ageing or ill parents or are unable to
cope in the family home. There is a lack of essential support care,
especially for those with intellectual disabilities. The HSE provides
limited, but insufficient, funding for this.

There is a lack of personal assistance and home support hours,
which prevents people with disabilities being able to take up social
housing to allow them to move out of the family home, or even
being offered it. A catch-22 situation exists where people with disabilities cannot secure housing from local authorities in the absence
of a sufficient support package. Many people with disabilities report
being on the social housing list for up to six years, and some even
up to ten years or more.

The real level of housing need is also significantly under-reported;
many people with disabilities are not on the housing lists. James

Cawley of the Independent Living Movement points out that there is a huge under-estimation of the real level of need, as many people with disabilities are not aware of what local authorities can provide, while others don't apply because of complex means tests. He says the government should fulfil its commitments made under international treaties. The Irish State has signed up to the UN Convention on the Rights of Persons with Disabilities, which commits to 'the equal right of all persons with disabilities to live in the community, with choices equal to others', including 'the opportunity to choose their place of residence and where and with whom they live . . . and are not obliged to live in a particular living arrangement', and 'have access to a range of in-home, residential and other community support services, including personal assistance necessary to support living and inclusion in the community, and prevent isolation or segregation'.

The potential of people with disabilities to contribute to society and lead fulfilling lives is being destroyed by the structural exclusionary barriers in housing. We are all losing as a result. People with disabilities have aspirations, desires and a determination to pursue education, find employment, live independently, fulfil life and career dreams and contribute to, and be part of, their communities and wider society. Irish society is poorer for its denial of this huge potential and capacity of disabled people.

Generation Emigration

We have had unprecedented economic growth since 2013, growth in employment, and huge progressive social change on foot of the marriage equality and Repeal the Eighth referendums. Yet despite this, in the last five years a phenomenal 150,000 Irish people emigrated. They were mostly in their twenties and thirties and many had a third-level education. In 2021 alone, 32,000 young Irish people emigrated. What is going on? It is the housing exodus. The housing crisis is causing tens of thousands of young Irish people to leave this country every year. It is heartbreaking that another generation is being forced to leave this country, so soon after we lost 250,000 young people who were forced to leave because of the crash and austerity between 2008 and 2014. Now, for the first time in Irish history, a generation is emigrating not because of a lack of jobs and opportunity, but because of the lack of housing, the dim prospect of securing a home, a future.

At the same time, though, the job market has also contributed towards this exodus. It is not so much the lack of jobs as the poor quality of jobs, low pay and lack of permanent contracts. We have one of the highest rates of low pay in the EU. This means those on lower incomes are disproportionately affected by higher rents and housing costs. There is huge inequality between those on higher incomes who can access mortgages or deposits and those on the minimum or average wages who cannot. There is also the pay inequality for public servants hired after 2011 who were put on lower pay.

Emigration is not a decision people take lightly. Most people emigrating from Ireland now are currently in a job. They have friends and family here, but they can't see the sense in staying in Ireland when the only future they can see is living at home with their parents, with the lack of independence and dignity that entails, or struggling in the unaffordable and poor-quality private rental sector. They see decision after decision being made in the interests of developers and investors, not their generation's need for homes. They see the lack of value placed on them, the erosion of communities, of creative and cultural spaces. They see a country obsessed with hotels and real estate funds, not affordable housing and community. This generation is at breaking point. For many, it is the housing crisis that has broken them.

A lot of creative people and artists have left – the arts in this country too often does not provide a viable career path, and the cost of rents makes it impossible to live in Ireland. As one creative in their late twenties who has decided to emigrate explained:

I can't see a future for myself here. I have to laugh out loud being told that getting a mortgage is the economically savvy option for me. But I am a single 27-year-old who couldn't get a mortgage even if I tried. It's back to 1950s Ireland where I'm reliant on having a partner to get a house. It's a bizarre situation that we are living in. It's time to go for me. It's sad because I love this country. I have great energy to try to enact change. But I can't stay here.

Hundreds of thousands of people like this who have a lot of passion and ideas for change and enterprise and desire to contribute to this country, are the new housing-fuelled brain drain. They face the dilemma of deciding to stay in Ireland and trying to make it a better place, or leaving and getting a better life for themselves.

Down through the years in Irish history, and during the recent austerity period, emigration has been used by the Irish State as a political pressure valve as it releases the societal pressure of the impacts of government failure. Rather than protesting and demanding change, young people have emigrated. Ireland has been stunted through the years because our young people left, and we remained a conservative, repressed, under-developed, unequal state for too long. Younger generations provide a dynamism and drive for change. That is lost when they leave. It may suit the government in power, but as a society, as parents, as family members, as communities, as a country, we lose our brothers, sisters, children, friends, neighbours, work colleagues. We lose our future.

There are many, many examples. Take Tom, a single gay man who is forty and working two careers. He had no choice but to move back home with his seventy-year-old mother because he cannot afford rents or a mortgage alone. He's an award winner in a small business and a manager in a four-star hotel. But he cannot afford to rent and save at the same time.

I cannot afford city rents and I can't afford a mortgage alone. Emigration is the only option open to me now. It's devastating to have to leave everybody behind, my heart is breaking, I don't want to leave but I can barely feed myself when all my insurances and taxes are paid. I'm being pushed out of my own country by my own government while [they are] telling me they are doing everything they can.

These people have good jobs, they are well educated, but they can't afford to live in Ireland. They can't get the most basic need of a home of their own. They feel they have done everything they can. They have saved. They have tried to get a mortgage. They rent. They have moved back home to their parents. They have a mortgage but can't find an affordable gaff. They feel their country has rejected them and there is no other option. They see no alternative but to emigrate.

Many Irish people living abroad have their own home and are able to start a family. Some would love to move back to Ireland and raise their children here, near their families, but they do not see it as viable because of the housing crisis, and other costs such as childcare.

It is just so illogical because there is a recruitment and retention crisis in public and private companies like the HSE and across the public sector and businesses in this country. They just cannot get workers to fill vacant posts, yet our educated and trained and talented people are leaving in their tens of thousands because they do not see a future here where they can afford a home of their own. The housing crisis has become an economic crisis – it has become another emigration crisis.

Chapter 8
Average Earners
Can't Afford an Average Home

For most people it's always been expensive to buy a home, and they had to work hard and scrimp and save. But it has never been harder to buy a home than it is in today's Ireland. Housing has never been as expensive relative to income and wages. And previous generations never faced trying to win a bidding war against global investor funds, wealthy 'cash buyers' and propertied landlords. Millennials are around half as likely to be homeowners as generations born only a couple of decades earlier. The age at which most Irish households owned their own home was just twenty-six at the start of the 1990s. By 2016, it had risen to thirty-five. Since the financial crisis, home ownership has collapsed among adults aged twenty-five to fifty-four. Housing has become significantly more unaffordable over the last decade. House prices have increased by 125 per cent since 2013. A home costing €150,000 in 2013 would now cost over €337,000. Property prices were four times higher than median incomes in 2013. In 2022, Property prices in Dublin are 11 times the median income; in Wicklow they are 10 times, in Kildare 9 times and in County Cork 8 times. All are classed as 'severely unaffordable'.

And property prices are still increasing exponentially across the country. In our main cities and in towns and rural areas. In the border counties prices increased by a phenomenal 23 per cent in 2021, in the south-east by 20 per cent, in the midlands by 17 per cent and in the south-west by 14 per cent.

The pressure from people freed up by remote working relocating to rural areas and coastal counties, combined with the ongoing purchase of housing as a 'property investment' to rent it out or let it as tourist rental, combined with the lack of attention and funding by government for local authorities to build in regional areas, has led to major house price inflation in rural and urban areas in Ireland. The housing crisis is truly a national one.

Let's look at some examples of the housing affordability challenge faced by workers who are essential for our economy and society to function. Let's start by looking at couples.

A couple, say a teacher on €50,000 and a nurse on €40,000, with a combined income of €90,000, can borrow €315,000. With a 10 per cent deposit of €35,000 (a lot of money to save), they could buy a home for €350,000. They could not afford to buy an average-price home anywhere in Dublin. You would need an income of over €130,000, and a deposit of €50,000 to qualify for a mortgage to buy an average-priced house – €500,000 – in Dublin. This means that you need to be in the top 15 per cent of income earners.

Take another couple, a Dublin Bus driver with an average salary of €40,000, and a supermarket manager, whose salary is €35,000. They could get a combined mortgage of €262,500, so if they had a deposit of 10 per cent (€29,000) they could afford a house for €290,500. Take another couple, a childcare worker on the minimum wage of €20,000, with a civil servant on €40,000. They could borrow a mortgage of €210,000. With a deposit of €23,000, they could buy a home for €233,000. Neither of these two couples could afford to buy an average-priced house anywhere in Dublin or its commuter counties of Wicklow (average price €448,000), Kildare (€354,000), or Meath (€319,000). So they're left with the option of trying to find a home in Louth, at an average price of €260,000, Offaly (€221,000) or Laois (€221,000).

It's happening again. Key workers, average earners, are priced out of Dublin, just as they were during the Celtic Tiger period, and have to be prepared for massive commutes in order to have a home of their own. But now that's completely environmentally unsustainable and they will pay the carbon cost price. That is utterly unfair. We have to provide affordable housing in our cities and across the country.

These examples were all couples with two incomes. Not one of those vital workers – a teacher, a nurse, a bus driver, a retail manager, a childcare worker, a civil servant – could afford, on their own, to buy an average-priced home in any city in Ireland, including Dublin or its commuter counties, or Galway, Limerick, Cork, Waterford.

A single teacher (or a teacher in a one-income couple) on a salary of €49,000 (that's point nine on the teachers' pay scale, which you would be earning around age thirty, if you started teaching at twenty-one) could buy a home for €200,000 if they had a deposit of €25,000. That would enable them to buy an average-priced home in only nine of the twenty-six counties in the Republic – Tipperary, Mayo, Sligo, Donegal, Longford, Roscommon, Leitrim, Monaghan, Cavan. So a teacher is locked out of buying a home in seventeen of the counties in Ireland and is locked out of every city in the country. It's a pretty big crisis when we can't provide homes for our teachers in every city and two-thirds of the country. If teachers can't afford to live in your city or county, who is going to teach your kids?

Special needs assistants are essential in our schools to provide extra education and supports to children alongside the teachers. In how many counties in Ireland can an SNA afford to pay the average price of a home? An SNA on point 10 of their salary scale (around €33,000, after ten years' working) could borrow €115,000. With a deposit of €13,000 they could buy a house for €128,500.

A single earner on the average wage of €40,000 (such as the bus driver or nurse) can borrow €140,000. That means they could buy a property of €150,000, if they had the 10 per cent deposit of €15,000. By April 2022, there was not one county in Ireland with an average price under €150,000. So the average earner cannot afford to buy an average-priced home in any county in Ireland.

Of course these examples do not include the significant fees that are also required, which can range from €5,000 to €25,000 (up to 15 per cent). And they are all based on the assumption of having the 10 per cent deposit, which is next to impossible to save if you are renting.

The REITs, the developers and the government are basically saying to millennials and Generation Z, get a partner, or try to buy in one of the four counties where the average-priced home is between €150,000 and €160,000 (Longford, Leitrim, Roscommon and Donegal) – or emigrate. It has echoes of Cromwell's famous, 'To hell or to Connaught', as he conquered and plundered Ireland. Now the REITs are plundering Ireland and telling millennials, 'Rent from us, or go and live in Longford, Roscommon, Donegal or Leitrim, or emigrate.' Now these counties are great places, and many people would love to live there. But even we need affordable homes *across* the country. And for many on low incomes living in these four counties, even these houses are unaffordable.

Housing wasn't always this unaffordable. A couple renting in 1989 would have had to save a quarter of their income, after rent and tax, over a year to raise a 10 per cent deposit. Today in Dublin, they would need to save 75 per cent of their disposable income to get a deposit. An utterly impossible task if you add in the wider cost of living inflation.

In the 1980s, a young couple would have had to allocate just 15 per cent of their disposable income to cover the mortgage. Today, an average young couple would have to allocate close to 30 per cent of their disposable income to mortgage payments in Dublin (which is the definition of unaffordable housing costs). We are back at Celtic Tiger levels of unaffordability of housing, at rates we saw in the mid-2000s when the Celtic Tiger bubble was rapidly inflating. This should be sending out warning signals. Housing is absolutely more expensive and more out of reach for those buying homes today.

If you are on a minimum wage, or work part time, or have a short-term contract, like some teachers and university staff, or waiters, cleaners, artists, or doctors, guards and nurses starting out – all those who make our cities and towns function – forget about it. You can't afford to buy a home in Ireland. So if those we rely on to make our society function can't afford to live here, how do we keep our economy and society going? Who will teach our kids, drive the buses and trains, keep hospitals functioning, police our streets, serve food in our restaurants, if these workers can't afford to live here, if they can't afford to get a home? Who will stay and work long term if they can't afford to get a home of their own? What talent will we be able to attract from abroad (including our emigrants) if they can't get a home? There is a recruitment crisis and policymakers are wondering, baffled, how did this happen? Well, the housing crisis you have ignored for a decade is a large part of it.

Housing policy claims it is all geared toward the 'traditional family', the so-called squeezed middle. But it's more like a squashed generation. There is a tiny proportion who have high-enough salaries and access to the bank of mum and dad, with enough wealth to provide a deposit, and additional loans to go above the mortgage limits and help their children to win in the bidding wars. This appears to be who housing policy has limited itself to addressing – just target the professional couple on high salaries. And ignore everyone else. And so the average couple on average incomes, the middle- and low-income earners who haven't a bank of mum and dad, the divorcees, the singles, the second-home buyer trying to move out of an apartment their family has grown out of, the family in overcrowding in need of social housing – they are ignored by policy and even in media debates. They are cast aside as the collateral damage of a housing system being built for the needs of developers, landlords, investors and banks, being built on reinforcing and worsening inequalities – between those who can buy homes and those who can't, between the 'have parents with cash' and the rest. Even worse, they are leaving the singles and divorcees, lone parents and migrants to the clutches of the real estate investor fund landlords and the regular Irish landlords – facing perpetual high rents and constant evictions and moving and looking for new homes.

As rents increased over the last decade, there was no consideration in government for how rising rents would make saving deposits impossible. As Leo Varadkar said, people like him could get a deposit off the bank of mum and dad. He conveniently ignored the fact that when he bought a home there were no Central Bank rules that required a 10 per cent deposit. It ignored the massive inequality between those who could get deposits from their parents or were on very high incomes, and most people who could get little or nothing, and therefore couldn't even get a mortgage to buy a home.

And many cannot get a mortgage as the banks claim they do not have the proven capacity to pay it back. Yet they are paying monthly rents substantially higher than what monthly mortgages cost. People are paying rents of €1,200 or €1,500 a month and the bank is telling them they can't afford a mortgage of €950 a month. For example, in Sligo the average rent is €890 a month, but if you bought a house at €199,000 (the average price in Sligo) the monthly cost of a mortgage would be just €745. In Louth, the average rent is €1,184. A monthly mortgage to buy an average-priced house in Louth (€260,000) would cost just €957. In north County Dublin, the average rent is €1,836. The monthly mortgage to buy an average-priced house there (€443,000) is €1,623. It's the same picture around Ireland. Monthly average rents substantially outstrip the monthly average mortgage cost for the average house price.

But even if people can get a mortgage, the rising property prices and competition with property investors mean that housing is being pushed out of their price range. And the lack of a supply of affordable housing means that people are competing for a limited supply of homes. They have a mortgage but there is nowhere available to buy in their price range. Then if they do see somewhere in their range and they go for it, they find they are outbid. Everywhere sales prices are going way beyond advertised prices.

Home buyers are competing against those who are seeking to buy a home as an investment – investor funds and Irish multi-property purchasers. Some buy just to flip the property. This is a well-known practice, and in a rising property market those who look at housing purely as real estate investment do this. A house might be bought for €350,000, then six months later put on the market again for an additional €50,000 or more. There has often been nothing done to the property.

We do not know the extent to which this happens because buying and selling property is not regulated adequately in Ireland. There is a property price register where the sale price has to be registered, but there is no regulation of the bidding process or who can buy the property, and there's no monitoring of bidding processes.

Many estate agents get bigger commissions from higher house prices and so are incentivized to get higher prices. Bidding wars is what they want to see. Rising house prices benefit them. This is fundamentally problematic for a home buyer. The odds are always stacked against them because the agent acting on behalf of the seller is pursuing the maximum price. This is a dysfunctional system. The property market is a rigged game and the first-time buyer can't even get on the pitch to compete; and if they do manage to get on the pitch, they are playing with their hands tied behind their back, the referee is paid by the opposing team and the more the opponent scores the more money he gets.

Home buyers who lose out in bidding wars feel devastated. Adding to their frustration, upset and anger are the raffles to win a house that have mushroomed in recent years. It seems that every local GAA club in the country has a house to raffle off as a fundraiser. As one home buyer who wasn't able to purchase a home in a local new development said:

> One of these houses is currently up to win in a raffle yet we can't buy one. How is it that we can enter a raffle to win a house, but if we have the deposit and mortgage we can't buy it? To say that my partner and I are devastated is an understatement. It was our light at the end of a very dark tunnel and now we continue to be stuck in this hell-hole we are living in. We have been together for 13 years (have shared a house throughout our entire relationship) and cannot even begin to imagine ever starting our own family. We are seriously considering emigrating to the UK as we are really struggling to see a future for ourselves here. It is the last thing we

want, but think it is our only option if we ever want to have a life for ourselves because right now we are certainly not living a life in the situation we are in currently.

The lending rules aren't the problem

The Central Bank rules have been necessary to avoid potentially unsustainable lending, and have actually helped to contain house prices to some extent in recent years. It is not the lending rules that are at fault, but the lack of supply of affordable homes. It is also the unfairness that there are constraints to borrowing by home buyers, and what first-time buyers can afford to pay for a home, but no lack of spending constraints on what non-household buyers – the property investors, the landlords, the funds – can borrow and spend. They face no limits on buying up property.

This is one of the fundamental points that many people, including economics commentators, have missed in recent years. They said we couldn't have rising prices and a property bubble because of lending constraints. But they completely ignored the impact of investor funds and landlords piling in cash from here and abroad into the housing market, thus fuelling massive price growth. It also shows up the futility of the suggestion that first-time buyers should go on strike, stop buying homes and wait. If they did that, investors and landlords would just buy up more. And people cannot wait while their lives and life possibilities are falling away. It is the investors and landlord and property cash buyers that need to be kicked out of the housing market, to create a properly regulated and price-controlled market. Taxing vacant homes, along with the State building homes on a massive scale, and making land and finance available for small- and medium-enterprise (SME) builders (with affordability requirements attached), for first-time buyers, and affordable housing providers at a sufficient scale, would ensure a supply of affordable homes.

The extent of profit gouging and exploitation in the property market is relentless. Did you know that if you are struggling to buy a home you can avail of a 'property coach'? They offer a 'property coaching session'. An hour-long session. One coach advertises their services, 'If you're feeling frustrated, unsure, stuck or completely disheartened during your property search then you're ready for one of my property coaching sessions.' During the call they will look at your experience to date, and identify 'problem issues'. For €145 for an hour. They also say that they will find a property for you to buy. You just have to pay a non-refundable €3,000 'briefing fee'. Then you pay a further €7,000 if they find you the property. How many more ways can home buyers be squeezed?

In 2021, 14,800 first-time buyers did manage to buy a home, just 30 per cent of all home purchases. That's 14,800 positive stories. They were more likely to be higher income earners and supported by their parents. There are homes to buy across the country, and some people will get lucky. But that is not good enough, and it is also not evidence that if some people can do it, everyone who tries hard enough can do it too. It is a tiny number in comparison to how many are actually looking for homes. At that current rate it would take twenty-one years just to provide housing for the 60 per cent of Generation Rent who want to buy a home (that's 200,000 homes) along with housing for Generation Stuck at Home aged twenty to thirty-five (125,000 homes). That doesn't include the thousands who are living abroad but want to return home. Estate agents report that since Covid they have seen an increase in the purchase of homes by expats living abroad seeking to return home. It also doesn't include the hundreds of thousands growing up in the coming years who will also need homes. It just shows how bad the lack of supply of affordable homes actually is.

These housing fissures are growing by the day. Where does this end? Where are we heading to? What hope and incentive are we giving people to stay in this country? The housing crisis has reached a point of social catastrophe. It is an earthquake ripping our society apart. It is the new faultline in Irish society: the struggle for a gaff. It is a trauma that we are inflicting on a generation. Generation

Rent is the new housing precariat, living with precarious housing and precarious work contracts.

Rising house prices aren't good for anyone

For the past twenty-five years, a quarter of a century, the dominant thinking in Ireland has been that rising house prices are a good thing and beneficial for all homeowners. Many started to question that 'common sense' after the Celtic Tiger and the role of property prices in the economic crash that devastated the country. But the government and policymakers (and all the property interests – land owners, lobbyists, banks, developers, estate agents) fed the narrative again from 2012 onwards that rising property prices are a good thing. They were needed, it was argued, to get people out of negative equity. 'Negative equity' is a term that homeowners are terrified of. Some people think negative equity is when the current property price is lower than what you paid for it. It is actually when the cost of your outstanding mortgage is more than the current property value. But negative equity only matters when you are selling your home, which is a very small proportion of home-owners at any one time. And it seems bizarre to make our entire housing policy oriented towards a scenario that affects a small proportion of people. But that's how policy has rolled in this country up to now, unfortunately.

The property lobby and government continued to peddle the narrative that rising property prices are beneficial. This completely ignored the impact of rising prices on making housing more un-affordable for people seeking to buy their home. It was generational shafting or 'pulling up the property ladder' at its most extreme. We property owners watch the value of our house prices rise while the generation looking for a home watch their chances of buying one fall. And it's our adult children living at home or stuck in private rental who are losing out. That connection didn't appear to be made by a lot of older homeowners until recently. A lot of the media feed the positive story of rising house prices – the property supplements and advertising they get is paid for by the property industry and estate agents. But there is a growing realization that this is largely a ruse that mainly benefits those who own multiple properties, and those who are engaging in 'flipping', and that in fact the overwhelming majority of people do not really benefit from rising house prices.

The ones who do benefit most from rising prices are the property industry (developers, estate agents, etc.) and the banks. Higher prices means higher mortgage lending and higher profits. While the economic orthodoxy considers rising house prices a good thing, adding to household wealth and GDP, there are economic downsides such as economic instability and reduced household disposable income, competitiveness and recruitment. The Economic and Social Research Institute (ESRI) identified the persistence in high inflation rates, of which housing costs is a key component, as a risk to the economy. Many workers cannot afford to live in Ireland, particularly Dublin. So stable house prices is better economics.

Rising housing costs dampen consumption in the wider economy as households have to allocate a high proportion of their income to housing. Rising rents and prices also exacerbate inequality between the property haves and have-nots, as the already wealthy and international shareholders of institutional property funds accumulate wealth from renters.

I'm surprised there isn't more pressure from business sectors for greater government intervention on housing. With the huge inflation of rents it is understandable why the ICTU has recommended its private sector unions seek pay increases.

There's a major bifurcation in the Irish economy, between housing and the wider productive economy. Housing has become utterly disconnected from the real economy. It is a site of speculative and predatory financialized investment. The housing crisis is now a fundamental risk to the wider economy.

For most people, when you sell your home, you have to buy a new one. If it's the same market, it's all the same. Of course, those who play the property game – the investors, the flippers – will argue that you can make a lot of money if you time it right. Sell high, buy low. Yes, that's true, if you are treating buying and selling housing as an investment asset – like the stock market. Only a tiny number make money in that game of real estate roulette. But our homes are not stocks and shares. And stock markets go through constant booms and busts. The winners extract huge profit but they have to be paid by someone. And it is the next generation of home buyers who are paying more and more.

Most homeowners who think they are winning from the huge rise in house prices have adult children living at home because they cannot afford to get a place of their own. That home is the parents' place to retire and enjoy their life. It is understandable then that 50 per cent of parents who live with an adult child would prefer it if they lived apart. It is okay to feel that. You have a right to your own space. So in fact inflated house prices do not benefit many homeowners either.

If you are a homeowner in your forties, or fifties, or older, I think it is really worth thinking about this. If you have kids, where are they going to live? How can they afford a house if prices are continuously rising? What is the point in leaving a high-value house to your children when you die, when they could be in their fifties or sixties, when their life formation chances are gone. These older parents need to join this conversation and be part of changing the housing narrative. Many are already joining the dots. From a wider societal and economic perspective, they realize rising house prices and rents aren't good for you or your kids. In countries with stable, more affordable housing systems, like Austria and Germany, house prices barely rise over decades. Your children need that stability. We need it as a society and an economy, rather than being stuck on this rollercoaster that rides every few years from dizzying highs of house prices that see home buyers filled with anxiety and worry, to crashing lows where those who got a home at the high point are left with high mortgages, struggling and depressed – and everyone loses as the economy crashes.

We have been administered a drug that we are told is a medicine but it has made us addicted to the highs of property booms – leaving us needing more when the effects wear off. And it is destroying our society as well – everyone is pitted against each other in the bidding wars, generation against generation. This is not how to run a functioning, cohesive society. It's destructive to all of us.

This must be challenged and stopped now, because there are hundreds of thousands coming up behind this generation who should not be made suffer in the same way. There are a million children in Ireland under fourteen and 325,000 teenagers who will need homes in the future. Are we just going to accept they will be put through the same as this generation? Where are they going to live? Will they have to emigrate?

You might not feel the housing crisis impacts on you if you are in your forties or fifties and you have your house and your kids are in primary school or teenagers – but it will if we allow this to continue. They will be stuck living at home with you, or they will have to rent – or they might just emigrate. You will lose them and potential grandchildren. You need to realize that, as a result of the housing crisis, you are losing your children to depression, to stress, to emigration.

You might want to downsize to a smaller home, more accessible to shops and services, or so that you can pass your home to your kids. But constantly rising house prices mean that anything you downsize to is also more expensive. Apartments, especially, are becoming ever more expensive as the investor funds are buying them up, and they are only available to rent – which, understandably, you do not feel is secure for your remaining decades. The fact that there are no affordable homes – and very little decent, affordable elderly sheltered housing (because it's not profitable for developers or investors) shows the crisis really affects you too.

You may not think you are affected by it. But you are. We all are. This is ripping our country apart and it's happening now.

It is important to put yourself in your children's position. Imagine what they feel. Their lives have been put on hold. They are seeing their future slip away from them. You might say, 'We're giving him a place to live', 'It's great she is still here with us in the house.' But they see it differently. You do not feel a failure as a parent – you provided, and continue to provide, a home for your children. But your children, because they cannot get their own home, do feel a failure, and feel shame and stigma, and poor self-esteem, particularly if they have kids themselves. This has a severe impact on them, but it impacts on you too. This is why it is so important that cross-generational conversations about the housing crisis happen more often.

The perceived political wisdom in Ireland is that rising house prices is a vote winner. But a seismic shift is under way in Irish attitudes to housing. Homeowners are realizing that rising house prices and rents are resulting in their twenty-, thirty- and forty-year-old children still living at home, unable to buy or rent a home of their own. An *Irish Independent*-commissioned poll in February 2022 showed that 75 per cent of Irish people wanted house prices to decrease. Of those, 50 per cent wanted prices to 'decrease by a lot'. Just 7 per cent wanted prices to increase, and 15 per cent wanted them to stay the same. A *Business Post*/Red C poll carried out in May 2022 showed an even bigger majority of 85 per cent in favour of house price reductions.

That is a cultural revolution in Irish people's attitudes to house prices and property. No longer are rising house prices viewed as a 'good thing'. The public want affordable, decent homes for their children, not rising property prices.

Chapter 9
Generation Homeless:
Ireland's Shame

In this 'decade of commemorations' when Ireland commemorated the 1916 Rising, the Proclamation of the Republic (which declared it would cherish all children equally), and celebrated the foundation of the State, more families, children and individuals were made homeless than at any point since the State came into being. There is nothing normal about the current scale of evictions and homelessness, which has worsened year on year since 2012.

There is a human face to homelessness that can be lost in the monthly press release from the Department of Housing. We need to see what housing policy failure is doing to ordinary people. It is inflicting a personal trauma on tens of thousands. The most frustrating aspect of this homelessness emergency is that it was, and remains, avoidable, and it could be solved, with the right policies and political will. Our response to Covid and the experience of other countries, including Finland, shows that we can solve and end homelessness.

Those who are made homeless suffer multiple traumas and losses. Stress and anxiety are caused in the weeks and months (and in some cases even years) leading up to being evicted or having to leave your home. Then there is the trauma of the actual loss of your home, the loss of safety, connections, stability, familiarity. Then there is the stress of trying to find somewhere to stay on an emergency basis, literally to try to find a roof for over you and your family's head for a night. You have to contact a local authority homeless service, or domestic violence refuge, hostel or B&B. Then, if you can even find somewhere, there is the fear of not knowing what it will be like, who you'll be there with. The experience leads to feelings of being degraded, dehumanized, of being invisible to society, with a pervasive lack of hope for the future.

The trauma of being made homeless

A mother rang RTÉ's *Liveline* in the lead-up to Christmas 2021. She was desperate. She and her family were being made homeless and had nowhere else to turn to. She told presenter Joe Duffy:

> We've been given notice to leave our property, we'd been renting for two years. The landlord is selling. We applied to over seventy properties but as of this coming Friday we are homeless. The council are placing us in emergency accommodation. I have four little girls, as well as my partner, and I don't know where else we need to turn to try and find somewhere for us to have a home.

This is an all-too-familiar experience in Ireland. Families and children up and down the country are being traumatized because the housing crisis is forcing them out of their homes, and pushing too many into homelessness.

What have we become as a country when people have no option but to ring a national call-in radio show to try to find a home?

The mother who rang *Liveline* also described the anxiety of the time leading up to becoming homeless, which had huge impacts on her children:

> My seven-year-old is starting to get really bad anxiety because of all of this. Her birthday is on the first of December. She said for her birthday she doesn't want anything; she wants a house. She just wrote her list to Santa saying that she just wants a house, a

forever home for her family. My kids as of Friday will be living out of backpacks, they've got their favourite teddies packed. My seven-year-old, she came home early from school yesterday, with her anxiety, because she believes if she is in school for too long, she will come home and she is not going to have a home.

Homelessness is a traumatic, adverse childhood experience that can have lifelong detrimental impacts. This is the reality of the unprecedented homelessness crisis in Ireland in the twenty-first century. This is Ireland's new Generation Homeless.

It is important that we listen to, and really hear, the human stories from people like the mother who rang *Liveline*. We must try to connect empathetically with them. Because if we don't, the danger is that we shut it out, we normalize it, we accept it, and it continues. Unfortunately, those in government have tried to downplay the impacts and normalize Ireland's unacceptable homeless emergency. Opening ourselves to the emotional impact of what is happening to these children and families, to actually feel the emotions it brings up in us, is more likely to lead us to not accept this, to try to help, and to demand of government that something must be done.

We must consider the young child sitting on O'Connell Street and eating their dinner off a piece of cardboard, a dinner that they and their family got from a soup kitchen because there are no cooking facilities in the emergency B&B or hotel accommodation. We should really think about it, try to feel their feelings – isolation, cold, shame. We need to consider the poor mother who died by suicide because she felt she had failed her kids by being homeless, because she blamed herself for not being able to provide them with a home and saw no prospect of getting a home.

We need to feel that this is not normal. It isn't. We need to open ourselves up to the centrality of home to all our lives, and the emotional impacts of not having a home of your own. We need to imagine the waves of upset and anger that must be inside those affected and really hear their experiences. We should let our own feelings of anger, upset and shame out too when we listen to them.

These feelings are the flame that can make us act to end homelessness. When we shut out their suffering we also shut down a part of ourselves. They are our fellow citizens, our fellow human beings. We are connected to them through our common humanity. We are also affected by the fear of losing our home, by the sense of shame that this is what our country does to people, by a sense of guilt. Homelessness does not just do terrible harm to those who are in it, it harms society, it destroys our common humanity, it reduces the humanity in each of us, it makes us all less. We all want to feel proud of our communities, cities and country. Yet we cannot be proud of this place that puts its most vulnerable through the trauma of homelessness.

The new institutionalization of mothers and children

A mother who was homeless describes the impact of living in emergency accommodation with just one room for herself, her partner and their two kids: 'It's hard to describe how tough it was, all of us in one room. The kids found it especially hard. My daughter cried every night saying she wanted to go home.' When they left their home, they had to leave most of their things behind. All their furniture and most of the kids' toys. Their youngest daughter was most upset because she had to leave behind a doll's house she had been given for Christmas. Focus Ireland supported the family to get a home; one of their workers helped them navigate the housing application process with the council, which can be incredibly complicated. When this woman got her home, she said one of the first things she did was to get her daughter a new doll's house.

In 2017, I wrote a report with my colleague, Professor Mary Murphy, documenting research we did with homeless families in Dublin. The report was read out to the then Taoiseach, Leo Varadkar, in the Dáil. It highlighted the severe impact of emergency accommodation on children: causing them to be consumed with feelings of anxiety and insecurity; leaving them unsettled and feeling out of control; unable to focus on and achieve typical childhood development milestones. We highlighted that the longer the time spent in emergency accommodation, the greater negative impact it has. The then Taoiseach and his government ignored the report, and ignored the devastating impact of homelessness on families and children. Half of all children in emergency accommodation in Ireland have been there longer than one year, and a quarter (25 per cent) have been there longer than two years. Think about those children spending the formative years of their lives growing up in emergency accommodation.

Doctor Ellen Crushell, clinical lead of the HSE's national clinical programme for paediatrics, has highlighted the increasing number of homeless children presenting at Temple Street Children's University Hospital in Dublin. Homeless children, she says, get more colds and ear infections, are more prone to skin infestations and are twice as likely to require emergency hospitalization. Homeless toddlers are particularly prone to burns and scalds, often from pulling over kettles in hotel rooms. I find the thought deeply upsetting and disturbing. Children, and families, living with all their possessions in one hotel room, cramped, trying to make breakfast, get the kids ready for school – and then a child, inevitably, pulls something like a kettle down on themselves. Over a third of homeless children have mental health or behavioural disorder of clinical significance. Being in temporary accommodation for more than a year trebles the child's risk of mental health issues. They and their families are trapped in inappropriate and psychologically damaging emergency accommodation of hotels, B&Bs, private hostels and Family Hubs.

A mother described the sad historical irony that one Family Hub used to be a Magdalene laundry. She said the rooms were so small and claustrophobic, 'you feel you can't breathe; the walls are closing in on you'. It felt like a prison. 'I know they are trying their best but it's not made for families to live in. I know it's not a prison, but sometimes you feel like you've done something wrong, or you are looked down on; you can feel yourself becoming institutionalized.'

The echoes and policy fingerprints of our institutional past that are evident in how we respond to families being made homeless, particularly those headed by lone-parent mothers, are truly shocking. Lone-parent families are much more likely to experience homelessness than two-parent families. Lone parents account for around 55 per cent of all homeless families but only 20 per cent of all families with children in Ireland. In Dublin, the majority (65 per cent) of homeless families were headed by a lone parent, of whom 86 per cent are women.

It is just so wrong. We know the trauma caused by the institutionalization of mothers and children, but we now have a new form of institutionalization – emergency homeless accommodation, where lone-parent mothers and children are being left with no option but to spend up to two years.

The mothers in Family Hubs described how they felt their parenting was being checked all the time, how they got warnings from staff, had their parental authority taken away from them in front of their children, and were spoken down to by staff. Mothers described this undermining of their role as a parent as a blow to their self-esteem and mental health.

Childhoods stolen by homelessness

Emergency accommodation also puts major limitations on children. It restricts their space and ability to play, to be, and they can't do simple things like have their friends over for a play date or a sleepover because visitors are not allowed in emergency accommodation. Imagine the feelings of the child in school listening to other children talk about play dates and going to each other's homes, and that homeless child knowing she cannot have her friends to her home because she doesn't have one.

Special times of the year, such as birthdays when they can't have a party, are particularly difficult for families and children in emergency accommodation. How emotionally hard it must be to even 'celebrate' your child's birthday in emergency accommodation. Or even to manage when you or your children are sick, with the lack of privacy and space, trying to manage the basics of washing dirty clothes and sheets when children get the inevitable vomiting bugs. Life is impossible in these institutional, congregated living settings.

It is at Christmas, more than any other time, when home is the centre of our hearts and lives and when childhood memories are made. Home is supposed to be magical, a place of wonder and warmth. We decorate and prepare for Christmas Day; families gather together. Yet these children are robbed of these memories of home at Christmas time. Memories will instead be clouded with darkness, of feelings of anxiety, sadness and stress, and of strange places that are the antithesis of home. That is why it is particularly traumatic for children and families to be without a home at Christmas. Rightly, there is a focus on homelessness at this time of year. While most children across the country are bursting with excitement about waking up on Christmas morning to their presents, homeless children and their parents are filled with dread about where they will be at Christmas. Thousands of children and their families will spend this Christmas in homeless accommodation in Ireland, and many more will do so year after year if policy continues as it is. Thousands more will have their childhood stolen from them by homelessness caused by government housing policy.

The exposure of families and children to the trauma of homelessness, both as loss of home and the damaging experience of emergency accommodation, is a form of structural violence being visited on these children by government policy failure. Structural violence is when social structures such as poverty and inequality harm people (in terms of higher death rates, increased physical and mental illness, and so on) by preventing them from meeting their basic needs. It is the avoidable impairment of fundamental human needs, a violence that results from society's structures.

Unfortunately, our 2017 report's recommendations for a strategy to eliminate family homelessness, and for a statutory limit on the length of time families spend in emergency accommodation, were not implemented. We will be dealing with the generation of children traumatized by homelessness for decades to come.

Homelessness is not the fault of people who are homeless

We have in recent years in Ireland seen senior state officials blaming those who are homeless for becoming homeless. Senior local authority officials responsible for housing those homeless said that people become homeless because of their bad behaviour. They said, in a public forum, 'Let's be under no illusion here, when somebody becomes homeless it doesn't happen overnight, it takes years of bad behaviour probably, or behaviour that isn't the behaviour of you and me.'

What behaviour of these families and children caused them to become homeless? It is disgraceful nonsense to blame them. The truth is that the overwhelming majority of people who became homeless since 2012 became homeless because of the massive rise in rents; evictions by landlords, investor funds and receivers; the lack of action by government to stop rising rents and evictions; and ultimately, the failure of governments over the last two decades to build social and affordable housing.

Investor funds and REITs bought up huge numbers of rental properties, evicted lower-paid tenants, and in some cases renovated the property, to get in higher-paying ones, and hiked up the rents. Receivers acting on behalf of NAMA and the banks took over buy-to-let rental properties in mortgage arrears and similarly evicted tenants to get in higher-paying ones or to sell the property. Regular private landlords hiked rents and evicted tenants as well.

And all the while governments just let this happen. They allowed, even facilitated, renters to be forced into homelessness to incentivize private investment and keep the landlords and investors happy.

The fact that governments consistently refused to put in place protection from evictions and rent hikes for tenants, despite knowing that it was pushing families and vulnerable individuals into homelessness, is a shocking dereliction of duty. It is, indeed, a violation of the Irish State's human rights commitments and it breaches government obligations under the Irish Constitution.

The further cause of homelessness, and really the fundamental root of the homelessness emergency, was the government's shift away from building social and affordable housing to rely instead on providing social housing through subsidies in the private rental sector. In the past, if someone was made homeless through eviction from the private rental sector or lost their home through family breakdown or violence, they would have got social housing through a local authority. But through the austerity decade from 2008 onwards, vulnerable people and those made homeless (including those already homeless and in emergency accommodation) have to try to get their housing themselves, with the HAP subsidy, from private landlords in the rental sector. But given the lack of supply of rental homes, they cannot compete with the new Generation Rent, who cannot afford to buy a home, and are relying on living in the private sector for much longer. They are also competing against tens of thousands of other low-income HAP-eligible households who are trying to get housing in the private rental sector.

So those in emergency situations facing homelessness are now at the mercy of private landlords and the private rental sector – they are trying to source housing in a market with limited supply, with unprecedentedly high rents and unprecedented competition from a generation of households with no alternative but to rent in the private rental market. Those made homeless are also discriminated against by landlords who refuse to take HAP tenants, even though this is illegal. Those on lower incomes, such as lone parents, or one-income families, face the problem of simply not having the wages to cover ever-rising rents, even with HAP. Massive childcare costs and the poverty trap of welfare cut-offs as you start earning make it even worse. Rising rents have also resulted in a growing gap between the rent available to be paid under HAP limits and the actual market rent. Government has refused to change the HAP limits since 2016, despite rents increasing massively since then. The rents for most of the homes in the private rental market are higher than what the local authority will pay to the landlord on HAP, so to get a property, people have to be able to pay top-ups over and above the rent. The more vulnerable lower-income groups such as young people, people leaving care, migrants, Travellers, those trying to leave direct provision, those with disabilities and mental health difficulties, and lone parents cannot afford these top-ups and so are excluded from even attempting to enter the rental rat race.

The most vulnerable in our society have been locked out of the private rental market, the only possibility of getting housing, and so are locked out of a home, and are locked into homelessness. They are stuck in the homelessness trap. They did nothing wrong but had the misfortune to be born in the wrong decade in Ireland. They are Ireland's Generation Homeless. Had they been born in previous decades they would not have been homeless; they would have got council housing. Housing policy has created this homelessness emergency.

Normalizing homelessness to justify privilege and inequality

Part of the reason why the government and the Irish State has not acted strongly enough to tackle the homelessness crisis is because many people in power believe that homelessness is, as the local authority official said, the result of individual bad behaviour. They see the cause of homelessness as being individualized – 'within the person' – rather than structural – arising from the problems in the housing system and policy. Of course they want to place the blame on individual issues such as family breakdown or addiction, because that takes the responsibility away from the policy and government failures that cause homelessness.

At an even deeper psychological level, there is a genuine belief among many policymakers, politicians, civil servants and even those working in housing and homelessness state services that those who are homeless are 'less-than', part of the 'undeserving poor', and in some cases are scamming the system to try to get a home (as if trying to get a home was something wrong!). Richard Wilkinson, co-author of *The Spirit Level*, speaking on my Reboot Republic podcast described how the view held by some of the privileged and powerful – that it is the personal failure of those who are homeless that explains their homelessness and poverty – justifies the privileged to be in their place of privilege in society. In this mythical meritocracy, the politicians and civil servants tell themselves that they deserve their place in society and the homeless deserve theirs. The truth is, of course, very different. It is the policies of the privileged and the structural inequalities in society that result in so many being left in poverty and allows a smaller group to gain their wealth and privilege from that inequality. This attitude bolsters the sense of self-esteem and self-worth of the privileged and does the opposite to those affected by homelessness and inequality – they internalize these neoliberal belief systems, blame themselves and feel inadequate and unworthy as a result. As Wilkinson argues, we shouldn't fool ourselves into thinking that homelessness exists because it is a very complex and difficult problem to deal with – because it isn't. It can be solved. Wilkinson argues that 'we have to accept that homelessness is there because governments tolerate it, and may even think it has some marginal worth for them.' He thinks governments and the privileged justify homelessness as normal as part of the 'self-serving theories the rich have about their superiority and the failings of people at the bottom. The rich see these as signs of the inferiority of the poor; they are homeless because they are lazy and stupid.' And that is what makes forms of deprivation like homelessness so psychologically painful and damaging to the wellbeing of those affected. As Wilkinson says:

> Talk to someone who is homeless and it's not just the physical discomfort of the sleeping out, or the coldness, or not having proper accommodation, it is feeling that your life has collapsed, and you are regarded absolutely as the dregs of society, looked down on by everyone. People have failed to see how important the psychosocial effects of inequality are.

Senior Fine Gael advisers and politicians such as Tánaiste (and set to become Taoiseach again in December 2022) Leo Varadkar have tried to minimize the homelessness crisis by claiming that Ireland's level of homelessness is 'normal' and lower than other European countries. They argue that there is homelessness everywhere, and Ireland's levels aren't out of kilter with other countries. It is a horrible argument to make, that there is some level of homelessness which is okay, which society should accept or tolerate as normal, and that Ireland's level of homelessness is acceptable. We just have to accept our levels of homelessness. What a defeatist, elitist view of society. And anyhow, that argument is factually wrong – other European countries experience much less homelessness than Ireland. And many countries measure their homelessness figures differently and include a lot more groups than Ireland does. They include those in domestic violence refuges, and couch surfers, which Ireland doesn't. So, statements about Ireland having less homelessness are not factually correct.

More to the point, surely as a society we should never tolerate or accept any level of homelessness as normal? Homelessness is a devastating experience for people. It takes away their basic humanity and leaves physical and mental scars that stay with them for their lives.

Homelessness could be the result of the breakdown of a relationship, escaping domestic abuse, overcrowding in a family home, job loss, illness, addiction, a mental health crisis, the loss of a child or a parent. These are all personal issues that lead to someone losing their home. People lose their networks of support, their community, their home. But then, they face the Irish housing market where it is impossible to get an affordable home or social housing, or they are evicted, and so they become homeless. The reason for someone becoming homeless is often described as that individual issue – the relationship breakdown, or the illness (including mental ill health), or the addiction. But that is a personal circumstance that makes someone vulnerable and potentially at risk of poverty, homelessness and social exclusion. It is then the structural problems in our housing system that turn a risk of homelessness into actual homelessness. A pathway into homelessness might be; (a) personal event/issue to (b) risk to (c) housing structure to (d) homelessness. This pathway could be broken and diverted if there was adequate affordable and social housing available in situation (c) housing structure. Then the risk would not turn into homelessness, but would take a different path. People would face a personal or financial crisis and be able to get a home, which would then enable them to deal with the traumatic event or issues and cope with, and hopefully recover from, that personal crisis. The alternative pathway would then be: (a) personal event/issue to (b) risk to (c) access to secure affordable home to (d) address personal issue/event with supports to (e) live life to full potential and with dignity.

The view that people become homeless due to their own behaviour allows policymakers and governments to avoid taking responsibility for their policies that have created a housing crisis and contributed to the structures of inequality and exclusion in our housing system that create homelessness. It is government housing policy and discrimination and profit-seeking by landlords (including investor funds and corporate landlords) that has created homelessness. This makes a nonsense of the outdated attitudes that saw homelessness as a 'within the person' problem. If sufficient affordable and social housing was available, along with sufficient support services, no one would be homeless.

Domestic violence

Some of our most vulnerable groups in society have been forced more than others into homelessness. Their marginalization and trauma has been exacerbated by the housing crisis and government housing policy.

Women make up a third of homeless adults in Ireland. That is 2,264 women. Many have experienced domestic violence. The need for safe housing, and the financial means to maintain housing, are often the most pressing concerns among women who are trying to leave an abusive home. A report published in December 2021 by Focus Ireland, 'Domestic Violence & Family Homelessness', by Dr Paula Mayock and Fiona Neary, found that

Parents further reported stressful and disruptive transitional experiences when relying on temporary accommodation and frequently expressed strong anxiety about exposing their children to multiple housing transitions and prolonged instability . . . .

Stakeholders working in domestic violence, homelessness and housing sectors

spoke about the multiple losses experienced by children, frequently drawing strong attention to the numerous ways in which homelessness accommodation, whether hotels, B&Bs or Family Hubs, exacerbated children's trauma. In general, stakeholders felt that current child welfare and mental health services fell far short of meeting the complex needs of children impacted by domestic abuse.

The report also found that mothers who have lost their home because of domestic violence are generally seeking private rental accommodation, but on leaving the unsafe home they become single parents, wholly reliant in most cases on rental subsidies like HAP, and with few or no safety nets in relation to income or other supports. They face the all-too-familiar problem of the lack of rental housing and finding landlords that will accept them.

Stable housing is essential for these mothers and their children to find a path to sustained safety and security. Without housing, they cannot see a way of moving forward with their lives.

As Louise Bayliss of Single Parents Acting for the Rights of Kids (SPARK) points out, 'Many people ask the question of those affected by domestic abuse, "Why doesn't she just leave?" Well, where does she leave to? At the moment many people are trapped in abusive relationships because the only places that are left for them are refuges, and after refuges they go into emergency homeless accommodation.' So many women face a horrific decision – to stay in a situation of abuse or make yourself (and your children too) homeless. What a country we are to leave traumatized women and children in such situations.

This is a key area for the government to act on its commitments to tackle gender equality and gender-based violence.

Disability and homelessness

The Census in 2016 showed that over a quarter of those homeless then (1,871 people) had a disability, one in ten homeless people had a chronic illness, and 180 people homeless in Ireland had blindness or serious vision impairment.

One example of the challenges faced by people with disabilities is of a young woman with a disability who was homeless in Dublin and could not even get emergency accommodation because there was no accessible emergency accommodation available. So she was left living out of her car. Two years before she became homeless her private rental accommodation was becoming unsuitable for her as she had deteriorating health needs. Then she was issued with an eviction notice by the landlord. She couldn't find any suitable private rental accommodation and her HAP payment was insufficient to cover the carer support she required. So she was made homeless. Without a home she lost her care provision, so she lost her occupational therapy and nursing support. She explained to the council that she had been at risk of homelessness, but they didn't act. She lives in pain, and if she didn't get appropriate housing, she was going to end up in a nursing home.

This shows how vital is it that the State provide accessible, suitable and secure tenancy housing for people with disabilities. A home is necessary to get the personal supports that enable people with disabilities to lead independent and fulfilling lives, to participate in and to contribute to the life of the community in which they live. From a crude economic perspective, it is more expensive for the State to accommodate a person with a disability in a residential care home than to provide them with housing.

And for those with disabilities, emergency homeless accommodation is also extremely challenging. A study in Dublin found that homeless accommodation led to severe psychological difficulties in carers and behavioural and developmental regression in children with intellectual disability and autism spectrum disorder (ASD). It also highlighted challenges for adults with autism in homelessness, who experience distress at not being diagnosed or supported to understand their ASD and are unable to access appropriate homeless services that recognize their individual support needs.

Othering in homelessness

We have a major problem of 'othering' some groups in society in relation to homelessness. In othering, certain groups and people are demeaned, given labels, descriptions, that de-humanize them, that disconnect them from 'us'. Homeless men, lone parents, Travellers, migrants and asylum seekers are othered, and these groups are viewed as undeserving of housing supports. Yet they have a human need of a home as much as anyone else. With a home they can become more included in society, and enabled to reach their potential.

There are thousands of asylum seekers in substandard and inappropriate direct provision accommodation. Many have been granted refugee status but are unable to leave because of the lack of housing available. They are working, they have families, their children go to the local schools. Yet they are excluded. Many who leave direct provision also go into hidden homelessness, sleeping in overcrowded houses and on friends' couches and floors. Their mental health suffers further. Landlords look for references, but how do you get references if you have been living in direct provision for years? They experience racism from landlords who ignore that these are healthcare workers, youth workers, retail workers, people we rely on and who are part of Irish society, who have rights and needs to a home just like us all.

Travellers are another group that is othered in Irish society. Some individuals and groups organize public protests and post on social media blaming migrants, Travellers, people of colour for the lack of housing. They say we should house 'the Irish' first. But refugees and people of colour are Irish too. Besides that, they are our fellow human beings and they have a right to live in dignity, and we have an obligation as a country to support them. Migrants, Travellers and asylum seekers are not the cause of the crisis; they are its victims. To blame them is to take responsibility and focus away from the real cause of the crisis and homelessness – the failure of the government and the market to deliver affordable and social homes. Far right groups are actively trying to use the homelessness crisis as a way to foment racism against refugees, people of colour and the 'new Irish'. This is deeply dangerous and damaging for social cohesion in Ireland, for our democracy, and it weakens the solidarity needed to get the voices of vulnerable groups heard and for common action against the common cause of the crisis.

Tent streets

Walk down a main shopping street late at night in any of our cities – Dublin, Galway, Cork, Limerick – and you will see our fellow human beings in sleeping bags, lying on sheets of cardboard, trying to sleep, or at least get through the night. Just imagine how cold and wet it must get when your only shelter is a doorway. Think of how you would feel if that was your home, night after night. How low your self-esteem and mental health would be as you watch the rest of society walk by. Your basic human dignity stripped from you. No shelter, no protection, no home. Between 100 and 200 people are sleeping rough on the streets of Dublin every night. Dozens sleep rough in cities and towns across the country. People are sleeping in their cars, in tents in fields and parks. We have no idea of the full extent of this 'hidden homelessness' crisis. Some of them face the challenge of not being from the local authority area where they seek emergency accommodation, and, for example, in Dublin sometimes they are refused entry into emergency hostels. They are given a number to phone, and they repeatedly call it but are turned down. They rely on the sleeping bags and meals provided by outreach workers. That might get them through the night, and the next night, but imagine the damage it does to one's self-esteem to be forced to rely on the kindness of strangers.

A life in hostels: unsafe and degrading

The number of individual adults in emergency homeless accommodation over doubled from 2,310 in July 2014 to 5,054 in May 2022. The number of emergency beds (hostel emergency accommodation) for homeless adults in Dublin rose from 617 beds in 2008 to 830 in 2014, but then increased to 2,245 in 2018. An increase of 263 per cent in the decade of homelessness. There are 3,519 individuals in homeless hostels in Dublin, and 1,535 homeless individuals across the rest of the country, in every region. There are 450 individuals in emergency homeless accommodation in Cork and Kerry, for example. Half of the people living in hostels have been there longer than six months.

Homeless hostels have been criticized for being dangerous, substandard, multi-bedroomed, with issues of drugs, violence and robbery, leading to physical and mental health problems for those who have to live in them.

Many rough sleepers and those staying in homelessness hostels had not experienced drug addiction before becoming homeless. But in homelessness, more end up addicted to drugs. As Mike Allen from Focus Ireland points out:

Very often, we look at people who are homeless and we see the drug addiction they have, and we think that that's the cause of their homelessness. But, in actual fact, many of the problems that people who are homeless have are consequences of their homelessness – and just the sheer misery and the sheer mental pressure of living in circumstances where you have no home and the security that should go with a home.

Homelessness exacerbates mental health issues such as depression and anxiety. In 2021, *RTÉ Investigates* surveyed 80 homeless people who slept rough or who used emergency hostels and found seventy per cent said their mental health issues had worsened since they lost their home.

Those living in emergency hostels describe how they feel the services do not see them. They feel invisible to society. And many are getting up in the morning in a homeless hostel and then going to work.

Emergency accommodation is the wrong response to homelessness – it is deeply damaging and makes people's exclusion and mental health even worse, yet it has been the main response of the Irish government to the homelessness emergency it has created. As the risk of, and number of people in, homelessness rose year after year over this decade, the primary response of government was not to invest in prevention or other solutions, but to channel most new resources into more and more emergency accommodation.

National expenditure on homelessness grew from €55m in 2013 to €226m in 2019. That is a total of a €1.5bn over the decade to 2022. And the majority of that, €1.2bn, was spent on emergency accommodation. Just a tiny proportion, 10 per cent, was spent on prevention – despite the proven success of prevention work on keeping people in their homes by the likes of Focus Ireland, Simon Communities and Threshold.

Covid response showed we can tackle homelessness

In March 2020, a range of protections were put in place for people affected by the Covid pandemic, including a ban on evictions and rent increases in the private rental sector. A new act set out that 'a landlord shall not serve a notice of termination in relation to the tenancy of a dwelling during the emergency period' and set a 'prohibition on rent increases'. These were in place until August 2020.

Then, just two months later, when another wave of the pandemic hit, another eviction ban and rent freeze was introduced, which was in place until April 2021.

The ban on evictions and rent increases had a dramatic impact on reducing homelessness.

April 2020, one month after the ban on evictions was introduced, saw the lowest number of new families (just 14) being made homeless since 2014. This meant a dramatic reduction in the number of people going into emergency accommodation. The collapse in tourism meant that some owners of property who were using it for short-term lets like Airbnb were willing to let it be rented out, and some homeless families were moved in, contributing to the numbers leaving emergency accommodation. The eviction ban stopped the flow into homelessness, and the increased supply of accommodation meant an increased flow out of homeless emergency accommodation, with prevention and support services working to support those homeless to get homes. And so, for the first time in Ireland in almost a decade, homelessness fell dramatically. A solution was found to end homelessness – stop evictions, provide homes and make sure homeless people get those homes.

The number of families in homeless emergency accommodation in Ireland began falling when the eviction ban was introduced in March 2020, and fell from 1,100 families in emergency accommodation to 856 in August 2020. But when the ban was lifted for two months, that reduction stalled. When the second ban was introduced in October 2021, the numbers fell again, down to a five-year low of 681 families, until the ban was ended in March 2021. That was a 38 per cent reduction in homeless families in a year. So just a year of these polices brought homelessness back to levels last seen in 2015. And then, depressingly, what we warned the government would happen if it lifted the ban and rent freeze, happened. The ban and rent freeze were lifted in April 2021 and the number of families being made homeless increased again and continued to increase month after month. By May 2022, it had increased to 1,366 families homeless, undoing the huge progress that had been made in the previous year.

The number of children homeless in emergency accommodation with their families fell to its lowest level in five years in May 2021, to 2,129 children. But by May 2022, that number had increased again, to 3,028 children homeless, up a disturbing 38 per cent in a year. Across the south-east and south-west of the country there was a 25 per cent increase in the number of children homeless between July and December 2021.

The reason for increased homelessness was straightforward: a huge increase in 'no fault' evictions in the private rental sector and no homes available for people when they were evicted. When the eviction ban was lifted in April 2021 landlords responded with a tsunami of eviction notices to tenants. Landlords issued 352 eviction notices in the first three months of 2021, increasing to a phenomenal 1,000 notices to quit (NTQs) in the last three months of 2021. That was the highest ever number since NTQs were required to be registered in 2019. There was a 62 per cent increase from 2020 to 2021 in NTQ, from 1,902 in 2020 to 3,038 in 2021. Just 7 per cent of these were due to a tenant breach of obligations. So over 90 per cent of evictions were for no fault of the tenant. Two-thirds were due to the landlord intending to sell the property. The majority of eviction notices were issued to tenants outside Dublin, showing that the crisis is affecting tenants all over the country.

The problem is that once tenants are evicted, there is nowhere to go, because of the lack of social and affordable housing, particularly the lack of rental properties, and especially if you are on HAP. Research by Simon Communities showed that in December 2021, in nine of the sixteen areas surveyed across the country, including Cork City, Galway, Limerick, Sligo and Waterford City, there was not one property available to rent within the affordability range of someone on a low income and eligible for HAP. Rising rents meant the gap between HAP limits and the market rent has grown even wider. And because of the cost of living crisis people have less money to plug the HAP rental gap.

Those working in low-wage sectors like hospitality were hit hardest by the Covid economic crash – they could not afford to pay rent, went into arrears, or could not afford to pay a higher rent sought, and have been served eviction notices or illegally evicted. As tourism returns, rentals are again being converted to Airbnbs and other short-stay tourist accommodation, taking supply away, making it even harder to find homes to help people leave emergency accommodation. Focus Ireland reported that their staff were seeing more families and individuals facing eviction from HAP tenancies due to soaring rents.

The increase in homelessness and evictions in the private rental sector in the second half of 2021 and into 2022 has been described by Focus Ireland as something they 'have never seen before'; people who had never been exposed to homelessness are now facing eviction and the prospect of homelessness. The number of tenants coming to Threshold for support increased by 25 per cent since the lifting of the eviction ban.

This is another tsunami of trauma for children and families in the rental sector.

The eviction bans and rent freeze, along with additional homes and supports as part of the State's response to Covid, showed that it is possible to significantly reduce homelessness. We cannot just pretend that this didn't happen and go back to business as usual. The pandemic revealed that it is possible to end homelessness in Ireland. We must take these Covid lessons, and combine them with the lessons from Finland, to make a new plan to end homelessness in Ireland, and make it happen.

Finland shows how to end homelessness

Dublin and Helsinki, the capital of Finland, have very similar population sizes. Yet their levels of homelessness are a world apart. In Dublin, there are 972 homeless families, with 2,259 children. Helsinki has just 72 homeless families, with 55 children. So Dublin's level of family homelessness is thirteen times higher than Helsinki's. Dublin's level of child homelessness is forty times higher than Helsinki's. There is nothing 'normal' about Ireland's homelessness crisis.

Finland did have a homelessness crisis in the late 1980s and 1990s. It had over 4,000 people living in emergency accommodation and sleeping rough, but it reduced this to just 512 in 2018. Its number of homeless families fell from 870 in 1989 to 200 in 2020. So how did it do it?

It set up a not-for-profit housing association, called the Y-Foundation, in the late 1980s, which was dedicated to providing housing for the homeless. At the heart of its approach was the Housing First model.

This started with a fundamental change in how it responds to, and thinks about, housing and homelessness. The usual approaches to homelessness, which we see in Ireland, is providing emergency accommodation as the main response, and for longer-term homeless with addiction or mental health issues, the 'staircase' model, whereby the homeless are first required to solve their 'issues' before they are offered housing. But Finland turned this on its head through their Housing First approach. Now its first, and main, response to homelessness is to provide a secure permanent home and support services as needed. This is based on the principle that having a place to live is a basic human right. The Constitution of Finland includes the right to social assistance, and the right to housing, stating that: 'Public authorities shall promote the right of everyone to housing and the opportunity to arrange their own housing.' The word 'shall' is central; it is an obligation, a duty. The Finnish Constitution also says that, 'Those who cannot obtain the means necessary for a life of dignity have the right to receive indispensable subsistence and care.' There are no such provisions in the Irish Constitution, law or policies. Irish housing and homelessness policy does not treat housing as a human right.

Housing First is a housing-led approach that also focuses on prevention, and the provision of adequate supports (addiction, mental health, family support) to people in their homes according to their needs. It provides a home, not as a reward that a homeless person receives once their life is back 'on track', but as the foundation on which the rest of their life is put back together. Finland gave a beautiful name to the plan – *Nimi Ovessa*, which means 'Your Name on the Door'.

It now provides long-term housing, permanent housing and adequate support services as the first response, so that everyone homeless is provided with a home of their own. Not a room, or a bed in emergency accommodation but, as the inspirational former CEO of the Y-Foundation Juha Kaakinen explains, 'a home with a key to their own apartment, and a permanent rental contract'. One of the most important aspects of this is that Finland ended the use of emergency accommodation. It shut the hostels, in contrast to Ireland, where we keep expanding emergency accommodation. The last big shelter in Helsinki, which was run by the Salvation Army, was closed down in 2019, and the building was completely renovated from 250 bed places into eighty independent flats for homeless people.

Kaakinen explains that they treat a homeless person as a fellow human being, listening to their needs. They start from the strength and capabilities of those who are homeless, not from failings and problems. They provide a home first, as this offers them 'the keys to their life, the keys to a future'. He says we should dream about a world without homelessness, and we can make this dream a reality.

What makes the Y-Foundation different is that it is a non-profit-making social enterprise housing association that specializes in, and focuses on, housing homeless people and vulnerable groups. The board of the Y-Foundation is made up of representatives from the local authority of Helsinki Social and Health Care Services, other local authority family and social services, Mental Health Finland and the Confederation of Finnish Construction Industries. The chair of the board is from the Finnish Construction Trade Union and the vice chair is from the Finnish Red Cross. It's a real cross-society social enterprise partnership. The Y-Foundation has remained focused on its core objective of providing homes for the most vulnerable groups of people in Finnish society.

The Y-Foundation developed its own expertise in building and construction. It builds units and renovates, and it purchases housing units and then rents them to homeless people through local authorities and local partners. It also manages some directly. The foundation and the local authority provide support services where needed to those being housed. Constructing and purchasing new, affordable housing has been central to the Y-Foundation's success, driven by the Finnish National Programme, in reducing long-term homelessness The Y-Foundation now has 18,000 homes across Finland.

These funded national programmes and plans, with clear targets and very concrete goals and strong political commitment to end long-term homelessness in Finland, have been central to the country's success.

Finland also took a wide definition of homelessness to include people in hidden homelessness, such as those temporarily living with friends or relatives due to lack of housing, and those in institutions, refuges and prisons, who need (or will need) housing. The Finnish response is based on prevention and solutions.

This approach of moving from temporary accommodation to permanent housing solutions is actually better value for money economically. Y-Foundation research found that giving a homeless person permanent accommodation can result in cost savings of at least €15,000 per person each year.

In contrast, in Ireland, we rely largely on emergency accommodation and insecure leases from the private rental sector via HAP for our homelessness response. Unlike Finland, we do not build and provide permanent homes to those who are homeless as a first response. While some homelessness charities like Focus Ireland, Simon Communities and the Peter McVerry Trust are building and renovating social housing for the homeless, this is still at too small a scale, and has not been the central response to homelessness in Ireland.

Finland is approaching functional zero homelessness, and its present government has an even more ambitious goal: to reach absolute zero homelessness by 2027. It is turning the dream of ending homelessness into a reality. It's time for us to do the same here.

What should Ireland be doing?

Homelessness is the most severe violation of the right to housing. As the United Nations Special Rapporteur on the Right to Adequate Housing described it:

> Homelessness is a profound assault on dignity, social inclusion and the right to life (survival and the right to live a life in dignity). It is a prima facie violation of the right to housing and violates a number of other human rights in addition to the right to life, including non-discrimination, health, water and sanitation, security of the person and freedom from cruel, degrading and inhuman treatment.

There is no inequality greater than homelessness. It is an egregious violation of human rights, threatening the health and life of the most marginalized. Homelessness is the unacceptable result of states failing to implement the right to adequate housing. It requires urgent and immediate human rights responses, according to the United Nations.

Yet the Irish response to homelessness does not even mention human rights. It does not use a human rights approach. The main homelessness response in Ireland has been the provision of emergency accommodation, which simply manages and maintains homelessness. Unlike Housing First. This is the fundamental difference between Ireland and Finland.

Ireland has begun to implement Housing First, but the current targets are completely inadequate for the scale of the crisis. The government's latest housing plan, launched in September 2021, has a nice title, 'Housing for All', but unfortunately the detail in the plan makes its title meaningless. The plan only targets 1,319 Housing First tenancies up to 2026. That's housing for just one in nine of all those currently homeless. In Cork City, for example, there are 450 homeless, yet the target is only 45 Housing First tenancies up to 2026, or 10 per cent of those currently homeless. Many of the Housing First tenancies are also via HAP in the private rental sector; they are not permanently secure homes. How is that a sufficient response to end homelessness?

The European Commission criticized the Irish Government for its 'unreliable and incomplete' statistics on homelessness, which were hampering planning and effective policy solutions. Unlike Finland, Ireland does not count as homeless some of the most at risk, including the hidden homeless: people with disabilities in inappropriate accommodation, young people and families couch surfing or living in overcrowding, those in domestic violence refuges, those in direct provision, care leavers, those in institutions and prisons, or Travellers in substandard accommodation. As a result, Ireland does not properly respond to the scale of housing insecurity and risk of homelessness because it doesn't count it as homelessness. We don't do prevention because we don't consider it.

Monthly homelessness figures from the Department of Housing provide a vital measure of those in emergency accommodation but we also need to adopt the European Typology of Homelessness and Housing Exclusion (ETHOS) devised by FEANTSA, the European Federation of National Organisations Working with the Homeless. Like the Finnish, ETHOS identifies four types of homelessness and housing exclusion: roofless (without any shelter, sleeping rough); homeless (with a temporary place to sleep, in institutions or shelters); living in insecure housing (due to insecure tenancies, eviction, domestic violence); and living in inadequate housing (in caravans on illegal campsites, in unfit housing, in extreme overcrowding). Ireland needs to implement the ETHOS framework to respond properly to those at risk of and in homelessness. We need to properly measure the level of homelessness if we are going to solve it.

It is utterly frustrating and disappointing after all the progress made during Covid, with the eviction bans, rent freeze and freeing up of homes for those homeless, that we were on our way towards reducing homeless and really tackling it in a major way. If the political will continued, we could have ended family homelessness within a few years. But instead, the government let the landlords, investors and property market get back to business as usual. The private property rights of landlords and profit requirements of investor funds trumped vulnerable families and children being made homeless.

Many of us have been making the case to the government that the bans on evictions and on rent increases should be reintroduced for an initial three-year period (aside from tenancies that have been validly terminated for antisocial behaviour, property damage, or wilful failure to pay rent) to give renters some stability and reduce homelessness. The eviction bans and rent freeze during Covid showed we can end homelessness. We know what can stop people being made homeless, so why are we not doing it?

The government argued that reintroducing the bans, and a rent freeze, would be unconstitutional as it would breach the private property rights of landlords set out in Article 43 of the Constitution. It also argued it would reduce the supply of rental property. Article 43 states that the Irish State, 'guarantees to pass no law attempting to abolish the right of private ownership, or the general right to transfer, bequeath and inherit property'. However, Article 43 also says that 'the exercise of the rights mentioned in the foregoing provision of this Article, ought, in civil society, to be regulated by the principles of social justice', and that the State 'may as occasion requires delimit by law the exercise of the said rights with a view to reconciling their exercise with the exigencies of the common good'. This means that property rights can be limited by what is deemed to be in the common good – for society as a whole and according to the principles of social justice, which means prioritizing the needs of the vulnerable. Introducing a three-year eviction ban and rent freeze would be constitutional as it would reduce the number of families and individuals being made homeless, clearly in the interests of the common good. It would reduce the number of families going into homeless accommodation and thus enable homeless providers focus on trying to find homes for those in emergency accommodation. It would give people more time to find a home. It clearly would meet the social justice principles of the needs of vulnerable people.

The constitutional protection of private property was not a barrier to the previous two temporary bans, and therefore would not be a barrier to another temporary ban. Neither would an eviction ban deter supply. In fact, it would increase the supply of rental homes by maintaining current tenants in situ – even if the rental home was sold by the landlord, the tenant would be able to remain – and thus maintaining more properties in the private rental sector.

However, the fact that the constitutional protection of the right to private property in Article 43 was cited by the Minister for Housing as a barrier to these measures shows the urgency for holding a referendum to enshrine the right to housing as a balancing principle alongside the right to private property and thus to enable policy such as longer-term eviction bans and removing the eviction of tenants on sale of rental properties.

The basic principle in homelessness is that if you are not stemming the flow into homelessness, you will not end homelessness. If you do not provide sufficient homes to get people out of emergency accommodation, you will not end homelessness. Evictions in the private rental sector are the main cause of flows into homelessness and there is little being done to address this.

As the UN recommends, and Finland has in place, a rights-based approach should be the cornerstone of all our state agencies' homelessness responses and policies. The Simon Communities Homeless Prevention Bill passed the Dail in December 2021. The Minister for Housing committed to progress it. While eviction notice periods have been extended, the key homeless prevention parts of the Bill remain to be implemented. In particular, providing local authorities with the power to intervene, both in advance of, and at a crisis point of eviction, to prevent homelessness. This would give those in crisis more time to secure a home with the support of their local authority and organizations like Simon Communities, Focus Ireland and Threshold.

The failure to stop evictions on the basis that more restrictions will cause more landlords to leave the market and reduce the supply of housing, and deter future supply of rental housing by investors, is a deeply flawed approach. Why is the government allowing landlords' investment decisions determine our social policy response to the human need of a home and the social emergency of homelessness? Allowing tenants remain in place on sale means the landlord can still sell the property.

This is the economics of the property market trumping social need. It is distorted, unethical and dysfunctional. It is facilitating landlords to take advantage of leases ending and getting in higher-paying tenants and selling up to take advantage of higher house prices, and then allowing another property investor get in new tenants at even higher rents. The ability of landlords to evict tenants when selling property should be removed. Who will lose out from this? Landlords will have to sell with the tenant in place, at perhaps a slightly reduced price. But are we really saying that maximizing their sale price on their investment asset is the priority over children being traumatized, over families and individuals losing their home? Local authorities should be purchasing the properties to keep tenants in place, and turn the properties into permanent social and affordable housing.

There is a massive potential and hope to be achieved for vulnerable and marginalized people in, and at risk of, homelessness by taking the Finnish Housing First approach. It will give people the stability to deal with other challenges in life, particularly if it is mental health or addiction or trauma.

Doctor Anne Doherty, a consultant liaison psychiatrist at the Mater Hospital and associate professor of psychiatry at University College Dublin, explained to me on my Reboot Republic podcast how getting a home, for those who are homeless, 'makes such a difference'.

It's really lovely when you see people getting a home, and getting that stability again, because you really do see it makes their ability to engage with everything so much better. I have seen quite a number of people, for example, who have been homeless for a number of years, but once they get into stable accommodation, often supported accommodation, often provided by charities, like Focus Ireland or Simon, or any of those organizations that do really sterling work in this area, but once they do that, their mental health improves quite dramatically, they are able to engage with the community mental health team, they are able to engage with substance misuse services, their lives are that little bit more bearable, because . . . they have that secure base, they have somewhere that is theirs, that is their own home that they can retreat to when they need to.

We can see from what happened during Covid and from Finland that homelessness is not normal, it is not inevitable, it is not the fault of those being made homeless; it results from policies, and it is a political and policy choice to allow homelessness to continue or to end it.

Providing emergency accommodation, the Irish State's main response to homelessness, is not the right solution. It makes the problem worse. The government hides it in monthly statistics, making it seem that it is addressing the problem, but it is not. It is merely maintaining homelessness and, in the process, inflicting severe trauma on those with no option but to live in emergency accommodation or in hidden homelessness.

No government can claim it did not know of the structural violence and trauma it has inflicted as a result of its housing policies; the devaluing and stripping of dignity that it has inflicted and continues to inflict on tens of thousands of individuals, on families and children; its decades-long failure to address Ireland's housing inadequacies; its creation of a generation of homeless people. Governments and successive Ministers for Housing, from 2014 up to the present day, including Ministers Phil Hogan, Alan Kelly, Simon Coveney, Eoghan Murphy and Darragh O'Brien – have left a terrible legacy: the normalization, the tolerance, the acceptance of child and family homelessness. It is another dark stain on our history. Let there be no doubt, Irish governments over this decade have been in clear violation of their international human rights obligations, constitutional obligations and ethical and moral obligations to those, including children, in homeless accommodation.

For me, this is the most important reason we need a right to housing in our Constitution. It would put an end to the Irish State refusing to take responsibility for homelessness. It would make it legally obliged to provide homes in emergency situations, so that it would be against our laws that a child is homeless in this country.

There is something fundamentally broken in a society, and fundamentally failed in a government, that leaves its most vulnerable exposed unnecessarily to such trauma. We need to act so that it is no longer acceptable, at any level, for a child or an individual to be left homeless.

It is not solved because it is not prioritized by government. Charity will not solve this. Homelessness is structurally caused by housing policy failures and our inadequate support systems for vulnerable groups in society.

If Finland can do it, so can we. Ireland can celebrate all its successes and talk about the wonderful 'quality of life' we have here, and wax lyrical about growth rates and employment. But it is all hollow, shallow, fake and meaningless to the thousands of children and their families who are homeless.

I'm deeply concerned that our level of individual and family and child homelessness has become normalized in Irish society. As a mother who was formerly homeless said, 'It will be a sad world if our children, our next generation, behave how this government are behaving, because this government have, and are, treating them as though they are invisible, as though they don't matter, when they do matter, very much.' I believe that homeless children do matter to most Irish people; most people in this country really care about homelessness, they are upset by it, ashamed of what has been allowed to happen in their name, and they want real action to solve homelessness. We can, we must and we will end homelessness in this country.

Chapter 10
REITs:
Creating a Permanent Generation Rent

There is a housing crisis in most major cities across the world, from Barcelona to London, from Boston to Berlin, and so – the government and others argue – the housing crisis in this country isn't just bad policy here. But the reason for the crisis across different countries and cities is the same – all governments have implemented, in one way or another, similar misguided policies.

First, over the last three decades, governments have stopped building social and affordable housing. Second, they have turned housing into a commodity, an investment asset – by inviting global real estate investment trusts, or REITs, into their housing markets, which have taken over housing and made it unaffordable everywhere. But the only reason these investor funds are taking over is because of the lack of supply by governments and the fallout of the 2002–2008 boom and crash that left many homeowners and buy-to-let landlords in arrears, banks constrained in their lending, smaller builders gone bust and the loss of key skills in the construction sector. This has created a housing shortage that the vulture funds and REITs are taking advantage of. Governments have created the market opportunity for property investors, landlords and global vulture funds around the world to profit from Generation Rent. But what are these REITs and investor funds, who are they and how are they making housing unaffordable?

What is a REIT?

Investor funds, or real estate investment trusts, are also known as vulture funds, cuckoo funds and, as I have named them, vampire funds. They are all private companies – businesses – that gather together lots of other people's money. Pensions, rich people's money, billionaires' and oligarchs' money, people's savings or people with a bit of money looking for somewhere to invest, and money made illegally through, for example, laundering, trafficking and drugs. The investor fund gathers all these little (and large) sums of money together into a giant lump called an 'investment fund' – a bank account containing a massive amount of money.

Then they use this fund to buy property. The property they buy is called real estate – it includes land (sites), hotels, shopping centres, offices and residential property. Residential real estate is apartments and houses – people's homes. These funds are mainly headquartered in the USA, Canada and Germany (that's where most of the money they make flows back to), but they also include money from Irish pension funds (that might include your pension). These funds go all over the world to see where they can buy up property that will give them the highest return on their investment (the biggest profit). They have huge bags of money in their fund so they can knock everyone else who is looking to buy property (such as a home) out of the way.

They also use the fund to lend money to local developers and investor landlords building apartments and houses. This lending is called private equity finance. So they fund the building and development of property as well – which means they have huge power over what type of homes are built in a country or city, both by what they fund and what they buy.

You might wonder when you see a new block of apartments or town houses built in your area, and you try to buy one, why none is for sale. What has happened is a global investor fund has already bought them up using their giant bags of money. You never even had a chance of a look-in. The investor fund probably 'forward purchased' the apartments. That means they essentially funded the development and bought the apartments before they were finished by the Irish developer who built them. So you were never going to be given an opportunity to even make a bid. The new apartments you might have been excited about in your community were never going to be forever homes for people.

And to make things worse, there are Irish investment funds and REITs as well, and some of the bags of money are coming from Irish pension funds – in a bizarre twist, your pension could be going to an investment fund or REIT to buy up property that you have no choice but to rent at an extortionate price. Your own pension could be locking you, or your children, out of having a home of your or their own.

The REIT and investor fund business model

The funds make their money, their profit, or 'return on investment', in a number of ways. First, the vulture-type funds buy real estate (property and land) cheaply (as they did after the 2008 housing and financial crash) and sell it on in a few years' time, when prices rise – and they make a profit from that 'flipping'. This is generally what the vulture funds do.

But since the 2008 crash the global investor funds have increasingly turned to buying property and then managing and renting it out over the long term, over twenty or thirty years (and even longer). These are the REITs. REITs have become massive corporate landlords, owning, managing and renting out millions of properties in cities across the world, including in Dublin. They are also looking to spread to Galway, Limerick and Cork. They also sell on their properties to other REITs, a longer term form of the flipping undertaken by vulture funds.

The REIT corporate landlords saw a new potential market in Generation Rent, who were locked out of homes during the final years of the property boom and the resultant financial crash, and the recession from 2008 onwards. They were being locked out of buying their own home because of being squeezed out by property investors (including 'mom and pop' landlord property purchasers), the lack of bank lending, unemployment, precarious wages, and the lack of affordable housing, so they have had to rely on the private rental market to get a home.

Vampire funds

REITs had been expanding in Canada, the USA and Germany and they, and the investor funds, quickly realized that the post-2008 Generation Rent, along with the huge amount of distressed property that was cheap after the crash, offered a potential gold rush that could provide investors a rental income from a generation being locked in perpetuity into living in their investment properties. And as younger generations would have to spend their income on rent, they would become even less able to buy a home, or at least they would spend longer renting, so the business strategy of the funds is to lock Generation Rent out of home ownership and into permanently renting from them.

That is why I call them vampire funds. They want to feed off your rent for ever. Instead of forever homes, it's forever rent from the REITs. They are sucking the life from us – our income, work, wages, our life dreams and possibilities, and feeding off it for their profits and returns to the wealthy investors, billionaires, pension funds and shareholders who put the money into the investment funds and REITs. And it is not just renters the REITs are after. They want to hoover up as a much profitable 'real estate' and public infrastructure as they can. They already own massive amounts of land in our cities; they are already building huge student accommodation developments (that no student can afford); they are building offices; and they are targeting elderly housing, social and affordable housing, primary healthcare facilities, and now even renewable energy. All because governments won't build these things themselves. Instead they're leaving the REITs to it – and the REITs are making huge profits. They want to turn as many of the buildings and as much of the infrastructure we need as they can into financial assets for them.

The REITs and funds, in partnership with our government, are taking us down a very, very dangerous road. They are playing an overly dominant, disruptive, distorting and disproportionate role in our housing market. They are making housing more unaffordable and not addressing housing need. They build what maximizes returns for their investors, not what will meet our population's housing needs. The investment funds are delivering not housing as homes to meet the needs of people in this country, but income-generating assets for their shareholders and investors. We have to understand that this is the business model of investor funds and REITs. They are not a charity; their aim is not to provide a supply of homes that will make housing affordable in this country.

The government and the property economists argue that we need these funds, and they are providing a supply of houses that meets people's housing needs – that provides homes and will reduce house prices. But it is not 'homes' they are supplying. Investor funds don't build gaffs. They build unaffordable housing units that do not meet the definition of what a home is and should provide for people. This is not housing that provides a home. It's not an affordable, secure place where someone can plan their lives, have space to develop and grow and belong, and be part of communities. These are soulless, money-making shoeboxes.

REITs need rents to keep increasing for ever

The investor funds are here to maximize their rate of return on their investment – they want to make as much money as possible for the people who put their money into the big bag of money in the fund. That is their sole purpose. In the main it's making people with lots of money and huge bank accounts even richer. The REIT business model requires a constant expansion to generate ever-higher returns, so they need to keep devouring more of the housing market so that they become the only option for people. And they want (as their shareholders and investors demand) rents to keep increasing. This has major implications for the future of housing in Ireland. If REITs continue to play a larger and larger role, given that rents are so high already, that means even higher and more unaffordable rents. Something will have to break. At the moment it is renters who are being broken. The REIT corporate landlords want to keep buying more and more property, building more and more build-to-rent developments, locking more and more people into their rental homes.

REITs want a permanent renting class

That is why the investor funds have made it clear that the most significant threat to their investments would be if the Irish government built affordable homes on a major scale. REITs buying up Irish property and developing the co-living and build-to-rent apartments don't want renters to have the option to buy or rent an affordable home. If they did have that option, most would not rent an expensive shoebox. REITs want us permanently locked into renting their micro-units. That is their global investment strategy – to create a permanent renting class.

Their business strategy is based on making Generation Rent bigger and permanent. The investment funds said it clearly: they 'like the private rented sector because of the increased propensity to rent and the unaffordability of housing markets generally'. They do not just want a niche role in Irish housing – they want to dominate it.

And our government is giving the Irish housing market to them on a plate, served with a side salad of tax breaks, and topped off with a dessert of guaranteed rent increases and lucrative social housing leasing contracts and HAP. Governments have for the last two decades refused to fund the state building of social and affordable housing. They have promoted rental as an investment commodity through buy-to-let landlords. They have given REITs tax breaks and allowed market rents to rise uninterrupted over the last decade. Through all this, government policy created the market opportunity for global funds and REITs that are turning renters into a cash cow for global and Irish wealth and pension funds.

Expansion of REITs and corporate landlords in Ireland

The rapid expansion of these investor funds in Ireland is nothing short of phenomenal. Since 2016, Irish and international investors have spent €7bn on purchasing and developing private rental sector apartments. In 2016, they bought up 6,266 homes. But in 2020, they bought 12,378 homes – a third of all homes purchased in that year. In 2021, they bought around 4,000 newly built residential units, 27 per cent of all the new supply of houses and apartments for sale in the country. In Dublin in 2021, 'non-household buyers' (mainly investor funds, but also local Irish property investors, Irish landlords, as well as the state through local authorities and housing associations) bought a half of all newly built homes (2,031 homes). That means investor funds bought almost twice as many newly built homes as did first-time buyers (1,060) in Dublin in 2021. The *Irish Times* described it accurately as 'foreign investors [flooding] into the capital's private rental sector market to avail of comparatively strong returns.' It continued into 2022. While 1,175 new homes were built in Dublin in the first three months of 2022, just 219 (19 per cent) were bought by first-time buyers; 739 (63 per cent) were bought by 'non-households' – mainly investor funds.

It is unclear exactly how many homes global and Irish investor funds and REIT corporate landlords now own. Residential Tenancies Board (RTB) figures state that investor funds and REITs own in the region of 18,000 private rental homes in Ireland. But Revenue property tax returns for 2021 show that large corporate landlords (owning 200 or more properties) own 45,600 properties in Ireland. That is up by 60 per cent from the 28,000 units they owned in 2017. At the current rate of expansion, within the next decade REIT corporate landlords and funds could own 85,000 rental properties in Ireland, or a quarter of all private rental homes in Ireland. That is a massive and dominant market share of homes, which would give them effective control over the rental market.

Who are the funds and REITs in Ireland?

In certain parts of Dublin, cranes dominate the skyline. New homes, mainly blocks of new apartments, are rising rapidly from the ground. Looking at them, for a moment you feel hopeful – at last, the housing crisis will be solved. New homes are being built. But a quick google of the names of the developers and who is buying the apartments will leave you depressed and frustrated. These will never be for sale. They will not be homes, just expensive rental units. Here are just some examples of who is building and buying them. Spoiler alert – they're not home buyers.

Hines is a US-based real estate investor worth €93bn, one of the largest in the world. Hines has a specific fund targeted at European cities, the Hines European Core Fund. Hines started investing in Ireland in 2011 and now has €3.7bn worth of 'assets' under management here. NAMA gave Hines one of its introductory offers to Ireland, when in 2014 it sold it the largest development site in south County Dublin – the 166-hectare Cherrywood site. Hines plans to build 1,221 apartments in Cherrywood. They will be build-to-rent. A Cairn Homes development of 107 apartments in Rathgar was sold to Hines in 2021 for at least €588,000 per apartment. No home buyer even got a sniff of them. Hines is also developing a gigantic development of 1,600 apartments in Drumcondra, and not one will be available for sale. Seventy per cent will be either studio or one-bed apartments. They are likely to be rented at unaffordable rates.

In 2021 and 2022, almost one thousand new apartments were built in three developments: Santry Place in north Dublin; Hampton Wood in Finglas; and Windermere in Clongriffin. Not one was sold to a home buyer. All were bought by Ardstone Capital, a property investment firm based in the UK and Ireland set up by former Friends First senior executives. It paid in the region of €500,000 per apartment.

A major new residential quarter of 435 apartments is being built by Irish developer Ballymore in the lovely Royal Canal Park in the north-west of Dublin. It is just 300 metres from the new Pelletstown railway station. Not one is for sale on the open market. A German investor fund, Union Investment, has forward purchased them all to be rented out.

There's also a new 166-apartment development being built in Dublin's much sought-after Harold's Cross area, in close proximity to Rathmines. They are a mix of one-, two- and three-bedroom apartments. Not one will be for sale. Germany's largest public pension fund group, Patrizia AG, as part of its European real estate investments, forward purchased the entire development for €93m. That equates to €560,240 per apartment. Tough to compete with as a home buyer. And Patrizia said, it will not stop there: 'Our aim is to push towards 1,000 units and become one of the city's largest private rented sector owners.' Why is Patrizia investing here? 'Our clients will benefit from the performance of the strong residential rental market in Dublin, which is characterized by an acute housing shortage.' It might be a crisis for people in Ireland looking to buy or rent an affordable home, but the housing shortage is an investment opportunity for these global real estate funds.

Lone Star, a multibillion US private equity firm owned by American-Irish billionaire John Grayken, also purchased assets from vulture funds' best friend in Ireland, NAMA. Grayken was ranked Ireland's third richest person in the *Sunday Independent* 2018 rich list, with a fortune of €5.8bn. The newspaper stated Grayken made his fortune by making a 20 per cent return on his investment in 'buying distressed assets in bombed out economies and flipping them as markets improved'. Lone Star also bought land in Cherrywood from Hines. In 2014 and 2015, Lone Star bought (with Cairn Homes) 687 hectares of prime residential land in Dublin from Ulster Bank. It also bought the UK development business Quintain in 2015. Lone Star is using Quintain to develop up to 1,200 units on the Irish land it bought, such as sites in Adamstown, Clonburris, Portmarnock and Cherrywood. Many are likely to be build-to-rent. Most profits made on building this Irish housing and from Irish renters of the property will be returning to the US fund Lone Star.

And there are lots of Irish real estate companies, big estate agents, real estate advisers, 'asset managers' and law firms who arrange and close out these deals and make their living from this trade. Big names involved in this include CBRE, A&L Goodbody, PriceWaterhouseCoopers, and Hooke & MacDonald. Cushman & Wakefield is a new entrant in this field in Ireland and you might see its 'for sale' signs on property and land across the country. It is a global commercial real estate services firm, headquartered in the USA, with revenue of $7.8bn in 2021.

Turning homes into stock markets

If you are a renter, you could use the few euro left over after paying your rent to buy some food, or you could take a bet and buy some shares on the Irish Stock Exchange. You might be surprised to find that you can buy shares in Ireland's largest private rental landlord, which might even be your own corporate landlord. You can effectively trade in tenants' homes, even your own home.

Irish Residential Properties REIT (IRES REIT), one of Ireland's largest private landlords, and the main REIT based in Ireland, is listed on the stock exchange, as are Irish developers Glenveagh Properties and Cairn Homes. IRES describes itself as specializing in owning and managing residential and commercial real estate assets located primarily in Dublin. It boasts that at the end of 2020, the group's real estate portfolio' consisted of thirty-five 'assets', which were 3,688 apartments, with a market value of €1.3bn. Its net income listed for 2021 is €53.5m.

So who are the shareholders who make the money from IRES REIT's tenants? The largest shareholder, with 18 per cent of their shares, is CAPREIT (Canadian Apartment Properties REIT), a Canadian-based REIT. Other large shareholders include US multinational investor Fidelity; another Canadian company, Vision Capital; UK-based hedge fund investment managers Landsdowne Partners; Irish investment funds such as Setanta Asset Management; and Irish pension funds including Irish Life Investment and Aviva PLC.

IRES REIT is pretty upfront about its purpose and intentions. It describes itself as 'a growth-oriented real estate investment trust focused on building a portfolio of residential rental accommodations . . . for the purposes of rental income located in major urban centres across the island of Ireland'. Its main objectives are to create 'growing cash flows through investing primarily in multi-unit residential properties in Ireland . . . to grow asset value and maximize shareholder value' and 'to provide investors with stable and growing dividends'.

So Irish homes have now become 'assets' for global and Irish investment funds. Renters are the 'growing dividend' for investors who want to maximize and grow their return. There's something deeply disturbing about Irish homes being listed on the Irish Stock Exchange and traded on global stock markets as commodities like stocks and shares. As more people are forced to rent from the funds and REITs, their rents rise. Subsequently share prices rise; and then profits rise. The purpose of housing is being warped into maximizing shareholder returns.

A dystopian future

This is the dystopian future we face. People won't be able to buy a home – they will become impoverished trying to pay the rent, and they won't have a decent-sized home to live in or raise a family in.

The investor funds are not providing a supply of affordable, liveable homes. This is not the future people want, and these are not the homes people need. These developments represent a housing dystopia.

So when the government says it's great to see the increase in the supply of new homes being built, and how they will be getting close to the targets of building 33,000 homes per year, we should take that claim with a pinch of salt. A lot of these are not homes that people want to, or can afford to, live in. If half of those new homes supplied are expensive investor fund apartments, that is not a supply of actual homes people need or will be able to afford. It's absurd and obscene. This is our future, and our kids' future, and our grand-kids' future – unless we do something about it.

The government and investor fund lobbyists make the point that this is what investment funds and corporate landlords do – they make money from property. But that is exactly my point. They are not in it to provide affordable homes. Their business model is based on maximizing profits by lowering building standards (building smaller units), constantly raising rents, renting out at the highest rent possible, and by the displacement and turnover of tenants. Their new rental properties are at extortionate rents, which set the new market rents, and thus propel overall rents upwards.

Some argue that these corporate landlord REITs are only a small part of the overall market and so do not have a major influence on rents. But they are expanding at such a rate that very soon they will be in control of the market. There are already some parts of Dublin where corporate landlords own up to 50 per cent of all private rental tenancies in the area. That means they get to set the local market rent. They have oligopolistic market control in these areas. And this is only going to increase in the coming years. Their current share will quickly become a much larger share.

REITs' business model of constantly increasing rents is utterly unsustainable for our society and economy. More and more of people's income will have to go on rents. That sucks money out of the Irish economy and sends it overseas, or it flows to those who already have money. It is also very risky for our economy to give these global funds a central role in housing provision in Ireland. It puts us at a higher risk of another property and economic crash; it is faulty economic logic. It's inherently risky, based on a flawed assumption of constant rising prices and rents, with a decline or crash inevitable. As the global and Irish economy falters, REITs' investment strategies will change. They are unreliable.

REITs have multiple business strategies to make as much money as possible out of their properties. These include 'rennovictions', where they buy a property, evict the tenants, renovate the property and then get in new tenants on much higher rents. They also find other ways of adding extra charges to increase the overall rent. They leave property vacant until they get the rent they want.

It might seem illogical to leave a property vacant when they could be getting a good rent, but rental yield – what they get each year – is only part of their business. The other part is what they call 'capital asset value appreciation'. For them, it is about the rising value of the property (the asset) over time – so when they sell the block of apartments in twenty years' time they will make much more than what they paid for it. Rising asset values also grow their investment and returns to shareholders. Their long-term game is to sweat the asset (maximizing rents at minimal cost of managing and maintaining properties) while they own it and then, at some point, sell it. They also use the value of these assets, the properties, to leverage more money into their funds, to invest further. For them, the long-term increase in property prices is important. Because they are investing in long-term assets, they can afford to leave rental property vacant. They treat property as an asset, not as a home. The ethical and human need side is never considered. It is a socially criminal act to allow property to sit vacant while our fellow human beings are homeless, living on the streets or stuck in overcrowded homes or in emergency accommodation.

The RTB interviewed a sample of corporate landlords and found that they 'typically buy in blocks with a minimum of 100 or 150 units'. They don't want to have units within the apartment blocks – they want to own them all, because 'having complete control enables them to brand, manage, control and handle the estate as an asset.' This has become an issue with apartment owners citing problems in blocks being taken over by funds. These landlords also say that their intention is to keep on devouring Irish homes. The RTB stated: 'These organizations are ambitious and growing. They all envisage managing property portfolios of several multiples of their current scale in the medium term.'

Cuckoo funds lock home buyers out

The investor funds have also been called cuckoo funds because of the fact that a cuckoo lays its eggs in another bird's nest, where the oversized cuckoo chick hatches and quickly elbows the original occupants over the side. In the same way, by buying up entire developments of new properties these cuckoo funds are crowding ordinary home buyers out of being able to get a home. Many big and small investor funds, REITs and investor landlords are buying individual and blocks of second-hand properties for sale as well.

Families are being outbid massively by these funds. The *Irish Independent* reported that institutional buyers paid up to 32 per cent more than the average price paid by household buyers in Ireland for each home they bought. Large investors paid €2.27bn for almost 4,900 private rented sector properties in 2021. That is an average of almost €430,000 a unit, €104,206 more than the average price of €325,502 paid by households who bought homes then.

Every unit bought up by an investor or developed as build-to-rent is a home lost. It is a house or apartment taken away from being a secure, affordable home and converted into an investment asset, locking some household into unaffordable housing for their lifetime.

Adding to growing inequality

Because these investor funds have a global reach, they provide a channel through which the trillions of dollars washing around in global hedge and wealth funds enters Ireland (the wealth funds of the global 1 per cent, the so-called 'high net worth individuals' – the billionaires). Through their local agents – Irish-based headquarters of the funds, real estate firms and estate agents, Irish developers, Irish investment and asset funds – this global wealth is funnelled in, and buys up, and profits from, the rents and property in this country. Through these funds renters are turned into global investment commodities that provide an ongoing stream of income to global wealth funds, pensions, rich investor and Irish pension funds and investors. This is creating an unprecedented generational transfer of wealth and adds to the growing crisis of wealth inequality. The investor funds buy up the homes that should be going to young people in Ireland, who now instead have to rent, and their rent makes the 1 per cent and the already wealthy and financially secure even wealthier and more secure, leaving others in a permanent state of insecurity, owning very little.

And because the funds are part of this global 'wall of money', they have an endless war chest of billions to keep funnelling into Irish property and to outbid Irish home buyers and affordable housing providers. International institutional investors went from investing nothing in Irish real estate before 2008 to investing 74 per cent of total real estate investment in Ireland in 2020. If that isn't game, set and match, I don't know what is. There is no limit to their purchasing of Irish homes and land and development of build-to-rent. They are not going to pull back or ease off unless we stop them. They will make housing permanently unaffordable in Ireland. They are also adding to another housing bubble.

Rents are low risk and high return

Another reason why rental property – residential real estate – is so attractive to global wealth funds is that it provides a guaranteed rate of return on their investment, and the higher the rents the higher the return. It is called a 'low-risk' investment. A country like Ireland that allows new rental properties (which is what the investor funds are now buying or building) to be rented out with no caps on the rent means the sky's the limit for the rent they set. And on top of that, they are then guaranteed a minimum 2 per cent annual increase in existing rents under rental legislation. This makes investment in residential property in Ireland a low-risk, high-return endeavour for global wealth and pension funds. It is the ideal type of investment. They don't want to invest in government bonds or, indeed, in many private companies because the return is lower and more risky. But the rent will always be paid. Governments guarantee it. They make laws that sanction the eviction of tenants who can't pay. So as long as you have a captive market of renters, your return will continue. This is why more and more wealth funds and pensions want to invest in residential rental real estate. They lobby governments to open up more and more housing markets to them. They are hungry vampires looking for more victims.

Ireland's low- to no-tax system for REITs

On top of the high rents, Ireland is so attractive to these funds because they can use our various tax avoidance and reduction schemes to pay as little tax as possible. The government has ensured that the vampire funds pay little if any tax on the massive profits they make. They access the various Irish tax breaks available for investment funds, such as Section 110. As the cherry on top, in 2013 the government brought in a specific tax break for REITs. So not only do the wealth funds get to extract rents from us, they get to make their profit more or less tax-free. And so the funds flow here, so that they can avoid paying tax in other countries, and some of it is criminal money.

While renters have to pay taxes on the wages they earn, their investor landlords pay hardly any tax on their 'income' from the rents. Property investor funds and corporate landlords took in the region of half a billion euros in rent from tenants in their 20,000 or so properties in 2021. They paid hardly any tax on that. That means the country is also losing a potential tax take (which could fund the building of affordable homes) in the region of €200m a year. The tax inequality between renters and REITs is pernicious and Dickensian in its level of injustice. And be under no illusion that the IFSC and the large accountancy firms, along with REITs, have the ear of our government about the importance of these no- to low-tax mechanisms for sustaining the flow of global investment funds into Irish real estate. Ireland is a pot of untaxed gold for these funds.

Irish government gifts social housing to REITs

Just when you think there surely can't be any more possible ways the Irish government has handed our country over to REITs and investor funds, the policymakers found another way to feed the vampires. It is through social housing. Despicably, it too has been turned into a profit-making asset for the funds and REITs.

The government's various rental subsidies for tenants, such as HAP, make Ireland even more attractive to funds and REITs as it further lowers their risk in investing in property in Ireland. They know if they own rental apartments, they will have the State as a potential tenant to guarantee their rent. It is similar with the social housing leasing schemes. Investors are building to rent and leasing the apartments to local authorities. The government is currently leasing 8,000 private market housing units as social housing. For example, the builder Glenveagh sold a development of 87 apartments near the Dundrum Town Centre in one block to German investor Realis for €55m (about €611,000 per unit). Realis then entered a 25-year lease agreement with Dún Laoghaire–Rathdown County Council, which will pay up to €3,000 a month to rent the properties to people on its social housing list.

This approach is hugely more expensive to the State than regular building of social housing, and it turns social housing into a profit-generating asset for institutional investors. If the government built social housing itself, Ireland would be less attractive to the REITs. But instead the government has acquired social housing through leasing and renting from the private market – a juicy treat for the REITs. The number of social housing units obtained through leasing has increased by 145 per cent in just three years, up from 1,100 in 2019 to 2,700 in 2021. This is because the government introduced new guidelines, following lobbying by investor funds, to allow local authorities lease rather than purchase social housing units obtained under the Part V measures that require private developers to provide 10 per cent of units as social housing. Investor funds wanted to keep all the units as one income-generating asset. Having to sell 10 per cent of the units under Part V to local authorities would have reduced their number of units, and therefore reduced the annual rental income stream they received. So the government obliged, and now contributes to the REIT income stream through leasing.

It is important to highlight that it's not just funds and REITs that are buying up apartments and houses. A small but not insignificant number of the new apartment blocks and houses being built are being bought by local authorities and housing authorities as social housing. Between 2016 and 2021, 12,000 properties were bought by the government to use as social housing. They are also buying existing housing (second-hand homes). Now, clearly it is infinitely better to buy property and use it as social housing than allow it to go to investor funds as unaffordable rentals. Nevertheless, it is problematic because local authorities and housing associations are swimming in the same purchasing pool as home buyers, investors and landlords. So more money is going into competing for a limited supply of housing, which inevitably adds to price inflation. It is another illogical housing policy. Purchasing housing in a market with low supply results in the Irish government pushing up house prices.

The government is doing this because it is another way they provide social housing without having to actually build it. Buying the units is an easy way to bump up its delivery of social housing. It makes its quarterly and annual announcements of 'new social housing' look much better. The Minister for Housing and the government look like they are actually providing new social housing. It's similar to the manner in which social housing provided through HAP in the private rental sector is used to inflate social housing delivery figures. But it's playing politics through spin. The government buys units built from the market and then includes it as 'new social housing' in the annual figures, making it look as though it's doing better on social housing building than it actually is. It's also been doing it as a way to 'incentivize' the market. If investors and developers know the State will buy or rent their homes they are more likely to get finance for it, as it's a guaranteed buyer and renter. It's bizarre, really, that the government is taking supply away from a market suffering a housing shortage rather than what it should be doing – adding to the overall supply by building social and affordable housing. But then that would add a supply that might bring down house prices and rents, and offer an alternative to people to having to rent from corporate landlord REITs and institutional investor funds. And who would want that?

Lobbyists

The government's role in bringing in the investor funds and providing them with tax breaks, with beneficial planning laws that reduce standards, and making general housing policy in their interests has been truly shameful and embarrassing. Government ministers and civil servants appear to have been utterly captivated by the investor funds, convinced by their lobbyists and wooed by their massive wealth funds.

The institutional property investors have dominated housing policy. They even set up a lobbying company to do this – Irish Institutional Property (IIP), which describes itself as 'the voice of institutionally financed *investors* with significant international backing in the *Irish* real estate market'. (emphasis mine) Among its members are investor funds IRES REIT, Kennedy Wilson, Hines and Lone Star's Quintain and big developers Cairn and Glenveagh.

According to the lobbying register (which provides records of who is meeting with public officials and government on policy), since September 2019 IIP lobbied officials and the government on forty-seven occasions. The lobbying register also shows that in 2018 Richard Barrett of Bartra Capital lobbied then Minister for Housing Eoghan Murphy for 'the inclusion of units developed under the Enhanced Long Term Social Housing Leasing Scheme as social housing for the purposes of development contributions' under Part V. The *Irish Times* reported that the company had been one of a number of groups lobbying the government to allow councils lease properties over the long term for social housing, instead of purchasing them under Part V. The *Irish Times* also reported that Bartra lobbied the government to cut the minimum investment required under the cash-for-residency scheme, the Immigrant Investor Programme, from €1m to €500,000. Chinese investors accounted for 1,088 of the 1,162 non-EU citizens who have used this scheme to get residency rights for themselves and their families since 2012. Bartra, the *Irish Times* reported, raises cash from investors through the scheme to build social housing and nursing homes. The company has aided about 200 Chinese citizens and their families to get residency in the Republic through the programme. Bartra, remember, is also the developer who received the contract from Dublin City Council to redevelop the public lands of O'Devaney Gardens. As of May 2022, it appeared that potentially up to 50 per cent of the 1,000 units in the development (on public land) could be sold to investor funds.

Because of the government's ideological unwillingness to use the likes of NAMA and local authority land to build social and affordable homes on a major scale, it turned in recent years to the investor funds as the key source of investment in providing the supply of new homes, including new social housing. The anti-public housing ideology and pro-investor, big developer and property fund beliefs led governments and civil servants to embrace the investor funds. The values and business model of the REITs aligned with the ideological beliefs of government. By hitching its wagon to the success of the vampire funds, the Irish government has become dependent on them. It really has been shocking to see our elected government and senior officials in government departments – who are supposed to represent the interests of the Irish people – argue strongly against taxing investor funds or restricting them. Instead they have made the case that we need the investor funds as they are providing a much-needed 'supply' to address the housing crisis. The most distressing policy that has protected the interests of funds and REITs has been the refusal of governments over and over to freeze rents or ban evictions (beyond the temporary Covid measures), because, it argues, that might deter the investor funds. It shows how the interests of the investor funds have come to control and influence our housing policy and impact on everyone in the housing market. A doubling in rents over the last decade has resulted from government policy prioritizing corporate landlord REITs and investor funds.

The narrative to justify this has been that there was no alternative. Just like Thatcher said. There is no alternative to the free market. No alternative to making our people homeless so that investor funds, landlords and REITs can get higher rents. Over the last decade Fine Gael- and Fianna Fáil-led governments have stated that there is no alternative but to hand over our housing to the global investment funds and REITs. It's a neo-colonialist mindset. They are playing the role of the quislings in Dublin Castle during colonization. The investor corporate landlords are our new absentee landlords. And they, along with the existing Irish landlords, have evicted tenants and raised rents to rack-rent levels. All backed by our governments and civil servants.

Another example of this is the way the state agency set up to provide funding to small-scale housing developments provided lending to investor funds. This state agency, Home Building Finance Ireland (HBFI), set up a €300m 'Momentum Fund' in May 2020 at the height of the pandemic to 'specifically help housebuilders commence large housing developments in prime locations in cases where funding may not have been available'. But it lent most of it – €242m – to large-scale developers and corporate investors. It should prioritise financing to small-scale affordable developers, such as Ó Cualann Cohousing Alliance, to build affordable homes. But the Irish State financed housing developers to build units that were then bought up by investor funds and corporate landlords. Of the 1,018 units constructed under the Momentum Fund, 841 are now investor fund rental, 92 went to private owner-occupiers, and just 85 went to social housing.

This raises two major problems as the long-term interests of investor vampire funds clash directly with the short-, medium- and long-term interests of Irish home buyers and renters. First, investor funds want and need rents and house prices to rise continuously – and they bake that in as an 'assumption' in their investment calculations. So if we want to freeze or reduce rents, or reduce house prices (which reduces the 'book value' of their asset), these guys are going to kick and scream, and lobby government to stop. Second, the more of the housing market they have and supply, the more influence they have over government. So there is a contradiction in government housing policy: on the one hand, it wants to make housing more affordable; on the other, it promotes a huge role for investor funds whose business model is to make housing more *un*affordable. As corporate landlord REITs become more dominant in housing, their interests have even greater influence over housing policy decisions, which are not the same interests as that of Irish renters and home buyers.

We have to get these funds out of the engine room of the housing policy train and get on a new track, with those in need of homes in the driving seat.

The flawed 'supply' argument

The argument is made over and over by government and the property economists that without this supply backed by global institutional investment we wouldn't have an adequate supply of new homes. But just any supply is not necessarily a good supply. Unaffordable, small, for-profit rental homes dominating the supply is not the right type of supply.

What is the point of the main supply of new homes being expensive rental homes that nobody can afford to live in, that will be left vacant, that will push renters into poverty and convert a generation into wealth generators for global wealth funds and Irish pension funds?

The most important thing about the new supply of housing is that it should be affordable. But in Dublin, new real estate fund developments are advertising two-bedroom apartments to rent at €2,500 a month. That rent would eat up over 70 per cent of the monthly take-home income of someone on €50,000 a year. How can they afford to live on that? These are not homes – when someone, or a family, is paying €2,500 a month in rent, and looking down the road thinking, 'How will I be able to afford this when I retire?' Where is the long-term thinking? These rents are not sustainable for renters. This is not a supply of affordable homes.

By being over-dependent on this 'supply', the government has made our housing system unaffordable for all, in order to make it profitable for a few vulture and cuckoo investors and property speculators. Our housing market has been deliberately made and allowed by our government to become unaffordable for most people so that it can make massive profits for a few investors and landlords – a small group of Irish and global wealthy investor funds. It's inequality laid bare.

The argument by some economists that we need these investor fund developments because they will add this supply that will (at some hazy point in the future) bring down rents is also flawed. The supply provided by these funds will never lead to reduced rents. It is trickle-down free market economics baloney.

There is not a city in the world where real estate funds have led to a drop in rents. They are building apartments now because there is an imbalance between supply and demand. They need that imbalance – they thrive in a situation of housing crisis and shortage. They want a permanent housing shortage, a permanent housing crisis. That is their business model. They will reduce their new building, as will private developers, as soon as it appears there might be a level of supply that could address that imbalance. Why would they build a sufficient supply of homes when that would mean rents and house prices would fall? These funds don't want to build to a point of saturation and flood the market.

The funds are able and willing to pay much more than home buyers because the returns from renting their properties are so high. They know that the more they lock people out, combined with the huge demographic demand, and the lack of building of social and affordable homes, the higher the return. But this completely contradicts the government's and property economists' arguments that the supply of housing by investment funds will reduce rents. How can that happen if the investor funds and REITs are investing on the basis that rents will not fall, and will in fact continue at these inflated levels and increase into the future? They will never allow rents to fall, unless they are forced to by policy and an alternative supply of more affordable rental properties (i.e. public affordable and social housing).

They will let the properties lie vacant so they don't have to rent them out at lower rates. You can see this in places like London. They can do that because, to them, these are assets; and they will hoard their assets to increase the capital value.

The funds and REITs also add to overall house price inflation through the massive global funds they channel in here. It is logical – if you have a limited supply. And these guys are bringing in an unlimited amount of global cash. They drive up the prices by being able to throw more and more cash at buying up property. The Central Bank lending limits, which are supposed to keep a lid on rising house prices and prevent another property price bubble, don't apply to them. So we are in another property bubble. During the Celtic Tiger it was banks lending excessively to buy-to-let landlords that started the locking-out of homeowners. Now investor funds are picking up where they left off, but they have even more money from the global funds, and homeowners have even less, because of Central Bank limits, and the supply is restricted too, so the investor funds are winning hands down.

The lack of an affordable housing supply in Dublin has knock-on impacts on housing around the country. People can't afford to buy in Dublin because investor funds have taken over so they are forced to try to buy or rent homes in the commuter counties of Kildare, Meath and Laois, which adds to pressure on rents and house prices there too.

Investor funds don't just outbid home buyers, they also outbid social and affordable housing providers trying to buy homes and land. The land issue is central. Because of the Build to Rent planning regulations – which allow you to put 1,600 shoeboxes in 16-storey high rise apartments on a site and every single one of them can be rentals – the most profitable way to develop land is through build-to-rent. So every piece of land becomes a potential build-to-rent site in the eyes of an investor fund or developer. And because they can pay much higher prices for land, they can outbid any small- or medium-sized Irish developer or builder seeking to build medium-density family homes, or housing associations or not-for-profit housing providers trying to get land to build affordable homes.

Land costs can be up to a third of the cost of a home, particularly in cities. By pushing up land prices further, they are locking out the potential for new affordable housing. So the level and reach of investor funds into the Irish housing market is distorted and disproportionate. It is making our housing system even more dysfunctional.

Market supply and demand

In classical economic theory, the supply of products such as computers and cars is best achieved through allowing the 'hidden hand' of the free market do its work without interference from the State. The market, according to economists, is the best way to allocate resources in the economy. The market works by allocating resources to provide a supply of a particular product that will meet the demand for that product. When supply is low and demand is high (such as in housing), prices are high. These high prices, the theory goes, then signal to the suppliers (the construction/development sector) that more supply is demanded, and they will produce it. The high prices mean that it will be profitable for suppliers to produce the products to meet the demand. The market theory then says that supply will increase, thus meeting demand, and at the point the supply and demand lines in the graph cross, prices will fall and stabilize. And efficient market allocation will result in a point of equilibrium, where supply equals demand on an ongoing basis that delivers the product, such as housing, at 'market prices' that make it profitable for the supplier and that the consumer (demand) can and is willing to pay.

But there are fundamental problems with applying the theory of free market economics to housing. First, demand is not just wanting to have something; demand only exists when a consumer has the ability to pay for the product. But many people don't have the ability to pay for a house, to get a mortgage, or rent, so they are not counted as a 'demand', even though they have a clear housing need. This is where the market and economics approach to housing runs into trouble. You can have a housing need, but the market doesn't see or respond to housing needs, it only responds to demand expressed through the amount of money you have to spend on housing.

Another assumption that free market economics makes that doesn't apply to housing is that there are lots of suppliers who compete with each other to lower the price. But in housing there are only a few suppliers (large developers, investor funds and REITs) who have enough funding and land to supply housing. Housing developments also take time; and they are risky because you are not guaranteed the price until you build the product, and that could be in a few years' time, when prices might have fallen, so unless you have access to large financing and lots of different projects that spread your risk, it is very difficult to do.

So the big developers and investors have a monopoly control on housing supply. They effectively control the market. And thus they don't face competition to reduce their prices or to provide a supply, even when prices rise. They also make their profit from the market in different ways. They can make a profit from sitting on their property or land, hoarding it for years, watching prices rise, and then selling it. They don't just make their profit from supplying homes to meet demand. This is speculation; speculative development that is essentially treating the housing market like a giant casino. The land is their chip, and they take a bet on it. Maybe let it sit there, maybe sell, maybe build. It is just a speculative asset.

An example of this is the huge number of planning permissions that developers and investors have for land, but that just lie dormant. There are literally tens of thousands of homes that have planning permission to be built, but their developers are not building them. This is because of the suppliers' speculation on the housing market. The property investors and developers are waiting for prices to rise further before they either sell (flip) that land with planning attached. Or because they are waiting until prices and rents go higher still to build on it, and again make higher profits. So they drip feed a supply onto the market, leaving a housing shortage in place.

And because they control the supply, they can control the market. They can produce just enough units – a supply that doesn't meet demand, but keeps prices and rents rising – to maximize their profits. These are also called supply-side distortions, and they are endemic in housing. People's need for housing is not a demand that provides enough profit for the market to supply housing. So people's housing needs are not met.

Because investor funds and developers are only building if rents and prices remain at a high level that gives them sufficient profit, as soon as rents and house prices fall, they will turn off the tap of supply, and try to retain high rents and prices. We can see this in the units that are left vacant or let out as short-term tourist lets rather than reducing the rents.

Government has over the last decade looked at all its housing interventions from the viewpoint of the market. It has focused its policy effort on developing measures to increase house prices to make a demand that is profitable enough for the investors and developers to provide the supply. Rather than make housing cheaper and more affordable, government policy has been making it more expensive.

Schemes like Help to Buy and the new 'First Home' shared equity scheme are run on that principle – we give home buyers higher mortgages so they can pay a higher price for homes that are sufficiently profitable for developers and investors, rather than we need to provide affordable housing and find out how we can bring prices down to achieve that. Policy should be about getting house prices and rents to fall, not pumping them up. The Croí Conaithe developer gift scheme is another example. Developers of apartments around the country will get up to €140,000 subsidy per apartment they build, with no requirement to sell them at affordable prices. They are a subsidy to keep the market propped up. While they are targeted at first-time buyers, they can be sold at market rates. It's like a state provided ATM service for developers, to enable them withdraw unlimited cash, with no strings attached, from the Irish exchequer.

The market on its own will never supply enough affordable housing to meet housing need. That is because a lot of people simply do not have enough money to provide a profitable demand, and so the market won't build housing for them. And because housing is so expensive to build and develop, there are a small number of suppliers in the market who essentially will control and manipulate the market in housing to maximize their profits from those who are trying to buy or rent homes.

It is important to highlight that market theory doesn't include the largest potential supplier of homes – governments and the State (through local authorities, not-for-profit housing associations, etc.) – because markets don't believe states are efficient. This is one of the biggest fundamental flaws in the market approach to housing. It ignores a key potential provider of housing in its models.

The perfect market has never and will never exist in housing. That is why the idea of the housing market being broken is flawed in itself. The housing market is always broken for affordable housing. If you leave housing up to market supply and demand, only those with money will get homes. We need an alternative way of delivering housing – the market supply and demand approach doesn't work. That's why governments need to intervene to provide a supply.

People are desperate for a home and they will pay whatever to try to get that home. There are no rational economic actors in the housing market. There is no point at which a person who needs a home says, 'Oh, I won't pay that rent or house price cost because I'm deciding I don't need a home.' They will bury themselves in debt to get a mortgage or go hungry to pay the rent because they need a home. The market cannot be relied on to meet that need. There has to be major government intervention in the market, through supplying homes. Abstract economic models do not apply to the real world of housing need. Housing is a basic human need and human right, so we cannot allow the economics of the free market determine its supply and demand.

We should not be trying to fix the housing market, because it cannot be fixed. Housing cannot be treated like markets for computers, cars, or oranges. The market does not work in housing. There is no equilibrium where supply meets need. It is always out of kilter because markets fail all the time in housing. It comes back to what is right and wrong. We need to ensure people have a home. Housing is a human right and everyone needs it. The market won't do it.

Instead, we need to realize that, just as in health and education, where we do not rely on the market to provide hospitals and schools – it is the government that provides – so too in housing – the government must play a central role in delivering affordable housing. Otherwise we will have a permanent housing crisis, going round in circles wondering why we can't fix the housing market, when the problem *is* the housing market.

Smoke and mirrors

The measures introduced to reduce the role of investor funds in buying up homes after the public outcry in May 2021 was just smoke and mirrors. The government had no intention of them ever working to stop investor funds. They were introduced to try to give the impression the government was doing something in response to the public clamour. But there was no substance to the measures. The stock market share values of IRES REIT rose significantly the day after the government's announcement. That said everything about the government's real intention and its impact. Investor funds and REITs continued to dominate the new homes market in the following months, and since. As soon as the public outcry died down, within a few months it was reported the Department of Housing was planning an international 'road show' to attract even more investor funds to Ireland.

The measures to reduce the role of big investment funds was restricted to what the government called 'traditional family homes'. Which basically means three- and four-bed semi-detached estates of houses, not apartments or duplex town houses. No measures were introduced to stop investor funds taking over apartments.

But apartments are homes too, especially for smaller households, singles, city workers and families.

What a horrible, 1950s, patriarchal, conservative, elitist view of what types of families should be protected from investor funds, and who should be left exposed to their exploitation. The queen of right-wing conservatism, Margaret Thatcher, would be proud of such a policy. Basically the nuclear family of two parents with two incomes – the only ones who currently have any chance of affording to buy a house – are the only ones being offered a figleaf of protection by the government from the investor vampire funds. But the single person, the lone parent (overwhelmingly women), the person with disabilities, the older person looking to downsize, anyone trying to buy an apartment or smaller town house or duplex – has been utterly ignored, abandoned by government to the clutches of the vultures. Even the Croí Conaithe is most likely going to benefit investor funds. Because the apartments can be sold at 'market prices', it means few first-time buyers will be able to afford them. As of May 2022, the government was allowing developers to sell the unsold units after one year to investment funds.

We can see the continued investor fund and REIT takeover of our housing system in the type of housing being granted planning permission. In 2021, the majority (60 per cent) of homes granted planning permission were apartments, a huge increase on previous years. They are all likely to be planned by investors fund and corporate landlord REITs to be rented out at unaffordable rents, and some as social housing. It shows how investor funds are coming to dominate the new housing supply. A total of 43,000 units were granted planning permission in 2021, but 26,000 were for apartments, and just 8,500 (one in five) were for scheme developments that will be houses people can buy. So just 20 per cent of the much-lauded 'new supply' that the government is banging on about will actually be homes that ordinary people can buy.

The REITs and funds are also targeting the Dublin commuter counties like Meath, Kildare and Wicklow, and they are extending their clutches to other main cities, Cork, Galway and Limerick. Galway's first build-to-rent apartment development is planned by US investment firm Quadrant Real Estate Advisors with Irish developer JJ Rhatigan. In Limerick, an investment fund called Novelty ICAV (an ICAV is an Irish Collective Asset-management Vehicle!) and Davy Global Fund Management Ltd are trying to develop a 14-storey build-to-rent tower block. Limerick Council granted planning permission for it, but permission was overturned by An Bord Pleanála as it was not considered proper accommodation.

The government's 2021 Housing for All plan is also completely dependent on the private market, and particularly on global investor and vulture funds. Of the €12bn a year required to build the planned 33,000 homes, €10bn will come from 'private capital sources'. Of this, 'the majority will be required from international sources . . . coming from well-established investors'.

So the private market and investors are to provide 83 per cent of new homes, with the State playing a small role, financing less than one-fifth of all new building. This is history repeating itself. The causes of the current crisis is the low level of state building of social and affordable housing since the 1980s. Now we have the addition of global funds that view Irish housing as the gift that keeps on giving.

It also seems inherently risky to hand over responsibility for the supply of social and economic infrastructure essential for our society and economy to function to global equity funds. Making ourselves dependent for housing on the investment decisions of investment and wealth fund managers in the USA, Germany and Canada seems a bit bonkers. Given the current global economic and geopolitical uncertainty it is not very sensible to be relying on a speculative flow of highly mobile international capital to fund and provide our people's homes.

Our very own government and Department of Housing are continuing to court global real estate funds to come to Ireland. They are leading 'engagement with institutional investors, including trade-show events, to communicate policies and encourage sustainable investment in residential accommodation'. A Department of Housing 'investment group has invited funding partners to attend and present to the group on their role and experience in funding residential housing delivery'.

It's not just the REITs either; there are Irish landlords, and large property owners and developers, who are also doing essentially the same things as investor funds – buying up land and homes, turning them into rentals, pushing up prices and locking people out of affordable homes. It's all the same: those with money to invest are turning homes into profit-generating investments – a commodity.

And adding to all this, in spring 2022 the government required young workers to auto-enroll into pension schemes. This is to cover their utter failure to provide affordable homes. As people will now be lifetime renters, as home ownership rates collapse, the issue has emerged of what to do when you retire and you are still paying high rents. The government's solution is not to build affordable homes for you, but to require you to put your wages into a pension fund that you will be able to use to pay your rent when you retire. But that pension fund is highly likely to invest your pensions into REITs and investor funds, which will then use your money to buy up more property and develop build-to-rents. So because of the government's unwillingness to build homes, your own money is likely to be used to lock you out of owning a home, and lock you into a lifetime of paying rent to the corporate landlord REIT. The pension scheme is so you can keep paying the REIT's rent when you retire.

It seems the private developers, landlords and REIT investor funds have a firm grip on the steering wheel in the engine room.

Berlin shows the danger of REITs

What has happened in Berlin gives us a glimpse of our future if we continue with REITs and investor funds. In Berlin, the large corporate landlords bought up close to a quarter of all homes in the city. About five of the big REITs own 250,000 homes. One company, Deutsche Wohnen, owns around 111,000 rental apartments. Some of the same corporate landlord investor funds that own property in Berlin are also now buying up in Ireland too (such as Patrizia AG and Union Investment). As in Dublin, rents have increased massively, tenants have been evicted and people cannot get an affordable home because the investment funds have taken over the market. That is where we are heading if we don't stop soon.

In Berlin, in 2020 the local government put in place a five-year rent freeze and rent reductions, but then the national court overturned this. So the local Berlin residents and tenants' unions organized a referendum that would require all corporate landlords with more than 3,000 properties to sell them to the City Council of Berlin and use a public agency to manage them and rent them out affordably. And they won it: 56.4 per cent of Berlin's residents voted in favour of putting the REITs apartments into a public agency to rent them out affordably. This has been the first major challenge to the drive of global finance.

There is another way

Some commentators claim that labelling investor funds and REITs as vulture funds creates a hostile environment and might put them off coming here. Well, I've explained pretty clearly why we do not need them and why they are making housing more unaffordable. So let's keep calling them what they are – vulture funds and vampire funds – and let's build a groundswell of support for a major policy shift that would eliminate their tax advantages and preferential treatment, and reduce rents, and build affordable homes. If they decide to stop investing, that would be a good thing. We have too many of them here already.

An Irish investor fund advisory firm pointed out that 'current housing policy has benefited both institutions and developers at the expense of individual buyers', and that the potential 'risks' for institutional investor funds like IRES REIT came from 'a potential change in government policy' such as 'a more interventionist approach aimed at improving housing affordability'. It is time for us to make that 'risk' a reality. Housing policy should benefit individual home buyers and renters at the expense of investor funds and developers. And government policy must become interventionist to make housing affordable.

If we put a high tax on all the vacant land they hold, they will have to sell it – which will lead to lower land prices, and small Irish builders and affordable housing providers could buy the land and build genuinely affordable homes on it. And we can also 'do a Berlin' on it if needed – buy back the units from the funds and sell the homes to people as affordable homes, and for social housing.

Our policy is currently being made on the basis of a manufactured fear among the public about what will happen if these funds up and leave. 'How will we provide a supply of housing?' the investor lobbyists, property economists and politicians ask pointedly of those of us who oppose the funds. It's simple. We will do it just as we did in the past – through the State funding and building housing, and through Irish developers and builders building it. Are we really saying we cannot provide homes for our people unless global real estate funds do it? Are we saying that we could build sufficient homes for our people in the 1950s and 1960s, when we were a much, much poorer country, but we cannot do it today, when we have the fifth highest GDP per capita in the world? Don't buy the manufactured fear; it is a narrative created so that we think we have no choice but to accept the dystopian future of unaffordable rents in the micro-homes of the investor funds and corporate landlord REITs. It's not true. There is another way.

Chapter 11
Affordable Sustainable
Gaffs for All

The climate and housing emergencies:
Solving them together

When we think of our homes and being homeless, we also need to think of our common home upon which we all rely as a global human species – our planet. Our planetary home is on fire and faces potential destruction. As humans, we have no other home. The billionaires who shoot off into space say there are alternatives. But earth is our only home. And all of humanity across the world is on the brink of becoming homeless. We are destroying the very home that gives us life and in the process we are threatening the potential existence of future generations. Humankind, along with millions of wonderful and vital plant and animal species, is faced with extinction. The climate of our planet is in turmoil, and we are causing it. Changing weather patterns, rising sea levels, floods, storms, heatwaves, rising global temperatures, and biodiversity and habitat destruction are all part of climate change caused by the burning and consumption of fossil fuels. This is already leading to the loss and destruction of millions of people's homes. And the homes of billions will be destroyed, and these people displaced, if we do not reverse the damage we are doing to our climate.

David Attenborough laid out starkly what we face in his speech to the COP26 Summit 2021:

> Ultimately the climate emergency comes down to a single number – the concentration of carbon in our atmosphere, the measure that greatly determines global temperature . . . our burning of fossil fuels, our destruction of nature, our approach to industry, construction, and learning are releasing carbon into the atmosphere at an unprecedented pace and scale. We are already in trouble – the stability we all depend on is breaking . . .
>
> [Is this] how our story is due to end? A tale of the smartest species doomed by that all-too-human characteristic of failing to see the bigger picture in pursuit of short-term goals.

Without rapid and massive fundamental reductions in our consumption patterns and emission of greenhouse gases, irreversible and catastrophic climate change is inevitable.

But there is still time to avoid a catastrophic future in which the human species makes ourselves permanently homeless. Climate change is real, it's happening, and it will have major impacts on us, but we can still survive and thrive, if we make radical changes now. And it is in our homes and housing that we can make huge changes to not just reduce but to eliminate the destructive consumption of fossil fuels, and achieve our climate change targets.

We can also solve the housing crisis and address the growing gulf of income and wealth inequality through a new green approach to housing.

We can achieve this through building affordable, zero carbon new homes, renovating vacant and derelict buildings, retrofitting existing homes, and planning and using our cities, towns and villages to deliver affordable, healthy, decent standard, sustainable homes that will also help us adapt to survive the changing weather of floods, storms and heat waves. Through these new green homes, we can also create new ways of local food production, caring economies, and societies in which everyone works together towards the common goals of our individual and collective wellbeing, and the wellbeing and sustainability of the planet.

The foremost global scientists on the UN Intergovernmental Panel on Climate Change in their 2022 report pointed out that meeting the 'needs for healthy, decent, affordable and sustainable housing' is 'a global opportunity' to plan and design housing and community infrastructure using social policy knowledge and nature-based solutions that are inclusive of all, in particular youth, women and the most marginalized.

David Attenborough named construction as one of the main areas we have to change. We need to go beyond the existing regulations and eliminate the use of fossil fuels in new home building. We need to make our homes energy-efficient, reduce energy consumption and switch to renewable energy. But the cost of major retrofitting of a home or making or purchasing a new sustainable home is beyond most people's means. Government is leaving individuals with the responsibility to pay for changes. Just as it has during the housing crisis, it is leaving the climate crisis response up to the private market. We have seen the disaster the market has made of housing. It will do the same in relation to the climate. The climate targets are insufficient and even those will not be reached under current policy approaches. The scale of change needed is transformative.

The current neoliberal market economic model is driven by the need for ever-rising levels of profit, which means a constant increase in production and more consumption. It funnels wealth to the top, and excludes a majority, resulting in massive inequalities. The relentless drive to get more markets, get people to consume more, all requires greater use of natural resources in a planet of finite resources. Each year the equivalent of the resources of 1.7 planet Earths are consumed, which means we are exceeding the regenerative capacity of our planet. Corporations and their billionaire CEOs have developed global consumption and production chains that are destroying our planet and our social bonds. Profit margins and shareholder returns are the overriding priority for them, as is the case with the majority of large developers and investor funds providing housing. These private companies will not make the necessary environmental changes unless they are regulated and their business model is fundamentally realigned with social and environmental needs.

It is in the building of new housing that the over-reliance on the private market to deliver housing is really problematic. The government has been reluctant to put in place higher building efficiency standards in order to keep costs down and profits high for real estate investment funds. High-rise developments are more environmentally destructive than mid-rise, compact, passive housing. But the private market, particularly Ireland's new build-to-rent landlords, the global real estate investor funds, want to develop massive high-rises, while developers want to build suburban four-bed semi-detacheds. Neither is sustainable.

We need to change how we live and to do this we need to change the economic and social model that is based on unsustainable consumption patterns, an unsustainable drive for continuous growth that produces unsustainable levels of inequality. We have to get off the runaway train, one being driven by a form of frenzied, financialized capitalism. We have breached our planetary, ecological, social, economic and political boundaries.

We must put all our effort into fixing our climate crisis, and with that radically transform our housing system, our towns, villages, city neighbourhoods, as a major part of reducing energy consumption and living sustainably in new ways. The path to having a sustainable collective home for everyone and for every aspect of nature is through making sustainable homes for all of us humans on this planet.

However, we will not achieve this if a majority of people are excluded. Unfortunately, the climate response and policy discussion has been dominated by how we as individuals need to change and take responsibility. This is of course vital, but it misses the large-scale fundamental and structural systems that have to be changed, such as in housing. And it ignores the one hundred largest multinational corporations (including massive construction companies, real estate investor firms, corporate landlords, and cement and concrete manufacturers) and lifestyles of the millionaires and billionaires who produce 70 per cent of all emissions. Too much of the climate discussion ignores social issues and inequalities such as the housing crisis. The story of the climate crisis, as Attenborough highlighted, 'is one of inequality, as well as instability. Today those who've done the least to cause this problem are being the hardest hit.'

These massive inequalities restrict the ability of many individuals to afford to make the necessary changes. Climate policy that is blind to inequality fails to recognize the differing capabilities of individuals to take part in the necessary transition to a zero-carbon future. And those left behind will understandably resist and oppose necessary change. Fundamental structural change and redressing inequalities need a societal and government response, rather than the individualization of blame.

When massive changes in society are required, the lesson from history is that it has to feel, and be, fair. A sense of justice and equality – that everybody is sharing the burden – must be at its heart. We haven't seen that in the climate transition so far. Those who are being hit hardest are young generations who can't get a home; the poorest, low- and middle-income families who can't afford energy costs, the cost of commuting or retrofits; the hard-pressed renters; the people affected by extreme climate events in the developing world. These are the ones paying the cost at the moment. In housing in Ireland, those with money can make adjustments and home improvements and gain the benefits. The gap between those and the majority of people who can't afford to make the changes and are paying ever-higher gas and electricity bills, carbon taxes, and being pushed into climate poverty, will grow. There will be a divisive inequality between those who can afford to buy A-rated zero-carbon homes and those who are stuck living in substandard high-energy-cost homes. If it is just left to the private market and individuals, the transition will be massively unequal. Climate inequality will grow.

Without bringing everyone along together – sharing the benefits – there will be an understandable backlash against the changes, which are essential. You can already hear it. People are saying, 'How can we afford the carbon tax, with the cost of energy? How can we think about the end of the planet if we cannot even afford to get to the end of the week, if we can't pay the rent, the electricity and gas bills, if we are going to lose our home?' Convincing people to come on board the climate transition requires the changes to be fair and benefit low and middle earners from the outset.

That is where state investment in homes – retrofitting and building affordable, sustainable new homes – could be a quick and hugely impactful win for society and the planet. The potential 'cost' of the public not getting behind necessary climate mitigation measures is not sufficiently considered by policymakers. That is shown clearly in the retrofitting plan that is dependent on householders shouldering the cost of changes to their homes. What if householders decide not to retrofit? What if they can't afford to? This isn't considered by a government removed from reality. The climate adjustment will be derailed if it doesn't have public support across society. People are already getting really annoyed at sweetly worded advertisements offering retrofit grants that will make your house 'warmer and more comfortable while also helping the environment' when they can't even afford the bills to heat their home now – or don't even have a home.

The change we need is being framed as our responsibility, but it's really meant to be internalized as our fault, and we will be 'punished' for our lack of income to make the changes, while those with the wealth to make the changes can feel even more virtuous. This is neoliberal social and environmental policy, blaming and making the poor pay for inequality and their 'lack' of climate action. It is the opposite of the climate plan's commitment to a 'just transition' where 'existing inequalities are not exacerbated'. How can youth do their bit to tackle climate if they can't develop sustainable homes of their own? When they're stuck in poor-quality and energy-inefficient private rental?

The political danger is that those people really hurting from the housing crisis and the cost of living crisis will be convinced by right-wing climate sceptics that the climate issue will be a massive unnecessary burden on them, and it's all a conspiracy of the elite. Housing is a central battlefield where we can open the hearts and minds of the public to the need for massive changes for the climate.

For people to make major behavioural change, they need to feel positively motivated. So we need to create ways of changing that are positively beneficial for people, society and the environment. Through delivering sustainable affordable homes in cooperative communities, they can gain and contribute at the same time. Solving the housing crisis must be at the heart of climate action, and it will also help lift people out of poverty and reduce widening generational and social class inequalities. Yes, we need to act individually to make the changes. It all starts with what you can do as an individual. But it is what we do as individuals together that can make the biggest difference. Acting together to change how we do things across the economy – with housing at the centre – can make the necessary transformative changes. It is about deciding to take action yourself, but we must do it with others, with our family, our friends, our neighbours, our communities, our towns, cities and across the country (and ideally the world) to get our governments and business to change fundamentally – and back us, back human need, back ecological need, to make the change.

A new value system for our economy

We need a new value system for a new economic model to solve the climate and housing crises. It has to be a value system based on creating economies where the principal focus is meeting human need and planetary climate needs, not obscene profit levels for equity funds. It requires a turning on its head of the current economic model and housing model. The idea of endless growth and hoarding of private property, land and derelict buildings when we face existential planetary and human survival crises is absurd. The developer- and investor-led model is broken – it is dysfunctional and it is no longer fit for purpose for the planet and for those in need of affordable homes. We cannot just build unsustainably on greenfield sites – we have to do infill; we have to provide affordable homes – involving people in community development. There's a major contradiction in promoting city and town living to reduce transport emissions and achieve the 'fifteen-minute city' while tax breaks and planning policy encourage build-to-rent investor funds to take over new housing provision and to provide unaffordable, high-rise, micro one- and two-bedroom units. Families are pushed into commuter belts to find affordable housing. What's the point in an unaffordable, unsustainable fifteen-minute city that no family or average earner can afford to live in? Essential workers, like nurses, doctors, teachers, having to make huge commutes because they cannot afford to live in the cities or towns where they work is not healthy for them or the environment.

We need new values in how we treat and deliver housing, driven by the delivery of a human right to a home which is environmentally sustainable, affordable, decent and lifetime-secure. Ireland has already signed up to this as part of the 17 UN Sustainable Development Goals (SDGs), which all UN members have agreed to work towards achieving by the year 2030. SDG Goal 11 is Sustainable Cities and Communities, which targets 'access for all to adequate, safe and affordable housing' by 2030. But to address the climate and housing crises together we need to get radical. We need to be visionary and take transformative action. We need to ensure the land and buildings in our towns and cities are put to use according to the common good – to meet human and planetary needs, not the narrow profit interests of private developers and investor funds. Providing homes close to work and school and reducing transport use, particularly car use, is vital. Yet we are pushing families and individuals out to the commuter belts when there are vacant sites and derelict buildings throughout our towns and cities. This is utterly illogical.

We have to reconstruct our values and our economies and societies with a new vision and purpose – one based on ensuring that everyone has their basic needs met in a way that enables planetary survival. One that ensures that everyone's human rights are met. That has to be the new driving principle of our economies – not profit maximization, shareholder stock value, wealth, or property values. And central to that new green economy is the provision of affordable, quality, environmentally sustainable homes, for all. And it is the central task and responsibility of governments, of the State, of people working in social enterprises to deliver that. That is why governments and states must invest at levels we have never seen before, on scales even higher than the post-World War welfare states and Roosevelt's famous New Deal. They must fund the provision of environmentally sustainable, affordable homes for all.

Addressing climate change while at the same time solving the housing crisis, reversing growing inequality and strengthening social cohesion is a profoundly powerful and radical idea. This is a vision for a new green and equal Ireland (and hopefully across the world too). Through changes to our homes, and how we live, as individuals, communities and society, we can provide quality green affordable homes for all that facilitate local economies of thriving, caring communities and food production networked together. Just as the garden city visionaries built groundbreaking, well-planned homes in the early twentieth century, we need a new vision for housing and living that ensures everyone, from the minimum wage workers to guards, teachers, consultants, nurses, to the unemployed, those with disabilities, single parents, Travellers, refugees, can have access to, and can be part of, green sustainable affordable homes in inclusive communities. We need to provide at least half a million new gaffs over the next decade and retrofit half a million more. This can be the decade of providing a million sustainable, affordable homes. These should be truly zero-carbon constructed and retrofitted without fossil fuels. They must be affordable. They should be built in ways that create homes and communities that provide local food production, biodiversity, connection to nature, community caring, and radically reduce car usage through building close to places of work, school and leisure.

There is a generation of young people stuck living at home. There is a generation of renters who feel they will never have a secure, energy-efficient home of their own. Imagine if we empowered them to be involved in designing, creating and building their own new green affordable homes.

We must approach this with the same vigour with which the Irish State rolled out electricity in the 1940s, delivered free secondary education in the 1960s, built local authority homes in the 1950s and 1960s; in the same way people worked together in cooperatives – the meitheals. We must tackle this as we worked together as communities during the Covid pandemic – all working together towards a common aim, the common good, our individual and collective wellbeing.

Everyone living in a sustainable, decent-standard, healthy, affordable, secure home in ecologically sustainable communities. Shouldn't that be the thing Ireland aims to be number one at in the world? Wouldn't it be incredible to be a beacon of hope for the world? Why don't we aim to be the place that shows what the future can be for climate sustainability and social equality, human rights and justice for all? That is a new vision for Ireland.

The old ways are no longer feasible. The planet is burning and through housing we can help save it, and provide affordable, warm homes for all. David Attenborough put it well: 'We're going to have to learn together how to achieve this, ensuring none are left behind. We must use this opportunity to create a more equal world and our motivation should not be fear but hope. Can we fix the climate problem in one generation? My answer would be yes, we have to.'

Real zero in housing and construction

Scientists say that we need to go beyond net zero carbon emissions to real zero. Net zero means we continue to emit carbon into the atmosphere, but we are extracting as much as we are producing. That still means we are producing huge amounts of greenhouse gases.

It also means that rich countries and big corporations of the Global North continue to pollute and burn fossil fuels, but they buy 'carbon credits' from poor countries in the Global South, or pay for tree planting or conservation projects to theoretically 'offset' carbon emissions. It's an accountancy trick. Basically, polluters in wealthy countries can effectively keep polluting by shifting responsibility for their pollution and adding more of a burden to already vulnerable communities suffering from the effects of climate change.

Getting to real zero means reducing and stopping carbon emissions before they get into the atmosphere. It means transforming our energy systems to 100 per cent renewable sources.

Housing and construction in particular is an area where we need to get to real zero, not just net zero. In 2018, the residential sector produced the equivalent of seven million tonnes of CO_2 (greenhouse gas emissions), or 10 per cent of the country's greenhouse gases. Three-quarters of our homes rely on fossil fuels for heat. Irish homes are very poor in terms of energy efficiency; three-quarters of our housing stock has a BER rating of C or below. Emissions from the housing sector actually increased in 2020 by almost 9 per cent compared to 2019. This highlights the need for our houses to become far more efficient, particularly in the context of broader home working.

The Irish Climate Change Advisory Council monitors how Ireland is achieving the transition to a low-carbon, climate-resilient and environmentally sustainable economy. It highlights that the government's proposed actions on the residential sector 'will not be sufficient to meet the target of 51 per cent emissions reduction by 2030, nor to eliminate emissions before 2050'. It says that 'ambition needs to be ramped up, and measures to accelerate the programme will need urgent consideration. There is no plan for a path to 2050.'

There is a fundamental flaw in Ireland's Climate Action Plan. It doesn't include in its targeted reductions the greenhouse gas emissions produced during the construction of homes; it only aims to tackle the greenhouse gases emitted from existing homes.

Construction is an incredibly carbon- and energy-intensive process. Greenhouse gas emissions caused by constructing buildings are known as 'embodied carbon emissions' and are a significant driver of climate change. They come from extraction, such as quarrying and mining, manufacturing, transporting building materials, replacement, demolition and disposal. Embodied carbon emissions account for up to 75 per cent of a building's total emissions over its lifespan. After burning coal and oil, cement manufacturing is the most carbon-intensive activity on earth. Cement accounts for 40–50 per cent of emissions related to the materials used in construction. And we need to build 500,000 new homes in Ireland between 2022 and 2032.

The size of homes is also significant. Larger homes can send carbon emissions through the roof. The average new-build detached house in Ireland has an average floor area of 241 square metres, an increase of 60 per cent since 2000, thus wiping out the 60 per cent improvement in energy efficiency in the same period. Large luxury homes are the biggest emitters.

To reduce the total greenhouse gas emissions from the residential sector by a half by 2030, as the climate targets require, means radically reducing embodied carbon as well – in the process of new building, and in how we provide 'new' homes, in particular the need to use vacant and derelict properties.

It is also important to point out that retrofitting also requires producing materials like insulation, heat pumps, solar panels, new windows, doors. All of these involve embodied carbon, which needs to be reduced, for example by using bio-based construction products and recycled materials.

Different types of building – high-rise apartments, semi-detached homes, offices – have different levels of embodied carbon. The embodied carbon cost of building commercial offices and high-rise apartments of 11–15 storeys is almost 40 per cent higher than building detached or terraced houses or low-rise apartments (3–5 storeys) and 56 per cent higher than building four-storey maisonettes and town houses. This is a real issue that needs to be addressed. As investor funds dominate our housing market, Ireland is building more high-rise apartment buildings than ever, and so the embodied carbon produced in construction will rise even further.

It also matters where we construct our new homes. There is a higher embodied carbon cost (and biodiversity loss) to constructing houses in 'greenfield' sites, where not just the housing has to be built, but there is also the use of materials to put in new infrastructure such as water systems, wastewater systems, new roads, pavements, even extending rail and bus infrastructure and services, etc. Building on existing 'brownfield' sites in towns and cities does not require the same level of new infrastructure and therefore has a lower embodied carbon cost than greenfield developments.

While retrofitting existing housing stock in line with climate and planning policies could reduce the carbon emitted by the residential sector by over a third (which still falls short of Climate Action Plan targets of 51 per cent), the embodied carbon of new building will increase. Embodied carbon emissions are predicted to account for 40 per cent of all emissions in the residential sector by 2030, offsetting many of the gains of improved reduction in emissions from the existing stock. If we build what is planned on the current basis, environment greenhouse gases from this sector could increase to three times the targeted level by 2030.

So what do we do? We could stop construction completely. But that is not feasible, given the need for new homes, which is only set to increase – the population is expected to grow from five million today to six million in 2050. We need to change what we build and how we build: the materials used (alternative materials such as timber, bio-based alternatives, modular); the type of housing; and how we provide 'new' housing by recycling existing buildings, vacant and derelict buildings, even making use of existing retail and office buildings. Vacant and derelict buildings can be retrofitted at a fraction of the embodied emission cost of new build. But we also need to look at radically reducing the construction of non-home buildings. We should reduce the construction of new offices, hotels and retail buildings, and assess how we could repurpose existing ones. Constructing new commercial buildings is a hugely significant emitter of greenhouse gases. Surely we should prioritize the construction of homes and care buildings, but also seek to reuse, adapt and repurpose existing buildings on a much greater scale. This is a challenge to the entire 'real estate' sector, as it means we need to map and identify all buildings, both privately and publicly owned, and assess them for their impact on climate and social need. All buildings should be treated as part of a new 'commons'; a common resource to be used and developed, not solely according to the profit interests of private owners, but to the social and ecological needs of society and the planet.

A new vision for sustainable, affordable homes

Belfast, like every city, has housing developments that did not involve or consider the local community, resulting in poor design, poor management and poor outcomes. The housing crisis there is getting worse every year, and new solutions are needed. A groundbreaking human rights community organization, the Participation and the Practice of Rights organization (PPR) has taken up the issue of homelessness and sought to involve communities in creating new sustainable, affordable homes on vacant public land. PPR worked with women and children living in a homeless hostel in the New Lodge in north Belfast and has been campaigning and engaging with local authorities for over a decade, including homeless families from across Belfast, in planning, creative protest and political engagement. Central to their approach is a participative model of involving those affected by homelessness in an empowering process of campaigning for, making and delivering change. It empowers those who are denied their housing rights – who are homeless or in hidden homelessness – with the language and policy of human rights to assert their needs in a public way.

In 2021, PPR created an innovative partnership, the Take Back the City coalition, with the expertise of the UK Town and Country Planning Association, an architect based in Queen's University and the homeless families it was working with. I am very proud to say that I have been part of the work of the campaign too. In an act of democratizing the land that is available for homes in Belfast, it made an interactive 'State of Belfast 2022' map of the public land and sites in Belfast that could be made available for housing but remain idle. One of the sites, the Mackies in west Belfast, is a 25 acre derelict public site. It has the potential for hundreds of social and affordable homes, yet it lies vacant. In the local area, there are seven homeless hostels accommodating people on the housing waiting lists.

Take Back the City has developed a participative masterplan that could deliver a sustainable and inclusive community on the Mackies site, and it has invited the wider community to get involved in a process of 'co-design'. But its plans go beyond delivering basic housing conditions to achieving healthy, zero-carbon communities and a non-sectarian housing policy based on meeting the needs of all the diverse communities of Belfast. The homes will be managed on a non-sectarian basis and with a strong culture of peaceful co-existence and cooperation. Its vision is a place that promotes respect and does not tolerate discrimination. And it wants the land to be transferred to a community-led housing body.

Communities can play a leading role in deciding how their homes are planned and designed. Normally it's developers who do this; but through co-creation and co-design processes communities work with planners, architects and engineers to develop a community vision of the future for an area. The heart of this idea is to put those who will live in the homes in the driving seat of the design process. This brings individual and community involvement in creating affordable, sustainable places from the outset.

There are also big opportunities for people to gain jobs and skills as part of these new sustainable home developments. Community-led housing can ensure that these opportunities go first to local people and local businesses. It can encourage and facilitate self-build homes. Community-led housing also generates employment from the management of the homes that are created and through a range of other social enterprises around managing community and food-growing spaces, or childcare. These can also combat loneliness and isolation.

The vision of community-led non-sectarian sustainable housing being promoted at the Mackies site offers a transformational potential for housing not only across Belfast, but also across this island. The social and community sustainable home-building cooperatives and social enterprises set up to deliver these schemes could also be used to support and finance the creation of community social enterprise to buy up and refurbish vacant and derelict housing schemes and land.

Homes as renewable power centres

Making renewable energy sources central to the development of new homes in communities can play a major part in the climate solution. At the moment, it is a very individualized approach to renewable energy – an individual homeowner, or social housing in some cases, might get photovoltaic (PV) solar panels or a heat pump. It might be able to offer excess electricity back to the grid, which a private for-profit company pays for. But there is no coherent approach that could fully utilize the potential for new and existing homes to generate energy that would be provided to communities and also reduce energy bills. In part, this is because the energy companies do not want this to happen as it reduces consumption, bills and their profits. They should therefore be mandated by government to pay, as they do in Portugal, a higher amount for excess electricity generated from renewable energy from individuals and communities.

All new homes and existing buildings should be provided by the State with renewable power generation in the homes themselves, like integrated solar or thermal panels in roofs. Wider district heating is another possibility. Homes could be used as mini renewable energy power stations. This offers a major potential to reduce carbon emissions. Again, leaving this up to individuals or private developers will mean it will only happen on a piecemeal and insufficient basis, and only those who can afford to invest will benefit. For example, solar panels cost in the region of €5,000 to €7,500, and additional associated works may need to be done on the roof, together with a heating system. Yet current grants are only a maximum of €2,400. Many people haven't a spare cent to put into anything beyond daily living costs. While there are some households who have savings and could invest, there are many who have no capacity to spend or borrow. They cannot take on the risk of investing in solar panels because they don't even have enough to cover life's unexpected costs like child illness or car costs.

It also passes the profits to the private energy companies, rather than using the opportunity to generate community benefits and help achieve greater social justice in the transition. It requires a major investment that the State (in partnership with housing associations, community cooperatives and social enterprise) has the capacity, ability and responsibility to deliver, and a change in supporting community energy production and mandating energy companies to facilitate and support this.

There is huge potential for developing community and cooperative energy developments that produce renewable energy on a significant scale. This is a real opportunity to achieve a just transition. We have privatized energy production, handing the profits from energy to a few corporations, when we should instead see energy as a human right and public good. Through local renewable energy production, we could massively reduce cost to individuals but also create a social and public good – public energy production – through our housing.

Irish community energy projects are few in number, but it remains notable that not a single project – planned or developed – provides energy at a low or cross-subsidized rate to local people in energy poverty. The potentially transformative, local wealth-building vision of community energy is reduced to a demand that people with private homes and disposable income can access the electricity grid to consume, produce and be publicly subsidized for energy on the same terms as multinational private interests.

The State should cover the investment for 500,000 households, low- and middle-income earners, in the cost of installing solar panels, and renewables, as part of retrofitting. They should also include it in renovating all vacant and derelict buildings.

Low-rise is better

If we are to make towns and cities where people can work, rest and engage in leisure activities, they have to be liveable and they have to be sustainable. They need to be high-density too, but that can be achieved without high-rise apartments. Three-storey duplex maisonettes, based on Victorian-type rows of houses, can provide eco-friendly, family-friendly, sustainable homes and communities and deliver more sustainable, better-quality, cheaper high-density and low-rise housing than high-rise apartment blocks.

A model proposed by Shay Cleary Architects sets out how three-storey buildings can achieve densities of 100–150 units per hectare. Reducing size reduces planning risks, and it is suitable for infill housing around estates, on brownfield sites, in derelict and rundown buildings in cities, towns and villages. It eliminates costly basement car parking and core circulation – lifts, etc. It provides a major reduction in development cost. It can be delivered using the modern off-site factory construction methods. On the ground floor there might be garden apartments of one or two bedrooms with private rear gardens. Above this level, and accessed by stairs, there could be a duplex maisonette with open plan living and a private terrace, and above that two ensuite bedrooms with access to a private sundeck.

One of the best examples of this is the award-winning development of Goldsmith Street in Norwich in England. It comprises 100 new social homes, built by Norwich City Council, which are the most energy-efficient houses ever built in the UK. They have beautiful brickwork, large windows, angled rooftops to ensure that, even in winter, each terrace will not block sunlight from the windows of the row behind, with walls curving gently around the corners of the street, and hidden rooftop patios. A planted alley runs between the backs of the terraced houses, which has communal tables and benches where neighbours can sit down together and socialize. These are homes built on streets, rather than giant slabs of apartment blocks. The architects reduced the width of the street, creating a human scale of development and fitting in more homes.

Dún Laoghaire–Rathdown County Council has completed a project with a similar vision, on a much smaller scale, though it is intended to be replicated and scaled up. It built four A1 rated social housing apartments at The Mews in Sallynoggin, within an existing estate. As the sustainable architecture magazine *Passive House Plus* describes it, the council and the architects achieved homes that are 'clean and modern in design rather than proffering the "shock of the new", and belong to the community in a general sense of not being jarring'. They 'were able to create a repeatable scheme that, if widely applied, could go some way to both easing the ongoing housing crisis and also improving the overall Irish housing stock'. Built on a garden site, the development helps address the issue of low density in the south Dublin suburb. As it is suitable for elderly or less abled inhabitants it has a further social function in that it promotes continuity and cohesion. It allows elderly residents to stay in their locality, rather than have to move out. It won the sustainability category at the 2018 Royal Institute of the Architects of Ireland (RIAI) Architecture Awards.

Climate inequalities in retrofitting plans

Most homes in Ireland have a poor energy efficiency – three quarters of our housing stock has a BER energy rating of C or less. They lose a huge amount of heat through poorly insulated walls and attics, and through windows and doors. Ireland's homes have almost double the EU average energy consumption level, making the cost of energy crisis so much worse here. Most average three-bed homes cost about €1,200 a year or more to heat, but an F- or G- rated home can cost up to €3,600 a year to heat. That doesn't include electricity or gas for cooking. And energy bills have increased astronomically. So reducing energy bills through retrofitting homes is a real opportunity to reduce energy poverty and achieve our climate reduction targets. A deep retrofit achieving a BER of B2 can reduce heating costs to as little as €380 a year, while an A1-rated home can cost only €200 a year to heat.

A retrofit or home energy upgrade involves carrying out multiple energy upgrade measures in a home, such as wall and attic insulation, replacing windows and doors, addressing airtightness and ventilation and installing a renewable heating system (such as a heat pump), as well as other renewable energy technologies (such as solar PV panels). A heat pump system harnesses energy from free renewable sources outside the building in order to both heat the house and produce hot water. Heat pumps are an environmentally friendly, decarbonized and extremely efficient alternative to oil, gas and solid fuel home heating systems. A deep retrofit involves doing all of these.

The government's plans for retrofitting homes is the principal way it proposes to reduce carbon emissions from the residential sector. Its Climate Action Plan aims to retrofit 500,000 homes to BER B2 standard by 2030. This is estimated to cost €28bn, but €20bn, or 70 per cent, of that is expected to come from householders deciding to retrofit their home.

The amount of money the government has allocated to retrofitting is completely inadequate to fund what is required. In 2023, the State will invest a mere €200m in retrofitting, enough for just 7,000 homes. At that rate it will take seventy years to retrofit the 500,000 homes, missing the 2030 target by sixty years. Just €400m a year is allocated to retrofitting between 2022 and 2026.

The plan is entirely dependent on 'homeowners'. There are no targets for retrofitting private rental homes. There is no mandatory obligation on landlords to invest in retrofitting rental properties.

The Climate Action Plan has completely ignored a million people: renters who make up one-fifth of households. It is delusional, and shows how disconnected from the reality of people's lives the government is, to think that most people can afford to pay for retrofitting their homes. Based on this approach, the climate plan will not achieve its targets, and in fact will worsen climate inequalities, as those with money to invest will be able to pay for retrofits and achieve lower energy bills, while hard-pressed families and individuals who cannot afford to retrofit, or are stuck in private rental homes, will be left struggling with ever-higher bills in a worsening cost of living crisis.

At the launch of the Climate Action Plan in late 2021 Tánaiste Leo Varadkar said, 'Nobody is going to force you to go out and insulate your home particularly when you can't afford to do so.' The message is clear – if you can't afford to retrofit your home, no one is going to help you either. If you can't afford the €50,000 to retrofit your home (which most households can't), you face a future of cold winters at home with rising energy bills. Is the Climate Action Plan restricted to the wealthy?

Vulnerable groups and those on lower and middle incomes who cannot afford to retrofit or build sustainable energy systems into their homes will lose out over and over again. They will be hit by increased carbon taxes and levies, higher energy bills, poor-housing-related ill health, and the incapacity to gain from producing renewable energy through their homes and neighbourhoods.

Individualizing the cost of climate action will inevitably exacerbate inequalities. This risks a public backlash against necessary climate measures. It could lead to massive resentment and potentially scupper the entire Climate Action Plan. Those unable to afford or access energy-efficient homes will see and hear advertisements everywhere encouraging them to 'act for climate change' by changing their behaviour, such as turning down the temperature in their home. Yet they have no choice. They are in cold homes, so if they turn the heat down, they will freeze and get sick. The advertisement blitz will add to people's sense of inadequacy; it will lead to a deeper disconnection and alienation from the climate transition.

Many homeowners can't afford the upfront cost or the loan repayments of a substantial retrofit. They cannot afford to take on even more debt. Renters cannot afford it either; many are struggling already with unaffordable rents, and are trying to save a deposit for a mortgage. Even if they could afford it, why would they invest in making a home energy-efficient when they could be evicted from it in a few months, and then the landlord will benefit from the uptick in property value from a retrofit?

The ESRI June 2022 research showed that energy poverty is at the highest ever with almost a third of households affected and the poor conditions of their homes, such as lack of insulation, is a significant factor. A third of Irish homes are affected by dampness. The St Vincent de Paul Society estimates that 140,000 children in Ireland are living in homes that have a leaking roof, damp walls, floors or foundation, or rot in window frames or floors. Over 240,000 people are unable to keep their house adequately warm. These include low-income families with children, lone parents, renters and people with disabilities. They cannot afford retrofitting. How can Irish households afford to fork out for retrofits when we have one of the highest costs of living in the EU, including rents, mortgages, energy costs and childcare?

A poll by the St Vincent de Paul in 2022 showed that a quarter of renters in the private rental sector and local authority housing have cut back on essentials like food in response to rising energy prices. A half of private renters and local authority tenants are worried about being able to cover their energy bills. Forty-three per cent of homeowners with a mortgage and 27 per cent of homeowners without a mortgage are worried about being able to cover energy bills.

The costs of retrofitting a home to bring it up to the recommended B2 level rating (which is still five grades lower than A1) is between €30,000 and €75,000. Even with a 50 per cent grant, that is a huge up-front cost for many households in this country, who are struggling to pay existing bills and often have nothing left at the end of the month. And the 'green' loans available from the banks have unaffordable interest rates. Forty-five per cent (765,000) of households have a gross annual income of less than €40,000. Twenty per cent of households (340,000) have a gross household income of less than €20,000. That's over a million households who are unlikely to be able to afford to retrofit or integrate renewable energy. And while some households have increased savings from Covid, many are worse off, having been hit by job and income loss, compounded by subsequent inflation and the associated cost of living crisis.

No retrofits for private renters

The fact that the plan does not have a target for private rental retrofits shows the government sees little being done by landlords to retrofit private rental homes. Minimum BER standards for landlords to achieve in their rental properties are not coming in until 2025. Yes, you read that correctly. We are in a climate emergency and landlords have no obligation to act until 2025. Are landlords writing the climate and housing policies? Even then, the requirements for minimum BER standards in the private rental sector have a get-out clause – they only have to be done 'where feasible'. So tenants will continue to be stuck with higher bills and no options. Are tenants to 'play their part' in reducing emissions by turning off the heat and freezing?

Tenants are afraid that landlords will start using retrofitting to avoid the RPZ rules, evict them and raise rents. Landlords can obtain the same grant as homeowners to retrofit their properties, so they can benefit from this state investment. But under current rental legislation landlords can also end a tenancy if they plan to carry out a 'substantial refurbishment' of their property. There is also an exemption available from rules limiting rent increases in Rent Pressure Zones (RPZs) if the landlord plans to make a 'substantial change' to the property, including substantially improving its BER. The new retrofit scheme will appeal to some landlords as a means of circumventing RPZ regulations. Landlords will get a state retrofit grant, then get their tenants to leave (where will they go?) in order to retrofit their property. Then they will put the retrofitted property back on the rental market at a substantially higher rent. There is a requirement for the landlord to offer the property back to the original tenant when it is complete, but if it is at a higher rent then the tenant is likely to not be able to afford it. This is all dependent on the landlord acting in good faith, and there is evidence that many landlords ignore their obligations and the rules. Without major policy change the retrofitting plan will add to rising rents and evictions in the rental sector. There needs to be a system of genuine enforcement by the RTB and local authorities.

In order to ensure the retrofitting of the private rental sector, the government must undertake a number of measures. First, it should bring forward to 2023 the minimum BER rating requirement and require landlords to provide a BER rating assessment and plan for retrofitting their property. In return for getting the state grant from the Sustainable Energy Authority of Ireland (SEAI) towards retrofitting their property, landlords should be required to offer their existing tenant a tenancy of indefinite duration, and the property offered back on the existing rent, including a long-term rent affordability and rent stability agreement, restricting rent increases. Evidence must be provided to the RTB and the tenant must confirm that this has been offered. Where the landlord is not in a position financially to undertake retrofitting, the State should fund the retrofit in return for rent affordability setting and lifetime tenancy for the tenant. If this is not viable for the landlord, the State should issue a Compulsory Purchase Order (CPO) on the property, undertake the retrofit and rent the property to the tenant on a cost or social rental basis.

A third of private rental tenancies (100,000 households) currently have the rent mainly covered by the State in various social housing schemes. These properties should be targeted for retrofitting as they are a form of social housing. Where a deep retrofit is proposed and the tenant has to temporarily relocate, the RTB must be notified, and alternative accommodation provided by the landlord or government while the work is done. Landlords cannot be allowed avail of state grants as a way to further increase rents and evict tenants.

A proper plan to get the private rental sector retrofitted will make much greater progress towards achieving our carbon emission reductions than is currently in the Climate Action Plan, given that the private rental sector is of such poor standard and energy efficiency, and there are no current targets for it in our climate plans. It is bizarre that this is ignored in current plans. Retrofitting the private rental sector will achieve energy efficiency in our worst carbon-emitting homes, and can also be used to provide lifetime tenancies for renters in retrofitted homes at more affordable rents.

Retrofitting social housing

Local authorities and not-for-profit housing associations own more than 250,000 social homes. That provides a massive potential to score a home run for delivering retrofitting and renewable energy production. The government is scoring an own goal instead. The number of local authority homes being retrofitted is absolutely minuscule. It plans to retrofit just 2,400 social homes in 2022 and in total just 36,500 local authority homes by 2030. That means less than a fifth of social housing will be retrofitted by 2030. And there is no clarity on whether that will include solar panels, district heating and other renewable generation options. At that rate of progress, it will take 120 years to retrofit our entire social housing stock. Way too late for solving climate change. The government doesn't seem to realize the enormity of the emergency that we face on climate change. Given the high levels of substandard accommodation – energy-inefficient homes that are also bad for tenants' health – the social housing sector should actually be a priority for retrofitting.

A major enhancement and an increased rate of retrofitting for the social housing and private rental sectors would provide the opportunity for a more socially just transition. Currently, the poorest and most marginalized in our society live in the most energy-inefficient homes that are the most expensive to heat. Providing them with warmer, healthier, sustainable homes and with low energy costs offers a real possibility to achieve a truly just transition.

Dealing with major climate events

As a small island nation we will have to deal with more climate-related weather events in the coming decades, including flooding and heatwaves, which have a particularly acute impact in cities due to the 'urban heat island' effect. Both coastal and river flooding is going to increase. That is not helped by the historical (and ongoing) issue of building on flood plains.

Sea levels could rise by as much as thirty centimetres by the year 2050, leading to an increased occurrence of flooding. It is expected to occur more than ten times as often as it does today. Coastal areas around Ireland are at risk of being partially submerged by flood levels within the next thirty years. That is within our lifetime. Homes in Dublin, Cork, Clare, Kerry, Louth, Limerick, Meath, Waterford and Galway are the most vulnerable, according to the data. Large parts of the coastline of the greater Dublin area are at risk, such as Portmarnock, Donabate, Swords, Howth, Malahide, Bull Island, East Wall, Clontarf, Ballsbridge, Sandymount and Grand Canal Dock.

Where will those made homeless by flooding go? They will need housing support elsewhere.

While it might be hard to imagine in Ireland, there will also be a greater risk of heat events in the future. This could cause health problems, including stroke. It's predicted that the demand for cooling for homes in summertime will increase, as people and buildings overheat. Therefore, the design of new homes, and retrofitting, also needs to consider cooling for adaptation to hotter weather.

We must tackle housing and climate crises together

My six-year-old son asked me if submarines run on petrol or electricity. 'I'm not sure,' I replied. 'Why do you ask?' He said, 'Because I want to use a submarine for my round the world trip, but petrol is bad for the environment, so I'll only go if it's on electricity from wind.' My six-year-old gets it – we have to change utterly to avoid disastrous climate change, and to save our environment, biodiversity and humanity's existence. But the government and business in the area of housing are still stuck in the old ways of continuous consumption thinking. There is a lack of a real strategy for ensuring new housing is a net zero contributor to climate emissions and for ensuring retrofitting is delivered for all.

The housing and climate crisis are two of the biggest issues we have to solve as a country. But while there is a sense of despair about climate issues, we need to realize that there is also hope. We have the opportunity to address the housing crisis and raise people's living standards through providing affordable sustainable homes for all, while also helping address the climate crisis.

Housing can make a major contribution to achieving a genuinely socially just transition, where people, particularly those struggling financially and most affected by the housing crisis, experience an improvement in their quality of life, while also addressing the climate crisis. If people see an improvement in their own homes, there will be greater public support for climate measures.

It is through a new vision for our housing system, based on ensuring environmentally sustainable, affordable, high-quality homes for all, that we can make a major leap forward to meeting our climate targets in a socially inclusive way.

Our current developer- and investor-led housing model is environmentally and socially unsustainable. Business as usual cannot continue. We have had enough greenwashing. Inequalities in housing have been ignored for too long. The vested interests of propertied speculators, investor funds, fossil fuel interests, and an economy based on endless growth in material consumption can no longer hold sway. We need a revolution in delivering energy-efficient, zero-carbon, affordable housing for all, not just as a luxury for the few.

We are not going to meet our climate targets based on the government's current approach to the building of new homes and retrofitting of existing ones. What should be done? The only way to guarantee it is for the State to fund it and to ensure that all the changes set out in this chapter are achieved.

We have to stop talking about the economic costs of retrofitting and building sustainable affordable homes and talk instead about the costs of not doing it. Isn't providing warm, decent-standard, healthy homes for all, saving our planet and ensuring the future of the human race priceless? There is no cost too high to achieve this. We have to instead talk about the social and environmental investment that is absolutely necessary. This is a necessary investment in our present and future generations and the future of humanity and the planet. In crude accounting and economic 'value for money' terms, by making a massive investment in sustainable homes, the State will reduce costs in health spending associated with poor housing (asthma, bronchitis, mental health impacts). Investing in improving the standards of housing can, along with addressing climate targets, also provide huge benefits in improving people's health, which boosts their own human capital and their ability to contribute to their family, community and country. It enhances the overall capacity of our society and economy. The current housing crisis results in a huge waste and destruction of human potential through negative physical and mental health impacts. Providing affordable, sustainable, healthy homes for all would be a major beneficial economic investment.

Substandard housing costs EU economies nearly €194bn per year in healthcare, social costs and lost productivity. Yet the cost of bringing the standard of housing up to an acceptable level across the EU would cost just €295bn. This investment in creating healthy homes would be repaid in just a year and a half. It would reduce the cost of the mental health impacts of the stress experienced by renters and the hopelessness of those stuck in their parents' home, of people disconnected from their communities, isolated and lonely. It would reduce welfare spending (many people are pushed into poverty because they cannot afford to pay their energy bills) and the €1bn a year we spend on housing subsidies to renters. It would also be an economic and social stimulus, as it would provide greater opportunities for people to become engaged in designing, delivering and managing sustainable homes, a caring economy, local food production and engagement with nature. It would provide a real opportunity to retrain and reskill workers in a new green economy. It would offer the opportunity to renew society and improve social cohesion. It would also offer, through individual and community production of renewable energy, greater energy security.

Currently the government has allocated just under €1bn a year of state funding for retrofitting. That should be doubled, to €2bn a year. That would pay for 51,000 retrofits a year. It could include, for example, 35,000 retrofits at €33,000 per home, and 16,000 at €60,000 per home. That would effectively double the level of retrofitting currently planned to be achieved by 2030. The State should provide 100 per cent grants for homeowners and grants for landlords who agree to the conditions of rents and indefinite tenancies set out above. It would fund retrofitting for low- and middle-income earners.

The State should also provide an additional €4bn annually toward the provision of new sustainable homes, through both new build and the use of vacant and derelict buildings and land. This would be focused on sustainable homes built by local authorities, housing associations, not-for-profit social enterprises and community co-operatives, and community-led housing groups.

Why do we allow our whole housing system to be dependent on private developers and builders? The government should set up a public home building agency. It should be a semi-state construction and housing development company to build and retrofit homes. This would guarantee that we'll get the workers to retrofit. We have to build a skilled workforce of qualified green technology and eco construction workers. To get construction workers to retrofit and build sustainable homes requires providing proper employment conditions and attracting them away from unsustainable and less essential construction projects such as hotels, shopping centres and offices. It must provide secure and well-paid employment to attract enough workers, and provide upskilling, training and apprentice-ships. If it is attractive enough, we will get the capacity to deliver. We don't leave the provision and delivery of our public health and education dependent on 'for-profit' private hospitals and private schools – why do we do it in housing?

The government currently spends €22bn a year on health, and only €4bn a year on housing. And of that €4bn, which the government trumpets is the 'largest spending on housing ever', less than €2bn is actually spent on building new homes (capital spending). Almost €1bn a year (a quarter of the entire housing budget) goes to private landlords and property owners through the various HAP, RAS and leasing schemes (current spending).

Yet decent housing is essential for physical and mental health, the economy and the environment. We should and could, therefore, be spending at least €8bn a year on housing, including sustainable housing, doubling the current housing budget. Decent quality, affordable housing is as vital as health to individuals and society. The market cannot be relied upon to deliver sustainable homes and meet social or environmental needs.

For those who say the government shouldn't be paying for this – 'We don't have the money', 'We can't afford it as a country' – I would say that we cannot afford not to do it. We need to look on it as a public service, a common good, a common necessity for all of us. If many cannot afford to retrofit their home, or are stuck in energy-inefficient private rental homes, or we don't build zero-carbon new homes, or we don't use derelict and vacant buildings, we all lose. The climate will lose, we won't reach our targets, our future generations will lose. We will cease to exist as a species.

If we do not do this there will be rising socially divisive inequality between those who can afford to retrofit their homes, and afford renewable energy generation, and those hard-pressed households unable to afford energy-efficient homes. Lower- and middle-income households will be paying the highest carbon taxes and suffer most from ill health related to poor housing. This includes tenants in very poor energy-efficient housing in the private rental sector, social housing and struggling homeowners.

We must approach policy decisions, not through narrow fiscal budgetary rules, the market, or investors' profit agendas, but through the collective needs of society and the planet today and its future needs. Policy should be seen through the lens of a common societal and environmental good. Business as usual cannot continue. The vested interests of propertied speculators, the fossil fuel interests, and an economy based on endless material consumption can no longer hold sway. We need a revolution in how we understand and approach housing, and its link to climate.

This approach is about supporting, empowering and motivating people to be part of designing, delivering, owning and managing new sustainable communities, where everyone will feel better off, and everyone will be a valued and included member of Irish society. That will lead to greater achievements, development and capacity as a whole country, as everyone will be enabled to contribute to their full potential, social divisions will reduce, trust will increase, crime and social problems will fall, civic involvement and solidarity and charity will increase. These are the benefits that more equal, more sustainable countries like Denmark, Sweden and Finland have achieved. Who wouldn't want that?

This is a vision and a pathway for us to deliver a new, reimagined state, society and economy in Ireland – through green homes, communities and social enterprise and cooperatives. It has to be about backing (financing and providing legislation, laws and human resources support) and empowering and involving people in designing, owning, managing, and in new forms of ownership. It's about government-led social enterprise, citizen- and community-led construction and social ownership of healthy, green, affordable housing and communities.

Involving homeowners and social and affordable renters in design of their homes is vital, not only to get homes that people will be satisfied and happy with, but also to get them to manage and maintain them over time, to buy into the home and the community, and to meet the specific needs of elderly people, children and families, people with disabilities, Travellers.

The State can borrow to do this. It can draw from the EU's Green New Deal funds, it can levy corporations and the wealthy. The economic prospects are looking uncertain, interest rates and inflation are rising. In that context, it is even more important, when the private market is likely with such uncertainty to stall its delivery that the State steps in with major financing to do this. The EU rules aren't blocking us; housing is a competency of each member state. The Irish State can do this, if it chooses.

The Covid pandemic showed that states have the money to spend if they want to – it is a matter of political will and political priorities. The response to Covid showed what was possible – not just government- and state-led financial support of individuals and businesses, but also the community spirit and solidarity when people came together to protect each other and wider society. We saw a thriving of solidarity and collective self-help. Covid showed that in order to respond adequately to emergencies and solve massive social crises – and the housing and climate issues are permanent emergencies at this point – a much bigger, caring state is needed to deliver and to fund communities, cooperatives and social enterprises, backing, involving and empowering individuals and society.

Social cohesion in these tumultuous times can be achieved through socially just policy interventions that ensure everyone is included and achieve better living standards for all. It is absolutely essential that those who are struggling today are not made to carry the burden of climate change disproportionately. They need to experience the benefit of the transition, and changes delivered in housing can achieve this. But if it's left to the individual and the private market, it will not work. People will not be able to afford the change, we will fail to meet our climate targets and social division and protest over the transition will lead to a dystopian future.

The great thing is, these ideas are already being realized in Ireland, if on a very small scale, such as in Cloughjordan and by Ó Cualann, Clúid, Respond and Cooperative Housing Ireland, some local authorities, and in community-led housing groups (check them out on the Self Organised Architecture website, soa.ie). They could be expanded to involve young people and Generation Rent in actually designing their homes and then managing and maintaining them as social enterprises and cooperatives. To be part of intergenerational and sustainable communities and have a sense of belonging. That needs to be done, so that people feel they have a future, a purpose, hope. A home is central to that. They need to be facilitated, organized, provided with local infrastructure, with funding. This is about moving our housing and economic system into the hands of the younger generations – away from the developers and investor funds and corporate landlords and banks. This is a green housing revolution – and it is the only way we can meaningfully and in a socially just way address the climate crisis, the housing crisis and inequalities together. It will nurture a generation to create their future based on values of cooperation, solidarity, caring for each other and for the planet. Young people's climate strikes show that they want to act on climate – they are motivated. This is their future. We have to empower them to deliver it.

We can end energy poverty through a just transition. We can improve the living conditions and standards of those struggling and living in poverty. We can achieve greater equality. We can solve the housing crisis.

Chapter 12
Delivering the
Human Right to Housing

Ireland can be the best place in the world to live. We have the most beautiful countryside, the most kind and warm people, who care about community, about social justice, about nature. Why don't we make it the best place for everyone living here? We can be a country where everyone has an affordable, decent-standard, warm, healthy, appropriate, lifetime-secure and environmentally sustainable home. Wouldn't we be so proud if that was the country we had? We would all feel better and more secure, as a society, if everyone had a home, a gaff of their own. We would feel better if everyone had a home that was carbon-neutral, energy-efficient and contributing to renewable energy, rewilding, biodiversity and even community food production. Our children would grow up without the existential worry about where they will live. They are growing up now unable to see a future. That fills them with anxiety and worsens the mental health crisis. Their worries are multi-faceted: Will I have to emigrate? Will I ever have a home of my own? Will I ever become fully adult? Will I ever be able to have a home to raise children in?

Home is the base for everything else in our lives. It is the launchpad for us to be as human beings, for us to become our true and fullest selves, to live the life we have the potential and desire to live.

By ensuring that everyone has a home we can give hope, meaning and motivation to all those currently stripped of dignity, those who feel hopeless and ignored in the housing and homelessness crisis. By making sure they have a home we can give them something to wake up for each day, feeling better about themselves and their society, supporting their physical and mental health, helping and nurturing them to be their best selves. Through providing a home for all we can give every child in this country the start in life they need and deserve. A childhood with a secure base of a home, a place to laugh, play, dream and create. Through a home we can enable people to do the jobs and hobbies they want to do, to be part of their local community, to get an education, to have and raise children, to grow old in security and warmth, to live their dreams, to be motivated to vote in elections, to engage in making their country better, to help those around them. Through a sustainable home with its own green space everyone can connect with nature, plant and grow food and flowers, contribute to their own wellbeing and nutrition and help tackle the climate and biodiversity emergency.

Guaranteeing a home for everyone as a human right would unleash a tidal wave of positive energy and creativity and love into our economy and society that would make us one of the most exciting, dynamic, inclusive, caring, environmentally sustainable, creative, climate-resilient, productive countries in the world.

How proud we would be of an Ireland that ended homelessness, that ensured everyone had a forever home of their own (whether owned or rented), and that put a right to housing in our Constitution. Where every child woke up each morning knowing that, in a world of uncertainty, their country will always ensure they have a home, at every stage in their life.

So how can it be done?

Gaffs for All: Ten key policies that can fix this crisis

The government called its latest plan Housing for All but as with previous housing plans rolled out in the 2010s and 2020s, it hasn't delivered. Central Bank figures suggest only 24,000 new homes will be built in 2022 – 25 per cent behind the government's 33,000 target set in Housing for All. They are still failing to get local authorities back to building new social housing. In 2021, local authorities built just 1,198 homes, 10 per cent less than in 2020. Homelessness has also increased. In the first three months of 2022, 728 families were made homeless across Ireland. This means that around 1,400 children experienced the trauma of the loss of their home in the first three months of 2022. The housing crisis is scarring a generation of children. Hundreds of thousands of children are growing up in this country not knowing what it is to live in stable, secure, safe homes. Their childhood is being stolen from them and their potential is compromised, due to the mental and physical ill health caused by housing stress. For renters, it is beyond a cost of living crisis – it is a cost of survival crisis.

We need a new vision and a new plan. I suggest it should be called 'Gaffs for All: delivering affordable, decent, green, forever homes'. But whatever its title, it has to ensure that everyone has a gaff of their own.

We can solve the housing crisis and achieve this vision with the following ten key solutions, real solutions that will actually work to deliver affordable green homes for all – not half-baked solutions that will leave us with a permanent crisis and merely benefit the property industry and investor funds as the current housing plan does.

1. Make housing a human right: Hold a referendum to put the right to housing in the Constitution;
   - The process of a referendum would be an opportunity for society to democratically debate, discuss and decide its values and approach in regard to treatment of housing. It would be a democratic deliberative process providing a clear social and political mandate for the State to deliver right to housing.
   - The constitutional insertion of right to housing will create the positive and progressive obligation on the Irish State to fulfil the right to housing – to deliver a right to housing in policy and practice, place *a responsibility on it to solve*

the housing and homelessness crisis on a permanent basis and enable and strengthen constitutional provision to implement measures to prevent homelessness, enhance tenant's rights and improve the supply of affordable housing.

- It would ensure the key aspects of the right to adequate housing, such as affordability, security of tenure and decent-standard housing are they key targets of housing policy.

2. A state-guaranteed delivery of a sufficient supply of life-time-secure, affordable, decent-quality, green homes for all using public land for 100 per cent actually affordable housing.
    - Provide 400,000 public affordable and social 'green' homes in the coming decade. That means 40,000 affordable homes per year (both new and using vacant/derelict buildings) on our state-owned lands (and CPO additional land as necessary):
        - 15,000 affordable home ownership (retained within a new affordable housing market)
        - 10,000 affordable (cost) rental homes
        - 15,000 social homes.

(Note that this compares to the government's current plan of providing just 14,000 social and affordable homes per year. Most of the 33,000 housing units per year in its plan is due to come from the private market – likely to be unaffordable, much of it build-to-rent, and possibly not even delivered.)

3. Set up a state construction company – as a semi-state enterprise – to develop and build affordable homes to buy and rent, refurbish vacant and derelict property, and undertake retrofitting.

4. Give adequate state funding to guarantee new affordable and social housing by:

- trebling state capital (new build and renovate derelict and vacant) funding from €2bn to €6bn a year for local authorities and housing associations
- setting up a €5bn national housing fund at affordable rates to finance and fund building of affordable homes by not-for-profits, community housing, cooperative housing and by SME builders with clear affordability requirements attached. Provide capital grants to higher education institutions for affordable, purpose-built student accommodation.

5. Make private rental real homes:
   - Make rents affordable – implement a three-year rent freeze, rent reduction mechanisms, rent controls on new units to the market.
   - Give renters security in their homes – immediate three-year eviction ban (of 'no fault' evictions); ban tenancy terminations for sale of property; remove the ability of landlords to evict tenants on sale and other 'no fault' evictions.
   - Airbnb/short-stay rentals should only be allowed to be used in your primary home, for less than thirty days a year, in areas of high housing need. Ban use of short stay rental/Airbnb for non-primary residences, unless you have planning permission for use as tourist accommodation. Proper enforcement and significant fines. Ban conversion of long-term rental homes to short-stay tourist accommodation.

6. End homelessness:
   - Develop new plan with clear timelines to end homelessness within five years.
   - Phase out the use of emergency accommodation.
   - Expand Housing First to provide permanent secure 'own door' long-term accommodation.
   - Implement legislation to prevent evictions into homelessness.

- Create a non-profit housing body to provide homes for those homeless on the Housing First model, modelled on the Y-Foundation in Finland, with the aim of providing homes and supports to those who are, or at risk of, homeless.
- Provide rent arrears supports and put the necessary funding into homelessness prevention services such as Threshold, Focus Ireland and Simon Communities, which identify and work with people to prevent them becoming homeless and support them out of emergency accommodation.

7. Stop the REITs, investor funds and property purchase as investment:
   - Remove the Real Estate Investor Trust tax incentive, and all other investor fund tax breaks and loopholes. Ensure REIT/corporate landlords pay a 40 per cent tax on all their rental income, similar to that paid by individual private landlords.
   - Require at least 40 per cent of all large private developments (including build-to-rent with planning permission already) are allocated for sale to home buyers.
   - Part V social and affordable housing obligation on build-to-rent developments should be purchased, not leased, for use as permanent social and affordable housing.
   - Levy a hefty tax on investor purchase of residential property to remove non-home buyers from the market.
   - Divest all state funding (such as the Irish Strategic Investment Fund) from REITs/investor funds/developers building for investor fund rental. Divest state pension funds and public sector pensions out of REITs/residential property investment funds.

8. Eliminate vacant and derelict buildings and land/sites:
   - Put in place an annual 'use it or lose it' tax, set at a percentage of the market value, on vacant and derelict property, land and buildings.
   - Empower local authorities to CPO 10,000 vacant and

derelict homes per year, and retrofit and convert them to social and affordable homes.

9. Ensure that all marginalized groups have appropriate, adequate housing, e.g. people with disabilities, victims of domestic abuse, refugees and asylum seekers, and Travellers. Put in place equality- and rights-based monitoring and implementation of all housing policy.

10. Green and retrofit all homes, including renewable energy, rewilding and food production, to make our housing system zero carbon in a socially just way. Make available a 100 per cent retrofit grant to low and middle income households.

The right to housing as the vision behind housing policy

For decades, housing policy in Ireland has prioritized the interests of the banking – property developer – investor nexus and has failed to provide affordable homes. The current housing market is unsustainable, another crash is inevitable (although significant house price and rent reductions are what's needed), and investors embed permanent unaffordability. A new value framework for our housing system and policy is required, one that can ensure adequate, affordable, secure housing for all. This is the human right to housing, which must be inserted into the Constitution in order to set a clear vision for our housing system and oblige the State to realize and uphold such a right through all its laws, policies and practice.

The market has no morals. The market does not care about affordable housing. Why are we building housing policy around the market when it does not care? The market only cares about profit.

The Irish housing system should as its primary goal and function ensure affordable homes for people and deliver housing as a human right – that is the ideology that should dominate.

The pandemic should have opened all our eyes to what really matters in our lives – our societal and individual health and well-being, and ensuring that no one is left behind. Yet in the housing crisis we are leaving an entire generation behind.

Rather than lurching from crisis to crisis, decade to decade, with housing policy unclear as to its ultimate goal and purpose, a right to housing in the Constitution would provide a clear and unambiguous policy direction and requirement for the government and Irish State. The Constitution is our guiding document for our country and sets the key principles to guide government and state action.

The first step, therefore, is to make the right to housing our guiding principle in policy and law. The current national housing plan does not mention the right to housing once. It should be its first principle. We should make the right to housing, as set out in the United Nations' rights-based housing strategies, the framework for a new national housing policy and plan. The right to adequate, affordable, decent and secure housing should be implemented in Irish housing policy and legislation and in its Constitution. This would make a rights-based housing system the aim of housing policy in Ireland, providing a vision and policy for housing that is underpinned by a wider vision of a society and economy that provides socially just economic development for all, a socially inclusive and active democratic citizenry, and an environmentally sustainable mode of development. This would require the Irish State to place the direct provision of public housing, not-for-profit, affordable rental and cooperative housing at the core of its function and responsibility, as with the delivery of health and education.

There is currently no legal obligation on the Irish State to provide housing. There is no legal obligation on local authorities to provide homes for a homeless family and children; and as a result thousands languish in emergency accommodation. We could change the legislation now to put that in place, and it should be done. But I do not believe that it will be enforced or delivered by this State until there is a clear, unambiguous, stand-alone right to housing in the Constitution. The Constitution includes the right to primary education. Decent, safe, secure housing is even more fundamental to us than education. Why does the Irish Government not accept the responsibility to ensure no child is homeless? Embedding the right to housing in the Constitution is a vital step towards changing the Irish housing system to one that meets people's housing needs.

We need this, because proposal after proposal to freeze rents, to ban evictions, to implement tax on vacant property has been refused by government on the basis of the Attorney General's advice that it would have a disproportionate impact on the private property rights of either landlords or property owners as set out in the Constitution. Putting the right to housing in the Constitution is a key part of solving the housing and homelessness crisis once and for all – it is a key part of ending our continual housing crises. It can give us the vision, the principles, the guide by which all policy would be assessed. It would become the target the government must achieve. Building social and affordable homes, and preventing people from being made homeless, is the core solution, but to get there we need the right to housing in our Constitution. This would have implications for the State, its responsibility for and expenditure on housing – if it didn't it would be meaningless. It should require greater expenditure on housing, better policy, more effective policy – and better intervention in the market.

A constitutional right to housing would permanently assert the State's responsibility to ensure access for all to adequate, safe and affordable housing and permanently propel the State to sustainable housing policies designed to ensure access for all to secure housing.

A constitutional right to housing would also support action on climate change, such as enabling us to put property and land, including private commercial property, to its most environmentally sustainable use. Using vacant and derelict property and land in our towns and cities is the best way to provide new homes. Derelict buildings, including commercial buildings, should be built and reno-vated as part of our climate response, yet this is not happening – in part because of property rights. Property rights must come second to the common social and environmental good and to social justice.

This would also strengthen government's hand constitutionally to improve tenants' protection from eviction, implement long-term leases and CPOs for vacant and derelict housing, and apply a stronger vacant sites levy.

Many pieces of legislation could be introduced immediately to effectively implement the right to housing in practice and make the private rental sector a secure, affordable housing option for tenants. These include laws to protect tenants from eviction, freeze rents, set rent affordability mechanisms and strengthen enforcement mechanisms of existing measures. Emergency legislation should also be introduced to make it illegal for landlords to evict tenants into homelessness. There should be increased powers and resources for the Irish Human Rights and Equality Commission and the Ombudsman for Children's Office to monitor, and ensure implementation of, the right to housing across the housing system. A rights-based policy would also ensure that housing and land in cities and towns are planned for people as homes. This requires policies to curtail speculative property investment, such as:

- implementing taxes on real estate investment
- abolishing the Real Estate Investment Trust Tax Incentive, and various forms of tax avoidance by real estate funds
- restricting and regulating short-stay online tourist platforms
- implementing the recommendations of the Report of the Committee on the Price of Building Land (1974), known as the Kenny Report, which made proposals to control the price of land for housing, including local authorities to be given the right to acquire undeveloped lands at existing use value plus 25 per cent
- restricting (or even removing) exemptions on the vacant site tax to force land owners to use or sell vacant land
- introducing vacant and derelict property tax for non-principal dwelling houses and small sites

- directing NAMA to use its remaining land, property and cash reserves for public affordable housing.

Rapid-build modular green social housing

More sustainable houses can be built quickly and affordably, applying modern industrial techniques and using low- and zero-carbon materials, including renewable and recycled materials. For example, prefabricated modular homes can be built in a factory in a week and assembled on site in four days. Factories in Carlow, Kerry, Cavan and Donegal are manufacturing homes for less than €200,000, and doing this at scale would reduce these costs further. Factory-built homes can be timber-framed or use light-gauge steel frames, made from recycled material and fully recyclable. Whereas a normal building site will generate multiple heavy transport movements with associated inefficiencies and a huge carbon footprint, the delivery of frames from a centralized manufacturing plant can be reduced to two or three trucks. These have already been delivered in new green social housing across Ireland. Unfortunately, these examples are too few and far between. The government should be funding them on a huge scale.

Dún Laoghaire–Rathdown County Council developed twelve beautiful terraced, own-door, high-density social housing units at George's Place in Dún Laoghaire, within walking distance of the sea front. The houses were built in a factory using a rapid-build timber frame system and have an A1 BER rating. Each home has its own front door and does not overlook its neighbour. The shallow-railed front gardens prevalent in the area offer a neat example of how to limit each house's external footprint, as does the small courtyard back garden. Splayed windows at the first floor also minimize direct overlooking of neighbours. Despite the fact that they are relatively compact, the new tenants say their house feels bigger, as there is great light through the windows. They were built for €249,000. This is a great example of what can be done on small brownfield vacant sites in our urban centres. These units will remain permanent social housing, and generation after generation of tenants will enjoy these extremely affordable, sustainable homes.

Another example of thoughtful redevelopment of small and tight urban brownfield sites to address housing and sustainability needs is the attractive two-storey New Street South apartments in Dublin 8 undertaken by the Peter McVerry Trust. It built eight high-quality homes – five one-bed apartments and three two-bed apartments – that are NZEB (Nearly Zero Energy Building) standard. These new homes will meet the long-term housing needs of single people and families experiencing homelessness.

Similarly, fifty-four BER A-rated family homes (three- and four-bed semi-detached) were developed in Ard Na Greine, Milltown, County Kerry by the not-for-profit housing association Clúid in partnership with Kerry County Council and funded by the Department of Housing. Milltown, with a population of around a thousand people, is a small town, so this development will make a big difference. The houses are located near local amenities, including transport, schools, shops, services and community facilities. They were built by the local sustainable building manufacturer Thermohouse, based in Killarney. It uses a unique low-energy system to manufacture homes in a state-of-the-art manufacturing facility. As well as being up to 60 per cent faster than traditional construction, the houses have superior levels of airtightness, considerably reducing their heating costs. The houses are NZEB compliant and cost just €220,000 per home to build. Why are we not doing this in every small town in Ireland?

Increasingly we are seeing innovative development of sustainable building materials using recycled materials. Insulation with a very low carbon footprint is being used in a new local authority housing estate in Cork. It is being provided by Ecocel, which manufactures cellulose insulation from recycled newspaper in its factory in Cork City. Timber can also play an important role in sustainable construction. It is a natural and renewable product, but we need to source and ensure a long-term supply of environmentally sustainable timber. This can deliver jobs in rural communities. Ireland has one of the best growing conditions for timber in Europe and this timber is suitable for use in mass timber construction here. There is a need to support a major expansion of the sustainable construction materials and recycling industry in Ireland too. This can all create jobs. But they should be set up as social enterprises, where the local communities gain, and the environment and social good is their priority.

Building affordable and social homes

The public housing sector in the Austrian capital Vienna is open to low and high income earners. More than half the population lives in either one of the 220,000 municipal homes or the 200,000 limited-profit housing association homes operating on an affordable cost-rental basis. They have large apartments and balconies, with community spaces and swimming pools inside the apartment blocks. Everyone wants to live in this beautifully designed public housing. In Denmark, public housing accommodates one million people in more than 8,500 estates owned by 550 different not-for-profit housing associations. It is financed by borrowing from the Danish Housing Investment Bank (funded by Danish pension funds). There is no income test – everybody is entitled to social housing. In Finland, the Helsinki council owns 60,000 social housing units, runs its own construction company and builds 7,000 new homes per year. The Housing Finance and Development Centre of Finland (ARA) plays a key role in funding social housing in Finland by offering grants and guarantees on long-term loans financing the provision of affordable rental housing. In addition, ARA monitors costs and quality standards, and promotes innovation and excellence.

A good target for Ireland if we are to solve the housing crisis permanently is to bring our stock of new 'public' (non-market social and affordable) housing up to the levels in countries such as Austria, Finland, Denmark and Sweden, which meet their citizens' housing needs much better than Ireland. That means increasing the level of public housing to a third of our total housing stock. It also means increasing home ownership, but providing home ownership that is actually affordable, that does not involve huge debt and that does not become an investment commodity.

We can see why we are in this crisis when we look at other countries that do housing well. The difference is how much more housing in those countries is delivered outside the market – by the State or by not-for-profit housing associations and cooperatives. In Amsterdam, 42 per cent of its housing is social housing – available to workers and those on low incomes; in Vienna, 50 per cent of its housing is public housing available to people on all incomes; in Copenhagen that figure is 28 per cent. In Denmark as a whole, 31 per cent of housing stock is outside the market – not-for-profit social housing or cooperative housing. In Sweden, 18 per cent is social housing and 23 per cent is cooperative- or tenant-owned; that means that 41 per cent of its housing is outside the market. In Ireland, the social housing stock comprises around 200,000 units – just 10 per cent of our housing is social housing. Ninety per cent is delivered through the for-profit market. And we wonder why we have a housing crisis.

Singapore provides another very interesting example of how to provide affordable housing. The State acquired huge tracts of land, so that it now controls the vast majority of development land, so it provides land cheaply for housing provision, massively reducing housing costs, and it provides cheap state loans to finance building and purchase of homes. There is a 90 per cent home ownership rate in Singapore, because a lot of housing is provided via the State, not the market. We could do this here too. The State could engage in a widespread CPO purchase of potential development land, and then lease it to affordable housing builders, who would build affordable homes and communities on it. But the land would always be retained in a 'community land trust', maintaining permanently affordable housing.

We have to consider how we get out of this current crisis and avoid getting back here again in the future. We need to create home ownership that is affordable, and that stays permanently affordable. How can we do that?

RORY HEARNE

Use vacant and derelict homes

We have a housing shortage and a crisis, but we don't *actually*, have a shortage of housing. The first principle is to use the existing stock of housing currently not being used as homes. The greenest, most sustainable building is the one already built. We hear all the time about the need to 'reuse and recycle'. Yet why do we not reuse and recycle housing and buildings? The greenest way to deliver new homes is to use existing vacant homes and refurbish derelict buildings. Ireland has a scandalously high level of vacant and derelict buildings in our cities and towns. Census 2022 shows the situation whereby 166,752 homes are vacant across the country. There is an additional 66,135 vacant holiday homes. Almost a third (48,387) of the vacant dwellings are long term vacant, being unused since 2016. Almost a decade of housing supply lies vacant. How is it fair and right that we leave thousands of people without a home, and hundreds of thousands stuck at home in parents' homes or in unaffordable rental accommodation, when there are enough homes for everyone already built? These homes are being left vacant by their owners, because they can, and they have no need for them. It is an unacceptable housing inequality, and unacceptable in terms of environmental costs. If we used vacant homes and holiday homes we could end homelessness overnight. And that is before we even think about the huge number of derelict buildings.

It is really important to realize that the 232,887 vacant homes are not the same as derelict properties. Vacant homes could be lived in today, but derelict ones have typically been unused for several years and require structural work or reconstruction before they can be lived in. The CSO explains that in identifying vacant dwellings their enumerators are instructed to look for signs that the dwelling is not occupied, e.g. no cars outside, junk mail accumulating, overgrown garden, etc. Enumerators call to the dwellings numerous times and ask neighbours whether a dwelling is vacant or used as a holiday home. Dwellings under construction and derelict properties were not included in the count of vacant dwellings. As a result, the empty housing units were classified as vacant house, vacant apartment or holiday home only if the dwelling was considered fit for habitation.

GeoDirectory measures the number of derelict (unliveable) properties. In 2021, it found a whopping 22,000 derelict residential properties. And this is an underestimation of the general number of derelict buildings as it doesn't include derelict retail or commercial buildings – the boarded-up shops and offices you see on most main streets. Ten counties had over a thousand derelict properties each. Mayo had the highest, with 2,924 derelict properties; Cork had the fourth highest, 1,448 derelict homes. While most counties saw a welcome fall in the number of derelict properties since 2016, in two counties, Sligo and Tipperary, the number of derelict homes actually increased. Sligo has 1,200 derelict properties, but just 20 properties advertised to rent on Daft.ie.

This is important given that the populations of our cities and towns are expected to see the most growth in coming decades, and this is where the vacant and derelict properties are. Dublin is expected to grow from 1.1 million currently to 1.4 million by 2040; Cork to grow by 50 per cent from 210,000 to 314,000; Limerick from 94,000 to 141,000; Galway from 80,000 to 120,000; and Waterford from 54,000 to 81,000. They will require a huge amount of housing. The most sustainable way is to use vacant and derelict homes, commercial, office and retail properties and the existing land in our towns, villages and cities.

Part of the reason we have this criminal level of vacancy and dereliction is that developers and investor funds make the biggest profits from developing huge new developments of apartments and houses. They don't own the vacant houses and have no interest in renovating them. Developers and investor funds have heavily lobbied government and have effectively driven housing policy, so their interests have been paramount among policymakers and governments in recent years. As a result, the housing policy effort and funding has been prioritized into initiatives, incentives and subsidies for new-build developments by investors and big developers, and very few measures of public funding put in to tackle vacancy and dereliction. Government has also been unwilling to tackle the issue of 'private property' rights of owners of vacant and derelict buildings and derelict and vacant land, as they are viewed by the large political parties of government as key groups in society who vote for them.

The massive scale of vacancy and dereliction has become normalized. We tolerate it. We don't even see it. A recent campaign led by Frank O'Connor and Jude Sherry of the Anois agency, in conjunction with the Community Action Tenants Union (CATU) and the Reclaim Our Spaces organization, have used social media to highlight how dereliction blights our villages, towns and cities under the hashtag #DerelictIreland. Frank points out that what motivated him to highlight this was 'the scale and significance of continuing waste, neglect and vandalism of historic centres like Cork, which doesn't need to be this way'.

Our children are growing up watching derelict and vacant homes and buildings crumble and decay around them while they can't get a gaff of their own. This is a viscerally pernicious inequality. Those without access to homes can literally touch and see derelict buildings abandoned because the owners have an excess of wealth and property. As one young parent living at home with her parents explained, 'I'm technically homeless (although lucky to have family). I live in a small bedroom, in rural west Cork, with a pre-schooler. There is not room for two beds. We share one. These empty buildings break my heart as there is absolutely nothing that I want more than a home.'

It is also utterly unacceptable when we face a climate crisis and the most sustainable way of delivering homes is using vacant and derelict ones in our towns and cities.

Local authorities

The lack of attention paid to vacancy and dereliction by governments is shown in the lack of funding given to local authorities, which are the key agencies with the responsibility to address the problem. Just three local authorities around the country have full-time vacant homes officers. Under the Buy and Renew scheme, in place since 2017, local authorities can use CPOs to buy vacant housing, which they can refurbish and let as social housing. However, since its introduction just 700 homes have been bought and used for social housing. That is well below the original target of 3,500 homes set by Simon Coveney when he was Minister for Housing. Interestingly, Louth County Council delivered 83 units, while Dublin City delivered just 58, and Galway City and Sligo delivered just one unit each. Clearly some local authorities are making this more of a priority than others. But it would be unfair to blame local authorities. As we have seen earlier, since the 1980s central government policy has underfunded local authorities, as it shifted to the private market to deliver housing. Local authorities were essentially told by government that they no longer had a role in housing. Now local authorities are being told to tackle issues like vacancy without the capacity to do so.

The government's latest housing plan, Housing for All, continues the inadequate level of ambition and funding for local authorities with a target of purchasing just 2,500 vacant units by 2026. It should have a target of triple that number – CPO buying vacant and derelict units, refurbishing them and then retaining as social housing, cost rental affordable homes, and selling as affordable gaffs to those trying to buy a home of their own.

Under the Derelict Sites Act 1990 local authorities can issue an annual levy and fines to the owners of derelict sites and property and CPO them rapidly. They are also required to maintain a public register of the derelict sites and properties. Yet a substantial proportion of derelict property is not being registered by local authorities. Kerry County Council does not have one derelict site listed on its register; Wicklow County has just three. Members of the public can contact local authorities to report derelict sites. The current lack of enforcement of the Dereliction Act is a clear problem. Some local authorities do not even collect the fines issued on the derelict sites they have registered. Cork County Council collected just €900 of €308,000 due from fines on owners of derelict sites.

Councils cite Article 43 of the Constitution, which sets out the right to private property and enables challenges from property owners to CPOs, as a major barrier and the 'elephant in the room' when it comes to CPOing vacant properties. An Bord Pleanála has also cited Article 43 in its rulings against local authorities attempting to buy up derelict property and sites. But Article 43 states that property rights can be 'regulated by the principles of social justice' and delimited in the interests of the 'common good'. The clearly defined rights to private property of developers and investors have continued to trump the rights of those who need a home.

The underlying problem – the vacant or derelict house, the decaying building, the dilapidated shop, the luxury and build-to-rent apartments left vacant – is that property is being treated as a commodity rather than a home. The government response has used market mechanisms to try incentivizing owners to either sell or lease the property to local authorities for social housing. But this doesn't stop owners just sitting on the vacant property as a speculative asset, watching property prices rise, and its value grow, even though they do nothing with it.

Derelict and vacant commercial buildings

There's a vacant building at the end of my street. It was used as a fitness studio until 2010. It has sat there idle, vacant, for over a decade. All this time it could have been a home for a family or two decent-sized apartments. But it's not counted in official statistics as a vacant property, and it's not listed on Dublin City Council's derelict register. It might be held by NAMA or the banks, or the property owner might be just leaving it vacant. It is part of the hidden dereliction crisis, the tens of thousands of derelict and vacant commercial buildings that are not included in the CSO vacant homes or GeoDirectory derelict figures. It highlights two key problems: the lack of data on the true scale of vacancy and dereliction; and the fact that property owners face no penalty that would pressure them to sell or rent their vacant or derelict properties. It also highlights the wasted buildings that could be used to provide sustainable homes. There is enough capacity above commercial ground floors for 4,000 apartments in Dublin. Research done by architect Ali Harvey as part of the Heritage Council's work on the Town Centre First initiatives found that just over one in four ground floor commercial premises in Tipperary town and Tralee were vacant. This is way higher than the 5 per cent levels of vacancy seen in cities and towns in Denmark and the Netherlands.

As people shift to remote working, there are tens of thousands of vacant offices and even entire office blocks that could be converted to homes.

A 'use it or lose it' tax

There is a heightened public demand to tackle the scandal of dereliction and vacancy that is blighting our towns and cities, particularly when there is a need to increase housing supply, with half a million young adults living at home and homelessness rising, and to tackle the climate crisis. There is a real potential in seriously tackling vacancy and dereliction to provide homes in a more sustainable way and to breathe life into towns and cities. To make our towns and cities places that people want to live in.

Owners of derelict and vacant homes and commercial buildings should no longer be allowed to leave their property unused. We need to disincentivize the holding of vacant and derelict property, effectively forcing property owners to sell. It is time to assert the principles of the 'common good' of society and the environment over the narrow individual private property rights of owners of vacant and derelict buildings and land. It should be a case of use it or lose it. A really heavy vacant and derelict buildings and sites tax is needed, along with a massive programme of local authority CPOs on vacant and derelict properties.

Property owners have been incentivized and nudged to use their properties through various schemes, but it hasn't worked. Grants for home buyers to purchase vacant properties might sound like a solution, but it's likely to just further push up prices of a limited supply of derelict stock for sale. As property owners see home buyers getting grants, they will ask for the additional value of the grant on top of their projected sale price. Vacant grants are also dependent on an individual or couple's ability to pay the cost of purchasing the derelict or vacant property, and to pay the refurbishment costs. This restricts it to those with higher incomes.

Rather than individual home buyers with a new grant just being fleeced by owners demanding market prices, the State must disincentivize the holding of vacant property, effectively forcing property owners to sell through a punitive vacant and derelict property and sites tax, and it should engage in the widespread compulsory purchase of vacant and derelict property.

An effective vacant and derelict property tax must include all property, – with some minor exceptions, such as if the owner is ill or in a nursing home – including derelict homes and commercial property. There is a real issue that current measures of vacancy exclude derelict properties and sites. The tax needs to be sufficient to essentially force the sale of the property or site, to make it financially unviable to hold on to it. The Revenue Commissioners should be given full powers to collect this tax and, where needs be, investigate cases of potential avoidance. They should not rely solely on the self-declaration of vacancy. The tax should scale upwards as the length of time of vacancy and dereliction increases. It should be set at a percentage of the market value of the property. It needs to be punitive to force either the use or the sale of the property. What we need is a flood of vacant and derelict homes and sites on to the market which would offer a stock of property for home buyers and affordable home builders.

Local authorities should be funded to purchase tens of thousands of vacant and derelict stock and sites. (Home buyers on average incomes cannot take on the risk and cost of this alone.) They could then transfer them to a public home building company, which would refurbish them and either sell them home at genuinely affordable prices to home buyers (not investors or landlords) or transfer them back to the local authority or a housing association for social or affordable rental housing. Where there are issues with CPOs, compulsory sales orders (CSOs) should be used to get this done rapidly.

Vacant and derelict land

Another area of vacancy and dereliction is land that is left idle in cities, towns and villages. There is a huge amount of both privately and publicly owned land that is close to existing transport, schools, community use, etc. and therefore ideal for building new homes on. The current vacant sites tax and derelict sites register, and fines, are ineffective. A 'use it or lose it' tax on zoned development land trumpeted in Housing for All is also not due to come in before 2028.

A vision of 'compact growth' is set out in the latest city development plans in which local authorities set out what our cities are aiming to achieve in the coming years. For example, Dublin City's development plan 2022–2026 has an inspiring vision: 'All development will be connected by exemplary public transport, cycling and walking systems . . . by 2050, Dublin will be a zero-carbon city with all of its energy coming from renewable energy sources. All of the city's buildings will have been built or retro-fitted to near zero energy building standards.' Cork City development plan has a vision for Cork to become 'a world-class city . . . growing as a resilient, healthy, age-friendly and sustainable compact city with placemaking, communities and quality of life at its heart'; while Galway City's vision is of 'A city that is environmentally responsible, mobilized to combat climate change and resilient to challenge . . . that offers sustainable and quality choices in housing, work, transport and lifestyle opportunities.'

These are wonderful ambitions. As a country we're great at plans and vision. But our problem is implementing them. With local authorities cash-strapped and underfunded, who is going to deliver these plans? They will rely, once more, on the market, on private developers, property owners and investor funds. Policy will bend over backwards to entice them. But what is needed is the State to deliver and to back communities and not-for-profit social enterprises and cooperatives to actually guarantee delivery.

National housing and economic policy and local authority planning has to become less about wooing and incentivizing private commercial building and landowners, landlords and investors and developers and more interventionist and directly involved in dictating what gets built, where, when and by whom, and delivering itself. For example, why are we allowing building of more hotels, luxury apartments and short-stay tourist lets when it is affordable, sustainable homes and community, nature, and work/art spaces we need? Why are we letting such levels of vacancy and dereliction when the environment and society necessitates their urgent use? Why are we allowing land in our towns and cities to sit idle?

The development of our cities, towns and villages should put people at its centre – the individuals in Generation Locked-out, all of us together – as communities and individuals working in a cooperative way to redevelop them in ways that nurture community and sustainability, ensuring people have homes in thriving, inclusive, nature-friendly urban spaces, rather than leaving people to suffer from a market-based, individualized, atomized, deeply unequal climate transition.

The shortage of housing in this country is an artificial scarcity. There is an untapped supply of housing and land being hoarded by property owners (including the State), who allow it lie vacant or derelict. Excuses are not good enough anymore, we need homes built and renovated now.

Remove the REITs and non-home buyers from the market

To reduce house prices we need to reduce the amount of money flowing into the Irish housing market that is being used to buy property as an investment. On a temporary basis, let's say for five years, until we get out of the housing emergency, we need to restrict the purchase of homes in areas of high housing need to anyone except a home buyer who is buying their principal residence. In cases where tenants are in situ, it can be bought for social and affordable housing. So we should restrict the sale of new and existing housing to individual home buyers and, where relevant, social housing providers. This would also stop the practice of 'flipping', where people with a bit of money are buying property and selling it again in six months for a much higher price and pocketing the profit.

We should also immediately implement Dublin City Council's Development Plan proposal to stop private developers from building 'rental only' schemes with no homes for sale. Build-to-rent schemes of more than 100 homes would have to have at least 40 per cent of properties available for sale to home buyers. It should be implemented on all existing planning permissions – not just new ones. On top of this we should introduce a 40 per cent tax on investor funds and large corporate landlords with more than fifty properties. A tax of 50 per cent on non-household purchases of property should also be introduced. We could start a process by which REITs would sell their existing holdings of land, by taxing the land to, in effect, force them to sell it.

If the investor funds and REITs significantly reduced their purchasing of new properties, many of the thousands of units being built would be available for sale to home buyers, apartment and house prices would fall, people could buy them, and land prices would fall massively also. The State could buy up that land and provide it to cooperatives and housing associations and Irish SME builders to build affordable housing.

If the REITs started selling up their apartments we would have more homes for people to buy. We would see a fall in house prices and rents. We would actually have affordable housing and other forms of private investment – Irish small and medium builders and affordable home builders that could buy REITs land cheaply and develop on it. We could 'do a Berlin' and compulsorily purchase REIT and large corporate landlord apartments that are not renting at an affordable rate.

The Build to Rent legislation should be scrapped. Planning density laws should be changed to enable mid-rise homes to be built for affordable purchase and rent. The investor fund bulk-buying stamp duty measures should include apartments, and the real estate funds should be served a hefty tax on their rent and profits.

Most important, the REIT tax break, and all tax breaks that investor and property funds are availing of, should be scrapped.

The governments of New Zealand and Canada have restricted non-residents from buying houses to dampen down prices and increase the supply available to people living there. The German government banned REITs from buying up residential property. Paris enacted a vacancy tax in 2015, assessing 20 per cent of the market value of rent, and tripled the tax to 60 per cent in 2017.

Make sure the private rental sector provides homes

Landlords need to understand that they are part of a wider social contract – the provision of homes for renters, not investment assets. Landlords need to accept that their property is rented to a tenant and it is the tenant's home. Buying houses as investments, benefiting from ever-rising rents, and then selling and flipping properties or evicting the tenant and convert the property to Airbnb is no longer ethically, socially, or economically acceptable.

We need emergency measures to stem the tide of the crisis while we build up our capacity to provide and find homes for those who are homeless in Ireland, and for refugees – including Ukrainian refugees, and, in the future, probably climate refugees – and those in direct provision. These should include a three-year ban on evictions from the private rental sector, a three-year rent freeze, and rent reduction measures. No-fault evictions such as on the sale of property should be removed. When a landlord is selling a property they need to notify the local authority and if the tenant wants to stay they are allowed to stay. Property should be sold with the tenant in place. You see it all the time when commercial properties are sold – 'tenant not affected'. We saw this work during Covid, so why are we not using what we know works? We need a ban on short-stay tourist lets, such as Airbnb, but also other companies doing this, for more than thirty days (currently ninety), and local authorities need proper resourcing to enforce it with the threat of, and imposition of, massive fines for breaches.

There is a lot of talk about what we must do to keep landlords in the market. But we are looking at this the wrong way. If a landlord wants to sell up, fine, but they have to leave the tenant in place. Also the State should set up a fund to purchase properties off landlords wanting to leave the market. The State could then rent it to the existing tenant as social housing or as cost rental if they are on a higher income. You, as a landlord, won't have to worry about it. If you don't want to be a landlord any more, that's no problem; the State will buy your unit from you. Policy should not be held hostage by landlords.

A state construction company

As a country we are completely dependent on the private construction industry and developers to provide the fundamental requirement of homes. The biggest reason we are in this crisis is because local authorities stopped building homes on a major scale. We handed housing over to the market. Is this not utterly illogical? Can you imagine if the delivery of our hospitals and schools was left up to private companies? Some might consider this a good thing, but most people know it would be an utter disaster resulting in care and education only being provided to those who could afford to pay for it and private companies only providing a service that makes profit for them. It is time to guarantee the provision of affordable housing in this country on a permanent basis by setting up a national house building company. This would employ all the key professions and trades people (architects, engineers, social and affordable housing experts, planners, quantity surveyors, brick layers, carpenters, project managers, financial experts, etc.) needed to plan, design, finance and build quality, sustainable, affordable homes. It would also deliver retrofitting of homes and the refurbishment of vacant and derelict ones.

Given the rising costs of building, materials and labour, it is a no-brainer to set up a semi-state company that would ensure we get best value for money in economies of scale through the sourcing and bulk purchasing of materials, and are not fleeced by the profit gouging of the private construction and developer industry, who always have the government over a barrell with construction contracts. The government is completely dependent on the private contractors, and so they just keep telling the State, costs are rising, we need more money, and the cost of delivery just goes up and up. A state construction company would give the country a cost-effective, guaranteed delivery mechanism for providing affordable homes for all.

It should be a semi-state commercial enterprise with regional delivery centres and offices, building excellently designed and planned public housing developed with and for local authorities, not-for-profit housing cooperatives, housing associations and the Land Development Agency. An enterprise such as this could build 5,000 homes per year and retrofit thousands more, scaling up rapidly, ideally to 10,000 per year. It would directly employ its workers and thus provide quality permanent jobs and apprenticeships to building and construction sector workers, and upskill construction workers.

The State employs 41,000 nurses and 64,000 teachers to guarantee delivery of quality public health and education. Yet housing is even more fundamental to our lives. Without decent housing we have nothing, and the quality, design and space of our homes are also essential. Yet there's no such state employment to directly deliver housing.

The company would also help overcome the shortage of skilled construction workers to build homes. Young people are reluctant to enter a sector with job insecurity, bogus self-employment and boom–bust bouts of unemployment and emigration. Construction workers have become part of the precarious gig economy with a shift from direct employment to subcontracting, particularly in the wet trades – bricklaying, floor and wall tiling, painting, plastering.

Only a minority (40,000) of the 150,000 construction workers in Ireland are actually building homes. Many are building hotels and offices. In a housing emergency, it seems illogical to have our skilled workers building luxury hotels when there aren't enough workers to build or retrofit homes.

Up to 70,000 of construction workers who lost their job during the 2008 crisis emigrated. Many want to return with their families but unaffordable rentals and little prospect of owning their own home are stopping them. The only way to attract construction workers in sufficient numbers, while also guaranteeing the capacity to deliver homes, is to create a state-owned building and retrofit company to deliver homes, and offer quality permanent employment and apprenticeships. Quality employment means quality service – which in this case would be the highest-quality homes.

There's a real opportunity to provide hope for the younger generations through a career in a new state building and development company, offering a future with quality employment, building the affordable and climate-sustainable homes we need. If we are serious about the housing crisis and retrofitting, we need to be serious about providing top-quality jobs to ensure we have the capacity and skills to deliver.

Look at the quality of work done by ESB workers, by our teachers, by our nurses – all public-sector or semi-state workers. We can treat our construction workers the same: pay them properly, give them permanent contracts, motivate them, get them inspired by their vocation – building homes for their communities, their families, their country. They will do what's needed to deliver the homes we need. And we need to set up this state building company because there will never be a time when we won't need more homes to be built or refurbished or renovated or retrofitted.

This is a key permanent solution. Build the capacity and skills in our country and we will never again be dependent on US investor funds or big developers to provide the fundamental need of homes to our people.

Deliver a new supply of genuinely affordable homes

The State, through the new public home building company, and in partnership with local authorities, housing associations and not-for-profits, needs to build genuinely affordable homes for sale and rent. An affordable home for an individual or couple with an income of €40,000 is in the region of €150,000. Government-provided 'affordable' homes at €350,000 or €450,000 are not actually affordable. A genuinely affordable rent for an individual or couple with an income of €40,000 is €640 a month. Cost-rental homes charging rent at €1,000 for a two-bed apartment is not actually affordable housing. Affordable housing should be about providing housing that is not taking up more than 25 per cent of people's take-home (net) monthly income. Affordable housing is not a price linked to some proportion of market prices, which are completely out of kilter and way too high. To provide genuinely affordable homes to rent and buy requires the State making a significant investment – providing a subsidy, through land and finance. That's what we need to do to fix this crisis.

We are developing affordable housing in Ireland such as cost rental and local authority affordable schemes. But it is not enough, and it is actually not even affordable in some cases.

Cost rental is a really important new form of affordable housing. This is affordable rental housing, provided by local authorities and housing associations that is available for those on higher incomes above social housing eligibility levels. The first cost-rental housing was built in 2021 by housing associations Clúid and Respond. Further schemes are planned by the Land Development Agency and by Dublin City Council in St Michael's Estate, Inchicore. It is vital that this cost-rental housing is genuinely affordable, and that it is delivered on a not-for-profit basis. Investor funds want to deliver and profit from new forms of affordable housing like cost rental, but the State must guarantee cost rental remains genuinely affordable and not-for-profit. That means providing sufficient land and finance to subsidise the delivery of cost-rental homes on a major scale.

We should also create a new form of home ownership that makes homes permanently affordable. Let's call this new, genuinely affordable scheme New Ireland Homes, or New Ireland Gaffs, whichever you prefer. The state construction company (or a private builder contracted by local authorities, the Land Development Agency, etc.), would build the homes. You would be then able to buy the house at a defined price related to your income – so it is income-related affordable housing. The cost of housing would be subsidized by the State (and you could be given a state loan to buy it) and it would be yours for ever, to do it up, to extend it, and yours to pass on to your kids. But if you wanted to sell it, you must sell it back to the State, such as the local authority or whatever state agency is tasked with delivering the New Ireland Homes scheme. They would buy it back off you for at least the price you paid, plus inflation and additional if you invested in the home. Then the home would be put back into the New Ireland Homes scheme and made available for another person to buy. If we built 5,000 of these homes per year, all around the country, within twenty years we would have a potential affordable housing market of 100,000 homes being kept affordable on a permanent basis. People could buy one of these homes if it came up for sale, and they could sell it at any point. The values would be guaranteed. But it would remove the property speculation aspect of the housing market. It would create a controlled affordable homes market, outside the private for-profit market. The scheme would prevent affordable homes being sold on the wider housing market and just becoming another investment asset and commodity. It would keep the state investment, ensuring that housing is affordable permanently. Around 10 per cent of our housing stock should be used for this purpose.

This would build affordable homes for teachers, nurses, guards, cleaners – homes that they can buy. The New Ireland Homes scheme could be delivered through community cooperatives like Poolbeg Quay and the Ó Cualann Cohousing Alliance.

We need to do what the investor funds do not want us to do. We need to build affordable housing on a major scale.

We have the land
Many countries would fall over themselves to get the amount of land we have to develop – and that includes the huge level of vacant

and derelict land in towns and centres. Land is one of the most important elements in the provision of affordable housing. The Irish State owns massive land banks, and this land should be used to build 100 per cent affordable, 'non-market' housing developments. Some land should be transferred under leasehold arrangements or agreements to not-for-profit cooperatives, housing associations and community land trust ownership schemes. There is also a need for private land to be compulsorily purchased (following the Singapore model) to provide an ongoing supply of affordable land to deliver public and private affordable housing. A proper punitive vacant land and sites tax is required to stop hoarding of land.

We have the funding

The Covid pandemic showed how fundamental home is for our health and wellbeing. Housing is as fundamental as health and education. Yet the State invests €9bn in education, €22bn in health, but just €4bn in housing. It's clear that we need a massive increase in public funding for housing. But housing doesn't require as much funding as education and health in the long term because over time it will provide a return to the State. Everyone pays something for housing – that is accepted. But that is the return the investor funds want to get hold of. We need to grab it instead and put it to creating the public good of affordable homes for all. The State can raise the funding needed in lots of ways, for example through a national wealth fund that would give us all a return on our investment. The thing about investing in housing is that it does provide a return – people pay rent or buy it. You make your money back – that's why investor funds love it! So why doesn't the State fund it, make its money back and recycle it into delivering more affordable housing? A virtuous cycle.

The funding is available to do this. Finance could come from the Housing Finance Agency, Home Building Finance Ireland (a private lender owned by the Irish State), the European Investment Bank, the Ireland Strategic Investment Fund (a €20bn state investment fund), credit unions (which have almost €1bn to lend) or state borrowing.

The State should increase the funding going into building, retro-fitting and refurbing new homes from €4bn to €8bn a year for local authorities, housing associations and cooperatives to plan and deliver affordable and social homes and to contract the state housing company to build green homes and communities in every village, town and city across the country.

We should also set up a €5bn national housing fund at affordable rates to finance and fund building of affordable homes by not-for-profits, community housing, cooperative housing and by SME builders. This should be where Irish pension funds are told to invest to get a stable, low, long-term return, and also to be a wealth and savings fund for Irish people – to get a social return.

There is a way to provide affordable housing that the government doesn't want you to know about. This is a model of housing that really cuts through the financial arguments that it is too expensive for the State to fund housing. It is provided by the Ó Cualann Cohousing Alliance, a not-for-profit provider that is the only body in the country to actually build affordable homes in the last few years. The State could support and ensure the building of 30,000 affordable purchase homes through the allocation of just €2bn per year (that's just double what we currently give to private landlords in HAP each year and we get no state asset or affordable home in return). These homes would then be for sale for between €150,000 and €250,000 per unit. Local authorities and not-for-profit housing providers like Approved Housing Bodies (AHBs) and Ó Cualann build the units themselves on state land, using the state building company and SME building contractors if necessary. If the land is subsidized or if a site services fund is made available, the State pays a maximum of €50,000 to €100,000 per unit toward the cost of these houses. The total maximum cost to the State is €2bn per year. But that cost actually reduces rapidly year after year because the State recoups €50,000 per unit in taxes from these homes and then, when the not-for-profit sells the homes, it recoups the money to invest in building more, so the state subsidy requirement falls. The not-for-profit builder can raise the finance from commercial banks and Home Building Finance Ireland at competitive rates. Institutional investor funds and buyers are not needed in this model. The beauty of affordable housing provision is that you don't need to involve big investors. The State borrows the money, and then recycles the capital through the developments as it sells them in phases. You build the first phase and sell it, and you have funding for the next phase. It's how private developers work. Except this would be providing genuinely affordable housing and ploughing any money made back into building more affordable homes.

These policies will make housing in Ireland affordable. They will increase the amount of housing and apartments owned and rented affordably by people. They will also create, for the first time, a large pool of permanently affordable homes for purchase and rent. But the State has to take the lead, as it did in the 1950s and 1960s. Tinkering around will not cut it.

This approach is not about removing private sector involvement in housing, but it would provide a dramatic increase in the state and non-profit sectors within the housing system, and would support small and medium-sized private builders and home providers with access to affordable land and financing.

We need to understand that best economic approach is for the State to spend as much as possible on directly building homes. Making housing as cheap and affordable as possible is sound economics. High rents mean the State has to pay more in subsidizing those rents. High house prices and rents means that people are not spending their money on the local economy, and many choose to leave the country because they can't afford to live here. We are losing our talent and educational investment to the new housing emigration wave. If rents and house prices fell by 50 per cent, that would free up a huge amount of money to be spent on local businesses. People would stay here and contribute, to the best of their ability, to making a thriving economy and society. This in turn means a reduction in physical and mental health-related costs, both to the public health system and to individuals. In terms of crude economics, this is better social and financial value for money for the State, society and the economy. The more the State spends on direct building of affordable housing, the more creative, productive, healthy and fully functioning our society and economy will be.

We have the human energy and capacity

We should involve our citizens in the change, through regional and local forums. There is hope in the energy of young people who are demanding that the housing crisis is solved. Their ideas and energy should be brought into the discussion and policy. Conventions on the housing crisis should be held across the country to generate ideas and find ways to get young people actively involved.

Our response to the Covid pandemic has shown what we can do as a country when we come together and put everything we have into addressing a crisis. We need a 'pandemic response' to the housing crisis. We can rebuild our country out of this crisis, and create sustainable, affordable homes for all – with communities central to the process. Let's get the hundreds of thousands of people who need gaffs involved in designing, planning and delivering them, as future tenants and homeowners, and reskilling and training those who want to get involved in construction. We should harness the wave of community togetherness and support we saw during Covid lockdowns. We have to do something radically different, and this would provide hope to the younger generations that their country wants them, values them, and is giving them a future here.

We can provide homes for everyone

The humanitarian crisis caused by the war in Ukraine comes on top of a pre-existing housing emergency in this country. It is the right thing to do, as a country, to provide refuge for Ukrainians fleeing the war. The government's response, however, has been to provide temporary accommodation in hotels and reception centres, and to investigate the use of vacant public buildings. However, after enduring the trauma of war, many of these refugees could be left living in this accommodation – in warehouses, tents and congregated settings – for years, just like those in direct provision and the pre-existing homeless in Ireland were left in 'temporary' emergency accommodation. The government should be providing a real emergency response to the pre-existing housing and homelessness emergency, and the additional humanitarian need of Ukrainian refugees. But a real emergency response – like the response we had to Covid – requires that you use every available resource you have to solve it. We have never seen that in the government's response to housing. We still haven't seen it, despite their claims and rhetoric. A real emergency response would provide structural long-term solutions to solve our multiple housing emergencies.

Given the depth of the housing crisis here, some people have expressed frustration that the government are putting 'more effort', as they perceive it, into housing refugees than they did into solving our pre-existing housing crisis. This sense of being left behind has been fuelled by the government's cynical narrative that has pointed to the Ukrainian refugee crisis as a factor in not meeting housing targets for 2022. This is dangerous and wrong. The government was repeatedly failing to meet its housing targets long before any Ukrainian refugee arrived here, and the reality is that the government is only doing the bare minimum for those refugees. We must not fall into the trap of believing it is a case of choosing between either housing the Irish living here, or housing refugees. Simply put, there are enough gaffs for all of us. Just look at the huge numbers of vacant and derelict properties and land available. The refugees did not cause the housing crisis. That responsibility lies squarely with Irish governments, banks, developers, and investor funds.

With a proper housing system based on the large-scale provision of social and affordable housing, we can ensure that everyone in this country – including refugees – has the basic dignity and need of a home fulfilled. A home for all is the foundation of an inclusive, tolerant, cooperative, multicultural, equal and socially just society. It is the country we all want to see. If we really tackled vacancy and dereliction, took emergency measures and built new homes, we could unquestionably 'house Generation Locked Out' and house refugees. We can, and must, do both.

Chapter 13
Taking Action:
What Can You Do?

There is so much you can do. We need to get a national conversation going about the housing crisis and the solutions. That starts with you. We need to get everyone talking about how the housing crisis is affecting people in real-life ways (sharing our personal housing experience – your story), about how the crisis can be solved (the ten key solutions), and then bringing everyone together into a gigantic tidal wave of a social movement (the power to pressure the government to make the change). We need to think big – a movement involving us all across the country – combining the best of the hope and love in marriage equality, the cross-generational conversations in Repeal the Eighth, the grassroots community protest of the water charges, the determination and energy of the climate movement, mixed with the spirit, community and reach of the GAA, with the concern and care of charities and the creativity of our musicians and artists. This isn't just about protest, this is about everyone who needs a home, and their communities, coming together to be an active part of the change – in raising our voice together, to say 'enough', that we are not accepting this as normal, we are not accepting this ongoing social devastation, we are not accepting another generation being forced to emigrate. And we need to come together to develop this new vision for homes and communities; you should be involved in designing, building and taking cooperative ownership over your new green homes and neighbourhood community spaces.

It starts with telling the stories, hearing them, really listening to them, and connecting with them at an emotionally empathetic level, just like marriage equality and Repeal successfully achieved change through people telling their stories and changing the way these issues were talked about, and thought about. Listening to people overcame prejudice and fear, and we were overcome by feelings of love, compassion and care. We need to do the same with housing. The housing social movement needs to bring about a national conversation where those affected by the crisis are able to tell their story, in their homes, among their friends and family and, especially, in the media. This can help lift the silence, shame and stigma felt by those affected by the housing crisis. Personal stories change people's hearts and minds. The values we hold dear – that everyone should be treated with love, compassion and care, and their rights should be valued and protected – were the ones we decided were important. We need to open up in the same way and hear people tell their housing story. Let's do it through our dinner table chats, our nights-out chats, our podcast chats, our Instagram and Twitter posts, our *Liveline* and radio talk shows. Let's do it through murals on our walls, our art, our plays and theatre, through songs, through dance, through public action and protest. Let's do it through a referendum to put a right to housing in the Constitution. Let's make our decisions on what needs to change in housing policy, on the referendum, on the basis of our shared values. As with equality, so too in housing. Let's create a massive tidal wave of change that everyone wants to be and can be part of.

We will face opposition. And in some ways housing is a more difficult equality issue to change fundamentally. Because those who gain from inequalities in housing make huge profit from it, they are massively wealthy: the global investment funds, the corporate landlords, large private developers, investor funds and financial advisors, estate agents and small-time landlords. This change will impact them. And so they will lobby hard, and create misinformation, and mislead, and pump in money to try to counter the value shift of turning property from investment asset into home, into a human right. To challenge this power of wealth we need to create an alternative. People power – the largest possible cross-society alliance that includes businesses, social enterprises, high-profile personalities, leaders, trade unions, artists, NGOs, civil society groups. People who understand that we need affordable homes for everyone so that our economy and society can function, so that people can thrive.

We will also face opposition from our State and government. Irish governments and the Irish State historically, and still today, has a deeply disturbing ability to ignore and hide away the suffering of stigmatized groups, and an ability to sacrifice younger generations in order to retain the status quo. From the way the Famine was used as an opportunity to evict the poor so that landlords could increase the size of their land holdings, to the Magdalene laundries, the forced 'assimilation' of Travellers, direct provision, the new institutionalization of families and children in homeless emergency hubs, and the forced emigration of younger generations, most recently in the austerity period. There is a culture among the top echelons of Irish society that considers it acceptable to sacrifice certain groups to keep the status quo in place. And that culture was encouraged amongst the wider population. It is there in attitudes you sometimes hear. We all need to ask ourselves, do we tolerate this? Do we think homelessness is normal? Do we accept the housing crisis, because it might not affect us or our family (yet)? I do not believe a majority of people accept it any more. And I know that the younger generation are going to make another historical breakthrough in this country. They will not tolerate the othering of marginalized groups, and they will not tolerate the sacrifice of those groups or themselves to maintain privilege and inequality in housing. Rather than being forced to emigrate, many will stay to change things properly. And that is where the hope for real change lies.

There is already a value shift in how we see and understand housing. We do not want a housing system based on the Celtic Tiger values that treated housing as something you made money from; as being about a 'property ladder'; as an investment; as something you 'add value' to; where you feel good about rising housing prices; where you think of your home as a stock or share with its value rising or falling and you wait to sell and make a profit. This cultural attitude to housing was excused because us Irish have suffered so long without owning our land and homes. The argument was made that it's in our genes to need to own property. But that's wrong. The desire to own a secure home was conflated and confused, deliberately, to justify making money from multiple property ownership, and to justify developers and property sellers charging eye-wateringly unaffordable house prices. We will pay anything to own our gaff. Even if we have to live in poverty for years. Or so we are told. But it doesn't have to be like this. What's in the Irish psyche and historical cultural memory is the need for a secure home, a gaff of your own, that you have control over, where you can feel safe, and plan your life, and have a family. And the only way you can do that currently in Ireland is to own a home, or through social housing. And we understand this; that is why we don't want a housing system where housing has been turned into a commodity and a financial asset that just makes huge profits for global and Irish investor funds. The financial asset-driven housing market has scarred and broken us. Younger generations, indeed all those affected by the housing crisis across the generations, see housing differently now. But in particular, for Generation Locked-out the property ladder is an irrelevance. They see housing as a home, not property investment. They want a home, a gaff, where they can live securely and affordably. Having being robbed of their home, denied a home, and facing the possibility of never having a gaff of their own, they realize the true value and meaning of home. It is somewhere to live. This is the value change – the cultural revolution – that is under way. Housing now is valued as what it fundamentally is – a home, somewhere people can live their life, that is affordable, that is of decent quality, size, is lifetime-secure and enables you to be part of a community. Government and policymakers are stuck in the old Celtic Tiger values. But those values have caused this crisis. So the values have to change. They are changing. The housing train needs a new driver and engine – and it is the human right to housing.

We need to ask people to think about housing differently, to think about the deeper meaning and purpose and value of home. We need to show how the housing crisis is causing a mental health crisis, causing another generation to emigrate, taking people's hope and future away, and even denying people's hope to have children. We are nothing without a home, everyone needs a gaff, and everyone has a human right to a home. The market, developers and the investor funds have failed over and over to provide it. Just like health and education, housing should be guaranteed to all. Housing needs to be seen as a fundamental responsibility of our government, our State.

You have political power

We need a tidal wave of people across the country demanding the government implement these solutions to the housing crisis. The main thing that politicians are worried about is getting re-elected. We need to show them that the majority of people in this country want these solutions done today, and that they will only get re-elected if they implement them.

There will be local and European elections in Ireland in 2024. The next general election has to happen by February 2025. But we don't have to wait until then to make politicians feel the pressure of the public demand for change. If we make the politicians realize now that we are watching them and our vote depends on what they do now, we can have an immediate impact.

And we have a huge potential political power bloc. There are around 300,000 households, at least 400,000 adults, in the private rental sector. There are 450,000 adults living at home with their parents. That's at least 850,000 potential voters. That's more than all the people who voted for Fianna Fáil in the last election. It's more than all who voted for Fine Gael. It's actually about the same number as the total number of votes both Fine Gael and Fianna Fáil combined got in the last election. The power is in your hands. But you have to register to vote, you have to let the politicians know you are going to vote on the basis of what they do on housing, and then you actually have to vote! Right now the government parties don't believe that younger people, renters, those in hidden homelessness, those who are emigrating, will come out and vote on election day, so they are not as worried about how their policies affect them. Remember the impact in Repeal and Marriage Equality when tens of thousands of young and not so young returned to Ireland to vote. Imagine if we could convince people to return home to vote for housing. It would be a game changer. Then imagine if you convinced your parents to vote for housing as well. Your parents are more likely to be Fianna Fáil or Fine Gael voters, and if those parties feel in danger of losing those votes, that will put them under serious pressure. If you are a parent of a child who is part of Generation Locked-out, isn't it time to make a stand for your children, for your grandchildren? Combining the cross-generational votes there is a potential voting bloc of well over a million people. That is an incredibly influential group. Organizing that into a movement of voters who want housing solutions implemented would be a real force for change.

The government, the Taoiseach and Tánaiste, the Minister for Housing, all elected politicians and policymakers (in the Department of Housing and local authorities) need to hear that message clearly now. You can do that by emailing them, especially your local elected councillors and TDs. This will make them realize that the next time they come looking for your vote you will be deciding who to vote for on the basis of what they do between now and then to deliver housing solutions. You will be letting them know that they won't convince you to vote based on promises they will be making at the next election but on the basis of what they do to deliver these solutions between now and then.

You can do this

We are at a crossroads in our housing crisis. The decisions made in the coming months and years will have historic ramifications for generations to come. Are we going to go down the road of a permanent dystopia of housing crisis, people locked out of being able to buy or rent an affordable forever home, of homelessness, of emigration, of rising inequality, of a mental health crisis? Or are we going to take a different road, and make the shift to a housing system that provides affordable, secure, environmentally sustainable homes, for everyone?

You should not be forced to emigrate, to live in substandard unaffordable rental, or be living in your parents' box room, because of the failure of politicians in government.

Don't let yourself be silenced. Take action. Nothing will change unless we raise our voices together and create a movement of change that government can't ignore. Nothing will change unless you change it. No matter what people tell you, you can change this. There are countless examples whereby citizens – whether as individuals or having come together – have taken action, stood up for their rights, and have achieved major change. You have the power to do this in housing.

You are the generation who broke the historical conservatism that strangled this country down the decades. That conservatism is still holding the power in our housing system. But you are the generation who delivered unprecedented, unimaginable social change based on love and compassion and believing in what is right. You created a new Ireland that we never thought was possible. You forged a new, progressive, positive future for everyone in Ireland. You can do the same in housing – so that you, and everyone in this country, now and into the future can have a home, a gaff of their own, the most fundamental human need and human right.

Ten things you can do

1. Tell your housing story. Break the silence and stigma. Talk to your friends and family about your housing situation. Post about it on social media using the hashtags #gaffsstories,

#gaffs4all and #right2housing. Come on my podcast Reboot Republic and tell your story, as many others have. Contact gaffs4all@gmail.com.

2. Take a photo on your phone of 'The policies that can fix this crisis' on pages 299–304 and send it to your family and friends. Share the policies and this 'Ten things you can do' list on social media, using the #gaffs4all and #right2housing hashtags, print them out and stick them up on coffee shop notice boards, hand them out as leaflets at work.

3. Sign the Gaffs4All petition calling on the Government to fix the crisis & implement the ten 'Gaffs for All' policies on https:// my.uplift.ie/petitions/gaffs4all. The more signatures, the more it shows the government how many people want action; the more signatures, the more pressure. Let's make this a massive one! Share the petition on social media, text it, WhatsApp it.

4. Join the campaign for a referendum on putting the right to housing in the Constitution, and let's make a real difference together. Check out www.homeforgood.ie

5. Register to vote in the local and national elections and email your local politicians, the Taoiseach, Tánaiste and Minister for Housing telling them you are going to vote on the basis of the housing solutions set out in this book.

6. Be part of the growing movement for housing. Check out Raise the Roof and the Homeless and Housing Coalition websites for detail of housing meetings, events and protests. Join the Community Action Tenants Union (CATU), a union for tenants and all those affected by the housing crisis, along with people who just care about housing and community. This is a really important organization to get involved with, especially if you are a renter or if you are living at home with your

parents, or you are homeless. It supports people by organizing meetings of those affected, informing them of their rights, and supporting people who are being evicted. Check them out at www.catuireland.org. Volunteer with a homeless organization such as Simon Communities, Focus Ireland, Mendicity, or the Peter McVerry Trust.

7. Stop financialization of housing – homes should not be pension funds. Stop Irish pensions turning homes into investment assets – ask for divestment of pension funds from residential real estate investment. Contact your pension provider, broker, or HR to ask them to stop investing in REITs/ investor funds/real estate residential property investment. Ask for ethical investing in genuine affordable housing.

8. Take photographs of vacant or derelict buildings and land in your area and put them up on social media with the hashtag #DerelictIreland. There is a new movement highlighting derelict and vacant buildings around the country.

9. If you are facing homelessness, eviction from your home, or issues with your landlord, contact Threshold, Focus Ireland, Simon Communities or the Mercy Law Centre. If you are facing discrimination by a landlord, for instance because you are on HAP, you can take a case to the Workplace Relations Commission (WRC). The Irish Human Rights and Equality Commission has support on this. See www.ihrec.ie.

10. Why not get involved in planning and delivering affordable housing, for yourself and others, as part of a community group or cooperative? You can find out more from Ó Cualann Cohousing Alliance (www.ocuallann.ie). There is also information about community co-housing groups at Self Organised Architecture (https://soa.ie).

Acknowledgements

With huge thanks to all who made this book happen. I could not have written it without you. Especially to Catherine and everyone at HarperCollins Ireland, for signing me up, believing in me and in the need to tell this story, and expertly guiding the process.

To my colleagues at Maynooth for their support. And to Lucy, Tony G (for all the *Reboot* Podcasts that spark so many ideas and provide the space for the human stories to be told), Lorcan, Hugh, Samantha, John, Sinead M, Davie, Rob, David, and Lisa.

To my family, the foundation to getting the book written, commenting insightfully on drafts and then pulling me out of the rabbit holes; *mo réaltaí*; Leo, Aisling, Keelan, Erin, *agus, go deo*, Sinéad.